Mastering Kibana 6.x

Visualize your Elastic Stack data with histograms, maps, charts, and graphs

Anurag Srivastava

BIRMINGHAM - MUMBAI

Mastering Kibana 6.x

Commissioning Editor: Pravin Dhandre
Acquisition Editor: Viraj Madhav
Content Development Editor: Karan Thakkar
Technical Editor: Sagar Sawant
Copy Editors: Dhanya Baburaj, Shaila Kusanale, Dipti Mankame, Laxmi Subramanian
Project Coordinator: Nidhi Joshi
Proofreader: Safis Editing
Indexer: Pratik Shirodkar
Graphics: Jisha Chirayil
Production Coordinator: Nilesh Mohite

First published: July 2018

Production reference: 1310718

Published by Packt Publishing Ltd.
Livery Place
35 Livery Street
Birmingham
B3 2PB, UK.

ISBN 978-1-78883-103-1

www.packtpub.com

mapt.io

Mapt is an online digital library that gives you full access to over 5,000 books and videos, as well as industry leading tools to help you plan your personal development and advance your career. For more information, please visit our website.

Why subscribe?

- Spend less time learning and more time coding with practical eBooks and Videos from over 4,000 industry professionals

- Improve your learning with Skill Plans built especially for you

- Get a free eBook or video every month

- Mapt is fully searchable

- Copy and paste, print, and bookmark content

PacktPub.com

Did you know that Packt offers eBook versions of every book published, with PDF and ePub files available? You can upgrade to the eBook version at www.PacktPub.com and as a print book customer, you are entitled to a discount on the eBook copy. Get in touch with us at service@packtpub.com for more details.

At www.PacktPub.com, you can also read a collection of free technical articles, sign up for a range of free newsletters, and receive exclusive discounts and offers on Packt books and eBooks.

Contributors

About the author

Anurag Srivastava is a senior technical lead since 11 years in a multinational software company in web-based application development. He has led and handled teams and clients since 7 years of his professional career. Proficient in designing and deployment of scalable applications, he has multiple certifications in ML and data science using Python. He is well experienced with the Elastic stack (Elasticsearch, Logstash, and Kibana) for creating dashboards using system metrics data, log data, application data, or relational databases.

About the reviewers

Saurabh Chhajed is a Certified Spark and Hadoop developer with 8 years of professional experience in the enterprise application development and big data analytics , using the latest frameworks, tools, and design patterns. He has extensive experience of working with Agile and Scrum methodologies and enjoys acting as an evangelist for various big data frameworks and machine learning. While not working, he enjoys traveling and sharing his experiences on his blog, SAURZCODE.

Sharath Kumar M N is the author of *Learning Elastic Stack 6.0* which was named as one of the *Best Elasticsearch Books of All Time* by BookAuthority (bookauthority.org). He has done his masters in computer science at The University of Texas, Dallas, USA. He is currently working as an big data architect at CA Technologies. He being an avid speaker, he has also given several tech talks in conferences such as the Oracle Code Event. His new interests are into DevOps and AIOps.

Packt is searching for authors like you

If you're interested in becoming an author for Packt, please visit `authors.packtpub.com` and apply today. We have worked with thousands of developers and tech professionals, just like you, to help them share their insight with the global tech community. You can make a general application, apply for a specific hot topic that we are recruiting an author for, or submit your own idea.

Table of Contents

Preface   1

Chapter 1: Revising the ELK Stack   7
  What is ELK Stack?   8
    Elasticsearch   9
    Logstash   9
    Kibana   11
    Beats   11
  Installing the ELK Stack   12
    Elasticsearch   12
      Installing Elasticsearch using a TAR file   12
      Installing Elasticsearch with Homebrew   13
      Installing Elasticsearch with MSI Windows Installer   13
      Installing Elasticsearch with the Debian package   13
      Installing Elasticsearch with the RPM package   13
    Logstash   14
      Using apt package repositories   14
      Using yum package repositories   15
    Kibana   15
      Installing Kibana using .tar.gz   16
      Installing Kibana using the Debian package   16
      Installing Kibana using rpm   16
      Installing Kibana on Windows   17
    Beats   18
      Packetbeat   18
      Metricbeat   19
      Filebeat   21
      Winlogbeat   22
      Heartbeat   22
  ELK use cases   24
    Log management   24
    Security monitoring and alerting   25
    Web scraping   25
    E-commerce search solutions   26
    Full text search   26
    Visualizing data   26
  Summary   27

Chapter 2: Setting Up and Customizing the Kibana Dashboard   29
  Setting up the stage   29
    Configuring Logstash to fetch data from the Apache log file   30
    Outputting the log data into Elasticsearch   31

Configuring Kibana to read the Elasticsearch index 32
Creating demo visualizations with Apache log data 36
Creating the dashboard 39
Customizing the dashboard 44
Editing the visualization 44
Changing the title by customizing the panel 45
Moving the visualization to full screen 46
Deleting the visualization from the dashboard 46
Changing the colors of the visualization 46
Dragging and dropping visualizations on a desired location on the dashboard 48
Resizing the visualization as per our requirements 48
Exporting CSV data from the visualization 49
Getting the Elasticsearch request, response, and statistics 50
Summary 52
Chapter 3: Exploring Your Data 53
Kibana Discover 54
Discovering data using Kibana Discover 58
Configuring Packetbeat to push packet data into Elasticsearch 59
Configuring Kibana to read the Elasticsearch index with packet logs 62
Exploring Kibana Discover to access packet data 65
Showing the required fields 67
Applying the time filter 69
Elasticsearch query DSL 70
Filter 72
Saving and opening searches 73
Saving the result 73
Opening the result 73
Sharing results 74
Field data statistics 74
Summary 75
Chapter 4: Visualizing the Data 77
Creating visualizations 78
Basic charts 79
Data 80
Maps 80
Time series 80
Other 81
Pie charts 81
Metric aggregation 81
Bucket aggregation 81
Creating a pie chart 82
Adding another dimension to the pie chart 85
Bar charts 86
Metric aggregation 86
Bucket aggregation 87

Creating a bar chart	88
Area charts	90
Creating an area chart	91
Data metrics	92
Creating a data metric	92
Data tables	93
Creating the data table	93
Tag clouds	94
Creating a tag cloud	94
Markdown	96
Creating a markdown visualization	97
Sharing visualizations	97
Summary	98
Chapter 5: Dashboarding to Showcase Key Performance Indicators	99
Creating the dashboard	100
Arranging visualizations	103
Moving visualizations	103
Resizing visualizations	104
Removing visualizations	105
Showing in full screen	106
Showing visualization data	107
Modifying the visualization	109
Saving the dashboard	110
Sharing the dashboard	110
Sharing the saved dashboard	111
Sharing the snapshot	111
Cloning the dashboard	112
Exploring the dashboard	113
The search query	113
Adding filters	115
Applying the time filter	119
Clicking on visualizations	122
Summary	125
Chapter 6: Handling Time Series Data with Timelion	127
Timelion interface	128
Timeline expression	129
.es function parameters	130
Chainable methods	131
.sum()	131
.avg()	132
.min()	133
.max()	133
.log()	134

.abs()   134
.divide()   134
.multiply()   135
.derivative()   135
.bars()   136
.color()   137
.label()   137
.legend()   138
.movingaverage()   138
.trend()   139
.range()   140
.precision()   140
Data source functions   141
Elasticsearch   142
    Static/value   142
    World bank   143
    Setting the offset for data sources   144
Saving Timelion graph   146
Timelion sheet option   151
Deleting Timelion sheet   152
Timelion help   152
Function reference   153
Keyboard tips   153
Timelion auto-refresh   154
Summary   154

Chapter 7: Interact with Your Data Using Dev Tools   157
Console   158
Copy as cURL   160
Auto indent   161
Multiple requests in console   163
Profiling queries   168
Query profile   170
Aggregation profile   172
Grok debugger   174
Summary   177

Chapter 8: Tweaking Your Configuration with Kibana Management 179
Index pattern   180
Creating the index pattern   181
Setting the default index pattern   185
Refreshing index pattern fields   185
Deleting an index pattern   186
Managing fields   187
    String   189
    Dates   190

Geographic point field 190
Numbers 191
Saved objects 192
Dashboards 193
Searches 194
Visualizations 195
Advanced settings 196
xPack:defaultAdminEmail 197
search:queryLanguage 197
search:queryLanguage:switcher:enable 197
dateFormat 198
dateFormat:tz 198
dateFormat:dow 199
defaultIndex 199
Reporting 200
Security 200
Roles 201
Users 202
Watcher 202
Creating the watch 203
Threshold alert 204
Advanced watch 206
Deleting the watch 208
Summary 209

Chapter 9: Understanding X-Pack Features 211
Installing X-Pack 212
Installing X-Pack into Elasticsearch 212
Installing X-Pack into Kibana 213
Features of X-Pack 214
Monitoring 214
Elasticsearch monitoring 216
Kibana monitoring 222
Security settings 224
Users 224
Roles 226
Machine learning 229
Other options of X-Pack 229
Application Performance Monitoring 231
Logging 232
Apache logs 233
MySQL logs 234
Nginx logs 234
System logs 235
Metrics 236
Apache metrics 237
Docker metrics 237

Kubernetes metrics   238
MySQL metrics   238
Nginx metrics   238
Redis metrics   239
System metrics   239
Summary   240

Chapter 10: Machine Learning with Kibana   241
Machine learning jobs   242
Single metric Jobs   244
Multi-metric jobs   245
Population Jobs   245
Advanced Jobs   245
Create a machine learning job   246
Data visualizer   248
Single metric Job   250
Managing jobs   258
Job settings   259
Job config   259
Datafeed   260
Counts   261
JSON   262
Job messages   263
Datafeed preview   264
Anomaly explorer   265
Single metric viewer   266
Multi metric job   267
Explore multi metric job result   270
Population job   273
Summary   275

Chapter 11: Create Super Cool Dashboard from a Web Application 277
JDBC input plugin   278
Scheduling   279
Maintaining the last SQL value   279
Fetch size   280
Configuring Logstash for database input   280
Creating a dashboard using MySQL data   283
Creating visualizations   287
Total blog and top blog count   287
Blogger-wise blog counts   288
Tag cloud for blog categories   290
Blogger name-category-views-blog pie chart   291
Tabular view of blog details   292
Create dashboard   294
Summary   296

Chapter 12: Different Use Cases of Kibana   297

Time-series data handling   298
  Conditional formatting   298
  Tracking trends   301
A visual builder for handling time series data   303
GeoIP for Elastic Stack   309
  Ingest node   309
  GeoIP with Packetbeat data   313
Summary   318

Chapter 13: Creating Monitoring Dashboards Using Beats   319
  Configuring the Beats   320
    Filebeat   321
      Configuring Filebeat   322
    Metricbeat   325
      Configuring Metricbeat   326
        Enabling the modules using the metricbeat.yml file   326
        Enabling the modules from the modules.d directory   326
    Packetbeat   327
      Configuring Packetbeat   328
  Creating visualizations using Beat data   330
    Visualization using Filebeat   330
    Visualization using Metricbeat   333
    Visualization using Packetbeat   334
  Creating the dashboard   336
  Importing Beat dashboards   338
    Importing dashboards in Filebeat   338
    Importing dashboards in Metricbeat   338
    Importing dashboards in Packetbeat   339
  Summary   339

Chapter 14: Best Practices   341
  Requirement of test environment   341
  Picking the right time filter field   342
  Avoiding large document indexing   343
  Avoiding sparsity   344
    Avoiding unrelated data in the same index   345
    Normalizing the document   345
    Avoiding types in Indices   346
  Avoiding wildcard searches   348
  Summary   348

Other Books You May Enjoy   351

Index   355

Preface

Kibana is a powerful visualization tool which can be use to solve different types of problems. The basic use of Kibana is log management and it is mostly used for the log management only because it is quite difficult to handle the logs without a proper tool which can help us to explore, filter, search and visualize the logs. We can also use Kibana in many other areas like for security monitoring and alerting in which we use the tool to figure out any suspicious activity or attack. Machine learning is another important feature which was introduced in Kibana 5.4 and provides us the luxury to apply the machine learning algorithm directly on the index pattern data without any other software dependency.

The objective of this book is to first introduce the reader with basics of Kibana like installation, functioning and log management etc and then to explain some complex topics like Timelion, Machine Learning etc and at last to provide some practical explanation to setup the dashboard like creating dashboard using Beats and then through RDBMS data. So we can say that this book is a complete package and covers almost every aspect of Kibana.

Who this book is for

This book is for system admins, data analysts, programmers, and anyone who need a powerful dashboard using any sort of data. If you want to get complete insight of Kibana and how we can use it to solve our data exploration problems, you can refer to this book. This book is not a Kibana manual but a solution oriented approach where readers can get the idea to solve their problem in hand after learning the basics of Kibana. No prior Kibana knowledge is required for this book.

What this book covers

Chapter 1, *Revising the ELK Stack*, this chapter will explain details of ELK stack which is now known as Elastic Stack. Although they've all been built to work exceptionally well together, each one is a separate project that is driven by the open-source vendor Elastic. Through this chapter reader will get complete idea of these three software and will able to figure out that how we can combine these to achieve different use cases.

Chapter 2, *Setting Up and Customizing the Kibana Dashboard*, In this chapter we will know how to customize Kibana visualization by adding title, resizing panels, change colors and opacity, modify the legends etc. This will also explain how we can embed the dashboard on our existing application, By tweaking these features we can create more meaningful and impact full dashboards.

Chapter 3, *Exploring Your Data*, Here we will come to know the Discover tab functionalities like Search Bar, Time Filter, Field Selector, Data Histogram and Log View. Discover option provide us the way to search and select required fields from our dataset. It provides us the complete picture of Elastic search data which is loaded into Kibana.

Chapter 4, *Visualizing the Data*, The Kibana Visualize page is where we can create, modify, and view our own custom visualizations. There are different types of visualizations, ranging from *Vertical bar* and *Pie* charts to *Tile maps* and *Data tables*. Different type of visualization can be created using Kibana Visualize option. Visualizations can also be shared with other users who have access to the Kibana instance.In this chapter reader will learn to create various types of data visualizations like *Vertical bar,Pie* charts, *Tile maps,Data tables and tag clouds etc.*

Chapter 5, *Dashboarding to Showcase Key Performance Indicators*, With a dashboard, we can combine multiple visualizations onto a single page. Here we can filter them by providing a search query or by selecting filters by clicking elements in the visualization. Dashboards are useful when we want to get an overview of logs, and make correlations among various visualizations and logs. We can also export the csv data from data tables of Kibana.

Chapter 6, *Handling Time Series Data with Timelion* , In this chapter we will learn about Timelion which is a time series visualization plugin for Kibana which enables us to combine independent data sources within the same visualization. As with normal visualizations in Kibana, we can visualize Timelion expressions from the Visualize tab. It provides us various features such as function chaining, analyzing trends, data formatting, and performing basic calculations.

Chapter 7, *Interact with Your Data Using Dev Tools* , in this chapter we will learn about **Dev Tools** which contains development tools that we can use to interact with data in Kibana. Console plugin of Kibana Dev Tools provides a UI to interact with the REST API of Elasticsearch. Console has two main areas: the **editor**, where we can compose requests to Elasticsearch, and the **response** pane, which displays the responses to the request.

Chapter 8, *Tweaking Your Configuration with Kibana Management,* in this chapter we will cover Kibana Management interface is used to perform runtime configuration of Kibana, initial setup and ongoing configuration of index patterns, advanced settings that tweak the behaviors of Kibana itself, and various "objects" that we can save throughout Kibana such as searches, visualizations, and dashboards.

Chapter 9, *Understanding X-Pack Features* , in this chapter we will come to know how to setup X-Pack and use different features like security, alerting, monitoring, reporting and machine learning. In default setup of ELK we do not have these features and for using X-Pack we need to purchase the license. X-Pack provide us the feature to secure the ELK stack will user role and permission.

Chapter 10, *Machine Learning with Kibana* , in this chapter we will learn about Machine learning which is the science of getting computers to act without being explicitly programmed. For applying machine learning on our dataset we need to use any programming language like R or Python but Kibana provides us a tab with X-Pack for creating machine learning jobs and managing them. We can apply machine learning in any time based dataset and can get the output in Kibana UI. We can detect anomalies, find root cause of any problem, easily forecast the future trends and find many answers from our data using machine learning.

Chapter 11, *Create Super Cool Dashboard from a Web Application* , in this chapter we will cover how we can create a super cool dashboard from an existing web application through practical example. Here I will drive through application data flow from database to Kibana and then from Kibana visualization to Dashboard. The dashboard can independently be used or we can embed it in our web application.

Chapter 12, *Different Use Cases of Kibana,* in this chapter we will cover different important use cases of Kibana like handling time series data where we will cover conditional formatting and tracking trends etc. After that we will cover how to work with visual builder to handle the time series data and then will cover GeoIP for Elastic Search and how we can plot data on maps.

Chapter 13, *Create Monitoring Dashboard Using Beats,* in this chapter we will learn about Beats which works as a data shippers. This chapter will explain to create a quick monitoring dashboard using Beats. We will come to know about different type of beats like Metricbeat, Packetbeat, Filebeat, and so on. Here I will cover each steps from Beats configuration to dashboard creation.In this chapter reader would be able to create quick monitoring dashboard using Beats.

Chapter 14, *Best Practices,* in this chapter we will cover different best practices which we need to ensure while working with Elastic Stack. By following these best practices we can get optimum performance from our Elastic stack setup.

To get the most out of this book

1. Although it is not required but it would be beneficial if you have basic knowledge of charts.
2. You should have a system access where you can install Elastic Stack and can follow the instructions given in the book.

Download the color images

We also provide a PDF file that has color images of the screenshots/diagrams used in this book. You can download it here: `http://www.packtpub.com/sites/default/files/downloads/MasteringKibana6x_ColorImages.pdf`.

Conventions used

There are a number of text conventions used throughout this book.

`CodeInText`: Indicates code words in text, database table names, folder names, filenames, file extensions, path names, dummy URLs, user input, and Twitter handles. Here is an example: "To run Logstash, we need to install Logstash and edit the configuration file `logstash.conf`."

A block of code is set as follows:

```
input {
    file {
        path => "/var/log/apache2/access.log"
        }
    }
```

Any command-line input or output is written as follows:

```
curl -L -O
https://artifacts.elastic.co/downloads/elasticsearch/elasticsearch-6.1.3.tar.gz
```

Bold: Indicates a new term, an important word, or words that you see onscreen. For example, words in menus or dialog boxes appear in the text like this. Here is an example: "To get the statistics, we need to select **Statistics** from the dropdown."

 Warnings or important notes appear like this.

 Tips and tricks appear like this.

Get in touch

Feedback from our readers is always welcome.

General feedback: Email feedback@packtpub.com and mention the book title in the subject of your message. If you have questions about any aspect of this book, please email us at questions@packtpub.com.

Errata: Although we have taken every care to ensure the accuracy of our content, mistakes do happen. If you have found a mistake in this book, we would be grateful if you would report this to us. Please visit www.packtpub.com/submit-errata, selecting your book, clicking on the Errata Submission Form link, and entering the details.

Piracy: If you come across any illegal copies of our works in any form on the Internet, we would be grateful if you would provide us with the location address or website name. Please contact us at copyright@packtpub.com with a link to the material.

If you are interested in becoming an author: If there is a topic that you have expertise in and you are interested in either writing or contributing to a book, please visit authors.packtpub.com.

Reviews

Please leave a review. Once you have read and used this book, why not leave a review on the site that you purchased it from? Potential readers can then see and use your unbiased opinion to make purchase decisions, we at Packt can understand what you think about our products, and our authors can see your feedback on their book. Thank you!

For more information about Packt, please visit `packtpub.com`.

1
Revising the ELK Stack

Although this book is about Kibana, it doesn't make any sense if we are not aware of the complete **Elastic Stack (ELK Stack)**, including **Elasticsearch**, **Kibana**, **Logstash**, and **Beats**. In this chapter, you are going to learn the basic concepts of the different software, installation, and their use cases. We cannot use Kibana to its full strength unless we know how to get proper data, filter it, and store it in a format that we can easily use in Kibana.

Elasticsearch is a search engine that is built on top of **Apache Lucene**, which is mainly used for storing schemaless data and searching it quickly. Logstash is a data pipeline that can practically take data from any source and send data to any source. We can also filter that data as per our requirements. Beats is a single-purpose software that is used to run on individual servers and send data to the Logstash server or directly to the Elasticsearch server. Finally, Kibana uses the data that's stored in Elasticsearch and creates beautiful dashboards using different types of visualization options, such as graphs, charts, histograms, word tags, and data tables.

In this chapter, we will be covering the following topics:

- What is ELK Stack?
- The installation of Elasticsearch, Logstash, Kibana, and Beats
- ELK use cases

What is ELK Stack?

ELK Stack is a stack with three different open source software—Elasticsearch, Logstash, and Kibana. Elasticsearch is a search engine that is developed on top of Apache Lucene. Logstash is basically used for data pipelining where we can get data from any data source as an input, transform it if required, and send it to any destination as an output. In general, we use Logstash to push the data into Elasticsearch. Kibana is a dashboard or visualization tool, which can be configured with Elasticsearch to generate charts, graphs, and dashboards using our data:

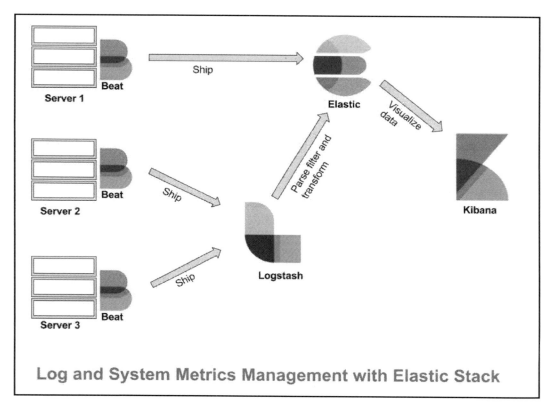

Log and System Metrics Management with Elastic Stack

We can use ELK Stack for different use cases, the most common being log analysis. Other than that, we can use it for business intelligence, application security and compliance, web analytics, fraud management, and so on.

In the following subsections, we are going to be looking at ELK Stack's components.

Elasticsearch

Elasticsearch is a full text search engine that can be used as a NoSQL database and as an analytics engine. It is easy to scale, schemaless, and near real time, and provides a restful interface for different operations. It is schemaless, and it uses inverted indexes for data storage. There are different language clients available for Elasticsearch, as follows:

- Java
- PHP
- Perl
- Python
- .NET
- Ruby
- JavaScript
- Groovy

The basic components of Elasticsearch are as follows:

- Cluster
- Node
- Index
- Type
- Document
- Shard

Logstash

Logstash is basically used for data pipelining, through which we can take input from different sources and output to different data sources. Using Logstash, we can clean the data through filter options and mutate the input data before sending it to the output source. Logstash has different adapters to handle different applications, such as for MySQL or any other relational database connection. We have a JDBC input plugin through which we can connect to MySQL server, run queries, and take the table data as the input in Logstash. For Elasticsearch, there is a connector in Logstash that gives us the option to seamlessly transfer data from Logstash to Elasticsearch.

To run Logstash, we need to install Logstash and edit the configuration file
`logstash.conf`, which consists of an `input`, `output`, and `filter` sections. We need to
tell Logstash where it should get the input from through the `input` block, what it should
do with the input through the `filter` block, and where it should send the output through
the `output` block. In the following example, I am reading an **Apache Access Log** and
sending the output to Elasticsearch:

```
input {
    file {
        path => "/var/log/apache2/access.log"
        }
 }

 filter {
     grok {
         match => { message => "%{COMBINEDAPACHELOG}" }
         }
 }

output {
   elasticsearch {
        hosts => "http://127.0.0.1:9200"
        index => "logs_apache"
        document_type => "logs"
        }
 }
```

The `input` block is showing a file key that is set to `/var/log/apache2/access.log`. This
means that we are getting the `file` input and `path` of the
file, `/var/log/apache2/access.log`, which is Apache's log file. The `filter` block is
showing the `grok` filter, which converts unstructured data into structured data by parsing
it.

There are different patterns that we can apply for the Logstash filter. Here, we are parsing
the Apache logs, but we can filter different things, such as email, IP addresses, and dates.

Kibana

Kibana is a dashboarding open source software from ELK Stack, and it is a very good tool for creating different visualizations, charts, maps, and histograms, and by integrating different visualizations together, we can create dashboards. It is part of ELK Stack; hence it is quite easy to read the Elasticsearch data. This does not require any programming skills. Kibana has a beautiful UI for creating different types of visualizations, including charts, histograms, and dashboards.

It provides us with different inbuilt dashboards with multiple visualizations when we use Beats, as it automatically creates multiple visualizations that we can customize to create a useful dashboard, such as for CPU usage and memory usage.

Beats

Beats are basically data shippers that are grouped to do single-purpose jobs. For example, **Metricbeat** is used to collect metrics for memory usage, CPU usage, and disk space, whereas **Filebeat** is used to send file data such as logs. They can be installed as agents on different servers to send data from different sources to a central Logstash or Elasticsearch cluster. They are written in Go; they work on a cross-platform environment; and they are lightweight in design. Before Beats, it was very difficult to get data from different machines as there was no single-purpose data shipper, and we had to do some tweaking to get the desired data from servers.

For example, if I am running a web application on the Apache web server and want to run it smoothly, then there are two things that need to be monitored—first, all of the errors from the application, and second, the server's performance, such as memory usage, CPU usage, and disk space. So, in order to collect this information, we need to install the following two Beats on our machine:

- **Filebeat**: This is used to collect log data from Apache web server in an incremental way. Filebeat will run on the server and will periodically check for any change in the Apache log. When there is any change in the Apache log file, it will send the log to Logstash. Logstash will receive the data file and execute the filter to find the errors. After filtering the data, it saves the data into Elasticsearch.

- **Metricbeat**: This is used to collect metrics for memory usage, CPU usage, disk space, and so on. Metricbeat collects the server metrics, such as memory usage, CPU usage, and disk space, and saves the data into Elasticsearch. Metrics data sends a predefined set of data, and there is no need to modify anything; that is why it sends data directly to Elasticsearch instead of sending it to Logstash first.

To visualize this data, we can use Kibana to create meaningful dashboards through which we can get complete control of our data.

Installing the ELK Stack

For a complete installation of ELK Stack, we first need to install individual components that are explained one by one in the following sections.

Elasticsearch

Elasticsearch 6.0 requires that we have Java 8 at the least. Before you proceed with the installation of Elasticsearch, please ensure which version of Java is present in your system by executing the following command:

```
java -version
echo $JAVA_HOME
```

After the setup is complete, we can go ahead and run Elasticsearch. You can find the binaries at www.elastic.co/downloads.

Installing Elasticsearch using a TAR file

First, we will download Elasticsearch 6.1.3.tar, as shown in the following code block:

```
curl -L -O
https://artifacts.elastic.co/downloads/elasticsearch/elasticsearch-6.1.3.tar.gz
```

Then, extract it as follows:

```
tar -xvf elasticsearch-6.1.3.tar.gz
```

You will then see that a bunch of files and folders have been created. We can now proceed to the bin directory, as follows:

```
cd elasticsearch-6.1.3/bin
```

We are now ready to start our node and a single cluster:

```
./elasticsearch
```

Installing Elasticsearch with Homebrew

You can also install Elasticsearch on macOS through Homebrew, as follows:

```
brew install elasticsearch
```

Installing Elasticsearch with MSI Windows Installer

Windows users are recommended to use the MSI Installer package. This package includes a **graphical user interface (GUI)** that guides the users through the installation process.

First, download the Elasticsearch 6.1.3 MSI from `https://artifacts.elastic.co/downloads/elasticsearch/elasticsearch-6.1.3.msi`.

Launch the GUI by double-clicking on the downloaded file. On the first screen, select the deployment directories:

Installing Elasticsearch with the Debian package

On Debian, before you can proceed with the installation process, you may need to install the `apt-transport-https` package first:

```
sudo apt-get install apt-transport-https
```

Save the repository definition to `/etc/apt/sources.list.d/elastic-6.x.list`:

```
echo "deb https://artifacts.elastic.co/packages/6.x/apt stable main" | sudo
tee -a /etc/apt/sources.list.d/elastic-6.x.list
```

You can install the `elasticsearch` Debian package with the following code:

```
sudo apt-get update && sudo apt-get install elasticsearch
```

Installing Elasticsearch with the RPM package

Download and install the public signing key:

```
rpm --import https://artifacts.elastic.co/GPG-KEY-elasticsearch
```

Create a file named `elasticsearch.repo` in the `/etc/yum.repos.d/` directory for Red Hat-based distributions or in the `/etc/zypp/repos.d/` directory for openSUSE-based distributions, containing the following code:

```
[elasticsearch-6.x]
```

```
name=Elasticsearch repository for 6.x packages
baseurl=https://artifacts.elastic.co/packages/6.x/yum
gpgcheck=1
gpgkey=https://artifacts.elastic.co/GPG-KEY-elasticsearch
enabled=1
autorefresh=1
type=rpm-md
```

Your repository is now ready for use. You can now install Elasticsearch with one of the following commands:

You can use `yum` on CentOS and older Red Hat-based distributions:

```
sudo yum install elasticsearch
```

You can use `dnf` on Fedora and other newer Red Hat distributions:

```
sudo dnf install elasticsearch
```

You can use `zypper` on openSUSE-based distributions:

```
sudo zypper install elasticsearch
```

Elasticsearch can be started and stopped using the `service` command:

```
sudo -i service elasticsearch start
sudo -i service elasticsearch stop
```

Logstash

Logstash requires at least Java 8. Before you go ahead with the installation of Logstash, please check the version of Java in your system by running the following command:

```
java -version
echo $JAVA_HOME
```

Using apt package repositories

Download and install the public signing key:

```
wget -qO - https://artifacts.elastic.co/GPG-KEY-elasticsearch | sudo apt-
key add -
```

You may need to install the `apt-transport-https` package on Debian before proceeding, as follows:

```
sudo apt-get install apt-transport-https
```

Save the repository definition to `/etc/apt/sources.list.d/elastic-6.x.list`, as follows:

```
echo "deb https://artifacts.elastic.co/packages/6.x/apt stable main" | sudo
tee -a /etc/apt/sources.list.d/elastic-6.x.list
```

Run `sudo apt-get update` and the repository will be ready for use. You can install it using the following code:

```
sudo apt-get update && sudo apt-get install logstash
```

Using yum package repositories

Download and install the public signing key:

```
rpm --import https://artifacts.elastic.co/GPG-KEY-elasticsearch
```

Add the following in your `/etc/yum.repos.d/` directory in a file with a `.repo` suffix (for example, `logstash.repo`):

```
[logstash-6.x]
 name=Elastic repository for 6.x packages
 baseurl=https://artifacts.elastic.co/packages/6.x/yum
 gpgcheck=1
 gpgkey=https://artifacts.elastic.co/GPG-KEY-elasticsearch
 enabled=1
 autorefresh=1
 type=rpm-md
```

Your repository is now ready for use. You can install it using the following code:

```
sudo yum install logstash
```

Kibana

Starting with version 6.0.0, Kibana only supports 64-bit operating systems.

Installing Kibana using .tar.gz

The Linux archive for Kibana v6.1.3 can be downloaded and installed as follows:

```
wget
https://artifacts.elastic.co/downloads/kibana/kibana-6.1.3-linux-x86_64.tar
.gz
```

Compare the SHA produced by sha1sum or shasum with the published SHA:

```
sha1sum kibana-6.1.3-linux-x86_64.tar.gz
tar -xzf kibana-6.1.3-linux-x86_64.tar.gz
```

This directory is known as $KIBANA_HOME:

```
cd kibana-6.1.3-linux-x86_64/
```

Installing Kibana using the Debian package

Download and install the public signing key:

```
wget -qO - https://artifacts.elastic.co/GPG-KEY-elasticsearch | sudo apt-
key add -
```

You may need to install the apt-transport-https package on Debian before proceeding:

```
sudo apt-get install apt-transport-https
```

Save the repository definition to /etc/apt/sources.list.d/elastic-6.x.list:

```
echo "deb https://artifacts.elastic.co/packages/6.x/apt stable main" | sudo
tee -a /etc/apt/sources.list.d/elastic-6.x.list
```

You can install the Kibana Debian package with the following:

```
sudo apt-get update && sudo apt-get install kibana
```

Installing Kibana using rpm

Download and install the public signing key, as follows:

```
rpm --import https://artifacts.elastic.co/GPG-KEY-elasticsearch
```

Create a file named `kibana.repo` in the `/etc/yum.repos.d/` directory for Red Hat-based distributions, or in the `/etc/zypp/repos.d/` directory for openSUSE-based distributions, containing the following code:

```
[kibana-6.x]
 name=Kibana repository for 6.x packages
 baseurl=https://artifacts.elastic.co/packages/6.x/yum
 gpgcheck=1
 gpgkey=https://artifacts.elastic.co/GPG-KEY-elasticsearch
 enabled=1
 autorefresh=1
 type=rpm-md
```

Your repository is now ready for use. You can now install Kibana with one of the following commands:

- You can use `yum` on CentOS and older Red Hat-based distributions:

```
sudo yum install kibana
```

- You can use `dnf` on Fedora and other newer Red Hat distributions:

```
sudo dnf install kibana
```

- You can use `zypper` on openSUSE-based distributions:

```
sudo zypper install kibana
```

Installing Kibana on Windows

Download the `.zip` Windows archive for Kibana v6.1.3 from `https://artifacts.elastic.co/downloads/kibana/kibana-6.1.3-windows-x86_64.zip`.

Unzipping it will create a folder named `kibana-6.1.3-windows-x86_64`, which we will refer to as $KIBANA_HOME. In your Terminal, CD to the $KIBANA_HOME directory; for instance:

```
CD c:\kibana-6.1.3-windows-x86_64
```

Kibana can be started from the command line as follows:

```
.\bin\kibana
```

Beats

After installing and configuring the ELK Stack, you need to install and configure your Beats.

Each Beat is a separately installable product. To get up and running quickly with a Beat, see the getting started information for your Beat:

- **Packetbeat**
- **Metricbeat**
- **Filebeat**
- **Winlogbeat**
- **Heartbeat**

Packetbeat

The value of a network packet analytics system such as **Packetbeat** can be best understood by trying it on your traffic.

To download and install Packetbeat, use the commands that work with your system (deb for Debian/Ubuntu, rpm for Red Hat/CentOS/Fedora, macOS for OS X, Docker for any Docker platform, and win for Windows):

- Ubuntu:

```
sudo apt-get install libpcap0.8
curl -L -O
https://artifacts.elastic.co/downloads/beats/packetbeat/packetb
eat-6.2.1-amd64.deb
  sudo dpkg -i packetbeat-6.2.1-amd64.deb
```

- Red Hat:

```
sudo yum install libpcap
  curl -L -O
https://artifacts.elastic.co/downloads/beats/packetbeat/packetb
eat-6.2.1-x86_64.rpm
  sudo rpm -vi packetbeat-6.2.1-x86_64.rpm
```

- macOS:

```
curl -L -O
https://artifacts.elastic.co/downloads/beats/packetbeat/packetbeat-
6.2.1-darwin-x86_64.tar.gz
 tar xzvf packetbeat-6.2.1-darwin-x86_64.tar.gz
```

- Windows:
    1. Download and install `WinPcap` from this page. `WinPcap` is a library that uses a driver to enable packet capturing.
    2. Download the Packetbeat Windows ZIP file from the downloads page.
    3. Extract the contents of the ZIP file into `C:\Program Files`.
    4. Rename the `packetbeat-<version>-windows` directory to `Packetbeat`.
    5. Open a PowerShell prompt as an administrator (right-click the PowerShell icon and select **Run as administrator**). If you are running Windows XP, you may need to download and install PowerShell.
    6. From the PowerShell prompt, run the following commands to install `Packetbeat` as a Windows service:

```
PS > cd 'C:\Program Files\Packetbeat'
PS C:\Program Files\Packetbeat> .\install-service-
packetbeat.ps1
```

Before starting `Packetbeat`, you should look at the configuration options in the configuration file; for example, `C:\Program Files\Packetbeat\packetbeat.yml` or `/etc/packetbeat/packetbeat.yml`.

Metricbeat

Metricbeat should be installed as close as possible to the service that needs to be monitored. For example, if there are four servers running MySQL, it's strongly recommended that you run Metricbeat on each service. This gives Metricbeat access to your service from localhost and in turn does not cause any additional network traffic or prevent Metricbeat from collecting metrics when there are network problems. Metrics from multiple Metricbeat instances will be combined on the Elasticsearch server.

To download and install Metricbeat, use the commands that work with your system (`deb` for Debian/Ubuntu, `rpm` for Red Hat/CentOS/Fedora, macOS for OS X, Docker for any Docker platform, and `win` for Windows), as follows:

- Ubuntu:

```
curl -L -O
https://artifacts.elastic.co/downloads/beats/metricbeat/metricb
eat-6.2.1-amd64.deb
 sudo dpkg -i metricbeat-6.2.1-amd64.deb
```

- Red Hat:

```
curl -L -O
https://artifacts.elastic.co/downloads/beats/metricbeat/metricb
eat-6.2.1-x86_64.rpm
 sudo rpm -vi metricbeat-6.2.1-x86_64.rpm
```

- macOS:

```
curl -L -O
https://artifacts.elastic.co/downloads/beats/metricbeat/metricb
eat-6.2.1-darwin-x86_64.tar.gz
 tar xzvf metricbeat-6.2.1-darwin-x86_64.tar.gz
```

- Windows:
    1. Download the Metricbeat Windows ZIP file from the downloads page.
    2. Extract the contents of the ZIP file into `C:\Program Files`.
    3. Rename the `metricbeat-<version>-windows` directory to `Metricbeat`.
    4. Open a PowerShell prompt as an administrator (right-click the PowerShell icon and select **Run as administrator**). If you are running Windows XP, you may need to download and install PowerShell.
    5. From the PowerShell prompt, run the following commands to install `Metricbeat` as a Windows service:

    ```
    PS > cd 'C:\Program Files\Metricbeat'
    PS C:\Program Files\Metricbeat> .\install-service-
    metricbeat.ps1
    ```

Before starting `Metricbeat`, you should look at the configuration options in the configuration file; for example, `C:\Program Files\Metricbeat\metricbeat.yml`.

Filebeat

To download and install Filebeat, use the commands that work with your system (`deb` for Debian/Ubuntu, `rpm` for Red Hat/CentOS/Fedora, macOS for OS X, Docker for any Docker platform, and `win` for Windows), as follows:

- Ubuntu:

```
curl -L -O
https://artifacts.elastic.co/downloads/beats/filebeat/filebeat-
6.2.1-amd64.deb
  sudo dpkg -i filebeat-6.2.1-amd64.deb
```

- Red Hat:

```
curl -L -O
https://artifacts.elastic.co/downloads/beats/filebeat/filebeat-
6.2.1-x86_64.rpm
  sudo rpm -vi filebeat-6.2.1-x86_64.rpm
```

- macOS:

```
curl -L -O
https://artifacts.elastic.co/downloads/beats/filebeat/filebeat-
6.2.1-darwin-x86_64.tar.gz
  tar xzvf filebeat-6.2.1-darwin-x86_64.tar.gz
```

- Windows:
    1. Download the Filebeat Windows ZIP file from the downloads page.
    2. Extract the contents of the ZIP file into `C:\Program Files`.
    3. Rename the `filebeat-<version>-windows` directory to `Filebeat`.
    4. Open a PowerShell prompt as an administrator (right-click the PowerShell icon and select **Run as administrator**). If you are running Windows XP, you may need to download and install PowerShell.
    5. From the PowerShell prompt, run the following commands to install Filebeat as a Windows service:

```
PS > cd 'C:\Program Files\Filebeat'
PS C:\Program Files\Filebeat> .\install-service-
filebeat.ps1
```

Winlogbeat

In order to install Winlogbeat, we need to follow these steps:

1. Download the Winlogbeat ZIP file from the downloads page.
2. Extract the contents into C:\Program Files.
3. Rename the winlogbeat-<version> directory to Winlogbeat.
4. Open a PowerShell prompt as an administrator (right-click on the PowerShell icon and select **Run as administrator**). If you are running Windows XP, you may need to download and install PowerShell.
5. From the PowerShell prompt, run the following commands to install the service:

```
PS C:\Users\Administrator> cd 'C:\Program Files\Winlogbeat'
PS C:\Program Files\Winlogbeat> .\install-service-
winlogbeat.ps1
```

 Security warning: Only run scripts that you trust. Although scripts from the internet can be useful, they can potentially harm your computer. If you trust the script, use Unblock-File to allow the script to run without this warning message:

```
Do you want to run
 C:\Program Files\Winlogbeat\install-service-winlogbeat.ps1?
 [D] Do not run [R] Run once [S] Suspend [?] Help (default is "D"): R

Status Name DisplayName
------ ---- -----------
Stopped winlogbeat winlogbeat
```

Before starting winlogbeat, you should look at the configuration options in the configuration file; for example, C:\Program Files\Winlogbeat\winlogbeat.yml. There's also a full example configuration file named winlogbeat.reference.yml.

Heartbeat

Unlike most Beats, which we install on edge nodes, we typically install Heartbeat as part of a monitoring service that runs on a separate machine and possibly even outside of the network where the services that you want to monitor are running.

To download and install Heartbeat, use the commands that work with your system (`deb` for Debian/Ubuntu, `rpm` for Red Hat/CentOS/Fedora, macOS for OS X, Docker for any Docker platform, and `win` for Windows):

- Ubuntu:

```
curl -L -O
https://artifacts.elastic.co/downloads/beats/heartbeat/heartbea
t-6.2.1-amd64.deb
  sudo dpkg -i heartbeat-6.2.1-amd64.deb
```

- Red Hat:

```
curl -L -O
https://artifacts.elastic.co/downloads/beats/heartbeat/heartbea
t-6.2.1-x86_64.rpm
  sudo rpm -vi heartbeat-6.2.1-x86_64.rpm
```

- macOS:

```
curl -L -O
https://artifacts.elastic.co/downloads/beats/heartbeat/heartbea
t-6.2.1-darwin-x86_64.tar.gz
  tar xzvf heartbeat-6.2.1-darwin-x86_64.tar.gz
```

- Windows:
    1. Download the Heartbeat Windows ZIP file from the downloads page.
    2. Extract the contents of the ZIP file into `C:\Program Files`.
    3. Rename the `heartbeat-<version>-windows` directory to `Heartbeat`.
    4. Open a PowerShell prompt as an administrator (right-click the PowerShell icon and select **Run as administrator**). If you are running Windows XP, you may need to download and install PowerShell.
    5. From the PowerShell prompt, run the following commands to install Heartbeat as a Windows service:

```
PS > cd 'C:\Program Files\Heartbeat'
PS C:\Program Files\Heartbeat> .\install-service-
heartbeat.ps1
```

Before starting Heartbeat, you should look at the configuration options in the configuration file; for example, `C:\Program Files\Heartbeat\heartbeat.yml` or `/etc/heartbeat/heartbeat.yml`.

ELK use cases

ELK Stack has many different use cases, but here we are only going to discuss some of them.

Log management

In any large organization, there will be different servers with different sets of applications. So, in this case, we need to have different teams for different applications whose task is to explore the log files for debugging any issue. However, this is not an easy task, as the format of logs is never user friendly. Here, I am talking about a single application, but what will happen if we ask the team to monitor all different applications that are built using different technologies and their log format is very different from other applications? The answer is very simple: the team has to dig through all the logs from the different servers and then they will spend days and nights to find the issue.

ELK Stack is very useful for these situations, and we can solve this problem easily. First of all, we need to set up a central Elasticsearch cluster for collecting all different logs. Now, we need to configure Logstash as per the application log so that we can transform different log formats that we are getting from different application servers. Logstash will output this data into Elasticsearch for storage so that we can explore, search, and update the data. Finally, Kibana can be used to display graphical dashboards on top of Elasticsearch.

Using this setup, anyone can get complete control of all logs coming from different sources. We can use Kibana to alert us to any issues in the log file so that the user can get the issue without doing any data drill downs.

Many organizations are using ELK for their log management as this is an open source software that can be built easily to monitor different type of logs on a single screen. Not only can we monitor all of our logs in a single screen, but we can also get alerts if something went wrong in the logs.

Security monitoring and alerting

Security monitoring and alerting is a very important use case of ELK Stack as application security is a vital part, and it costs if there are any security breaches in the application since security breaches are becoming more common, and most importantly, more targeted. Although enterprises are regularly trying to improve their security measures, hackers are successful in penetrating the security layers. Therefore, it is very much required for any enterprise to detect the presence of security attacks on their server, and not only detect but also alert them so that they can take immediate actions to mitigate their losses. Using ELK Stack, we can monitor various things, such as unusual server requests and any suspicious traffic. We can gather security-related log information that can be monitored by security teams to check any alerts to the system.

This way, security teams can prevent the enterprise from attackers who have gone unnoticed for a long time. ELK Stack provides a way through which we can gain an insight and make the attacker's life more difficult. These logs can also be very useful for after-attack analysis; for example, for finding out the time of the attack and the method of attack used. We can understand the activities the attacker performed to attack, and this information can provide us with a way to strengthen that loophole easily. In this way, ELK Stack is useful for both before attack prevention and after attack healing and prevention.

Web scraping

In ELK Stack, we have different tools to grab data from remote servers. In traditional **Relational Database Management System (RDBMS)**, it is quite difficult to save these types of data because they are not structured, so either we have to manually clean the data or leave some part of it in order to save it in the table schema. In the case of Elasticsearch, the schemaless behavior gives us the leverage to push any data from any source. It not only holds that data but also provides us with a feature to search and play with it. An example of web scraping using ELK Stack is a Twitter to Elasticsearch connector, which allows us to set up hashtags from Twitter and grab all the tweets that used those hashtags. After grabbing those hashtags, we can search, visualize, and analyze them in Kibana.

E-commerce search solutions

Many of the top e-commerce websites, such as eBay's, are using Elasticsearch for their product search pages. The main reason behind this is the ability of Elasticsearch in full-text searching, building filters, facets, aggregations, fast response time, and the ease it provides in collecting analytic information. Users can easily drill down to get the product set, from where they can easily select the product they want. This is just one side of the picture, through which we are improving the user's experience. On the other side, we can use the same data and by using Kibana, we can monitor the trends, analyze the data, and much more.

There is a big competition going on among e-commerce companies to attract more and more customers. Being able to understand the shopping behavior of their customers is a very important feature, as it leverages e-commerce companies to target users with products that they had liked or will like. This is business intelligence, and using ELK Stack, they can achieve it.

Full text search

ELK Stack's core competency is its full text search feature. It is powerful and flexible, and it provides various features such as fuzzy search, conditional searching, and natural language searching. So, as per our requirements, we can decide which type of searching is required. We can use ELK Stack's full text search capabilities for product searching, autocomplete features, searching text in emails, and so on.

Visualizing data

Kibana is an easy-to-use visualization tool that provides us with a rich feature set to create beautiful charts (such as pie charts, bar charts, and stack charts), histograms, geo maps, word tags, data tables, and so on. Visualizing data is always beneficial for any organization as it helps top management to make decisions with ease. We can also easily track any unusual trends and find any outliers in data without digging into the data. We can create dashboards for any existing web-based application as well by simply pushing the application data into Elasticsearch and then use Kibana to create beautiful dashboards. This way, we can plug in an additional dimension into the application and start monitoring it without putting any additional load on the application.

Summary

In this chapter, we covered the basics of ELK Stack and their characteristics. We explained how we can use Beats to send logs data, file data, and system metrics to Logstash or Elasticsearch and that Logstash can be configured as a pipeline to modify the data format and then send the output to Elasticsearch. Elasticsearch is a search engine built on top of Lucene. It can store data and provide functionality to do full text searching on data. Kibana can be configured to read Elasticsearch data and create visualizations and dashboards. We can embed these dashboards on existing web pages, which can then be used for decision-making.

Then, we discussed different use cases of ELK Stack. The first one we mentioned was log management, which is the primary use case of ELK Stack and which made it famous. In log management, we can capture logs from different servers/sources and dump them in a central Elasticsearch cluster after modifying it through Logstash. Kibana is used to create meaningful graphical visualization and dashboards by reading the Elasticsearch data. Finally, we discussed security monitoring and alerting, where ELK Stack can be quite helpful. Security is a very important aspect of any software, and often it is the most neglected part of development and monitoring. Using ELK Stack, we can observe any security threat.

.

2
Setting Up and Customizing the Kibana Dashboard

In this chapter, you will learn how to set up and customize Kibana visualizations by adding titles, resizing panels, changing colors and opacity, modifying the legends, and so on. This will also explain how we can embed the dashboard on our existing application. By tweaking these features, we can create more meaningful and impactful dashboards.

Before creating the visualizations, we need to push data into the Elasticsearch index, and using that index, we can create visualizations and dashboards.

In this chapter, we will cover the following topics:

- **Setting up the stage**: Here, we will cover all the configurations required to get the required data in place in order to use it for dashboard creation
- **Creating dashboard**: Here, we will cover the practical aspect of dashboard creation by creating different types of visualizations in Kibana and then integrate them to create the dashboard

Setting up the stage

In the previous chapter, we discussed the basics of Elastic Stack and its installation, but after the installation, we need to understand the process of creating different visualizations in Kibana. So, I am going to create our first demonstration for working with Kibana in which I will cover the complete flow through which you will be able to understand how Kibana can read log data and create beautiful dashboards from bulky, unorganized log files. For this demonstration, I am going to use Apache log data, and to get that data, we will follow these steps:

1. Configure Logstash to fetch data from the Apache log file
2. Output the log data into Elasticsearch

3. Configure Kibana to read the Elasticsearch index
4. Create demo visualizations with Apache log data

Configuring Logstash to fetch data from the Apache log file

The Apache web server is widely used for serving different websites worldwide, and by monitoring this data, we can solve different issues in our web applications. However, if we try to monitor it by reading Apache log files, it will be quite difficult to get the exact issue, as we need to read the log file line by line. For these types of situations, Kibana is a very handy tool that can solve this problem if we can feed it with this data. Here, you are going to learn about the process of feeding data in Kibana. So, first of all, we need to configure Logstash to read Apache log files.

We have to create the Logstash configuration file (`logs-apache.conf`) under the `/etc/logstash/conf.d/` location. In the Logstash configuration file, there are three sections: input, filter, and output. For now, we can use the input and output sections.

For Logstash input, we need to pass the Apache log file location and other details, such as the file path and file type. So here, in our example, we need to pass the file path as `/var/log/apache2/access.log` and the file type as `apache-access`. For the output section, we need to provide details such as Elasticsearch `hosts`, `index`, and `document_type`, as shown in the following screenshot:

```
user@KELLGGNLPTP0129: ~
input {
    file {
        path => "/var/log/apache2/access.log"
        type => "apache-access"
    }
}

output {
    elasticsearch {
        hosts => "http://127.0.0.1:9200"
        index => "logs_apache"
        document_type => "logs"
    }
}
```

In this way, we can configure Logstash to take inputs from Apache log files and output the data to the Elasticsearch server. In this setup, we are not going to configure the filter option, but we will cover that at a later stage.

Outputting the log data into Elasticsearch

The next step is going to be to execute the configuration so that Logstash can start reading logs from the Apache log file. In order to execute the Logstash configuration file, we need to run the following command:

```
bin/logstash -f /etc/logstash/conf.d/logs-apache.conf
```

The following screen is showing us the result after executing the preceding command. Once the command is executed successfully, we will get a message, such as Successfully started Logstash API endpoint {:port=>9600}:

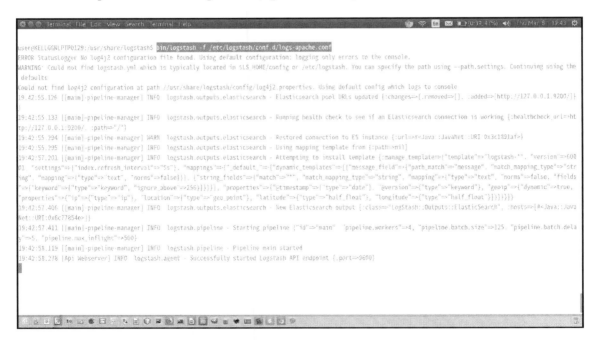

When we execute the Logstash configuration, it connects to the output source, which in this case is Elasticsearch. This starts the pipeline so that it reads the data from the log file and puts it into Elasticsearch.

To test this setup, we need to open the browser so that we can open some `localhost` websites that are served through the Apache server, as this will provide some data for writing to the Apache log file. To test whether the logs have been pushed to Elasticsearch, we can open the Elasticsearch index and check the logs:

```
http://localhost:9200/logs_apache/_search?pretty
```

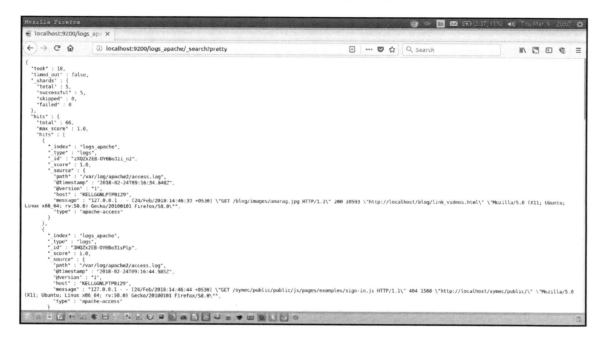

In the preceding screenshot, we can see that Logstash is reading the Apache logs and pushing them to the Elasticsearch server.

Configuring Kibana to read the Elasticsearch index

As the Elasticsearch server index has been created and the Apache logs are getting pushed to it, our next task is to configure Kibana to read Elasticsearch index data. We need to open Kibana using its default port number: `http://localhost:5601`.

This will load the default page of Kibana. Now, we need to click on **Management** from the left menu, which will open the following screen:

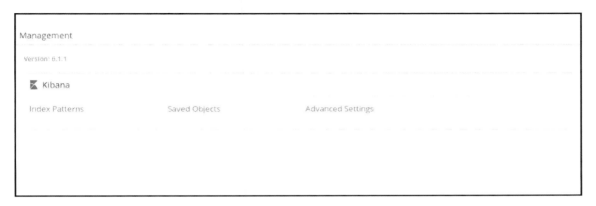

In the previous screenshot, we have three options: **Index Patterns**, **Saved Objects**, and **Advanced Settings**. For setting up a new index, we need to click on **Index Patterns**, which will open the following screen:

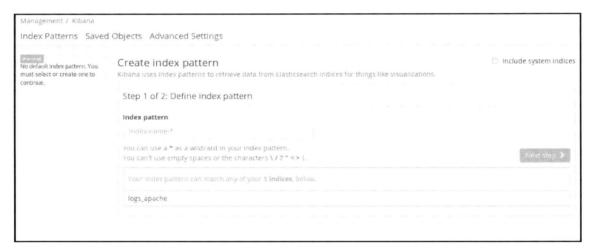

In the **Create index pattern** screen, there are two steps. In step one, we need to provide the index pattern in the given textbox:

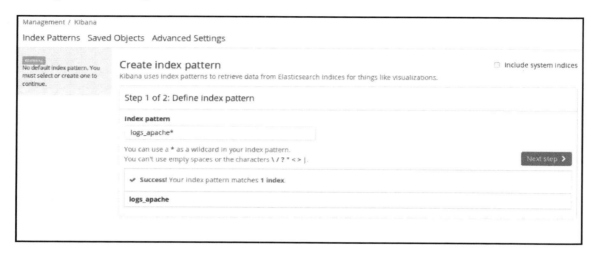

This textbox accepts a wildcard so that we can provide initial characters of the Elasticsearch index. This will automatically pick up the name by providing the dropdown and show the message Success Your index pattern matches 1 index. This will show you the count of indexes that are matched with given wildcard characters. Now, from the dropdown, we can select the index and click on the **Next step** button, which will open the following screen:

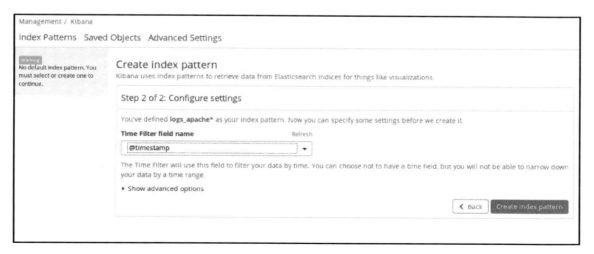

For the second step of creating an index pattern, here, we need to configure the settings by providing the time filter field name. This dropdown automatically picks all date fields from the Elasticsearch index. We need to select the field to use time filters. Now, we have to click on the **Create index pattern** button, which will open the following screen:

This is the final screen for the Elasticsearch index setup in Kibana. At the top, we can see the index name, and below that, the index fields with **type** and additional details, such as whether they are **searchable**, **aggregatable**, and **excluded**, with an edit icon to modify parts of these details.

We also have the option to delete the index from Kibana using the delete icon on the top-right section of the screen. We can also click on the refresh icon to refresh the index. We can refresh the index in Kibana if any changes have been done in Elasticsearch for the index. Apart from delete and refresh, there is a star icon, which can be used to make the index a default index. Whenever we open Kibana, the default index is loaded automatically.

In the index field display, we have the option to filter the fields on the basis of field types. By default, it is set on all field types, which we can change as there are different options, such as `date`, `string`, `number`, and `_source`.

In the **Except fields** tab, we have two more tabs: scripted fields and source filters. Scripted fields are computed from the data on the fly, and we can set them by clicking on the **Add scripted field** button. The **Source filter** tab is used to filter the field from search, as sometimes we may want to exclude certain fields, and at that time, we can use this option. I will cover these options in detail in later chapters.

So, we have covered how to set up Logstash to read Apache logs and output them in the Elasticsearch index. Then, we set up Kibana to read the index and display its data type with additional details.

Creating demo visualizations with Apache log data

Now that we have our Elasticsearch index configured in Kibana, we can verify it by clicking on the **Discover** tab on the left menu. By default, it shows data from the last 15 minutes, which we can change by clicking on the top-right link for duration. We can see our data with the `time` and `_source` columns. This view can be customized by adding the available fields from the left menu.

Now, I will create a very simple visualization option in order to explain the customization options. Later, I will explain these in detail. To create a visualization, we need to click on the **Visualize** link from the left menu, which will open the following screen:

This will show us all of the visualizations that we have created along with a button named **Create a visualization** for creating a new visualization. As we have not created any visualizations yet, there is only the button for creating visualizations. So, now, we are going to create our first visualization, and for that we need to click on the **Create a visualization** button, which will open the following screen:

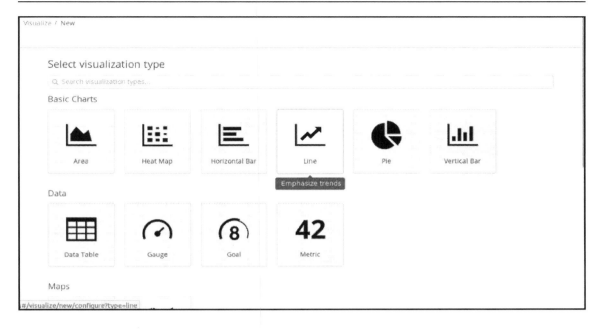

This screen is used for selecting visualization options. There are five categories, and these are **Basic Charts**, **Data**, **Maps**, **Time series**, and **Other**. Under **Basic Charts**, we have **Area**, **Heat Map**, **Horizontal Bar**, **Vertical Bar**, **Line**, and **Pie** charts. Under **Data**, we have **Data Table**, **Gauge**, **Goal**, and **Metric** options. Under **Maps**, we have coordinates and **Region Map**, whereas under **Time Series**, we have **Timelion** and the **Visual Builder**. Finally, under **Other**, we have controls, markdown, and tag cloud options available. We will cover these in later chapters, so for now, I will create a basic metric visualization under the data option. For that, we need to click on the **Metric** link, which will open the following screen:

In the previous screen, we can see two options: one from a new search and another from a saved search. For now, we will click on the index name from the first option, which will open the following screen:

Here, we can see the preview of metrics data and on the left part of the window, we have **Data** and **Options**. Here, we are going to create a very simple metric to count the number of log entries. For creating the count metrics, we need to click on the **Metrics** link from the left side of the window, which will open the following screen:

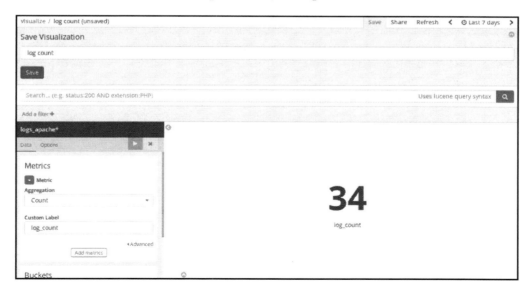

In this screen, from the **Aggregation** dropdown, we have to select the **Count** option, and in the custom label, we need to provide the label of the metrics display. Now, our metrics data display is ready, which we need to save in order to use it further. We need to provide the name of the visualization and click on the **Save** button, which will save the visualization. Now, we can verify it by clicking on the visualization link from the left menu, which will open the following screen:

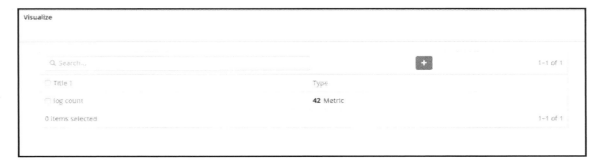

Here, we can see the link for the metrics data visualization that we have just created with a plus button so that we can add more visualizations if we desire. For now, I have also created a test bar chart visualization named ANC_data, which I will use with the metrics data visualization to create the dashboard.

Creating the dashboard

Now that we have created the visualizations, we can create the dashboard using these visualizations. To create the dashboard, we need to click on the **Dashboard** link from the left menu, which will open the following screen:

This will show an empty screen with a **Create a dashboard** button, since we haven't created any dashboards yet. When we create dashboards, this screen will list the name and links of those dashboard along with a create dashboard link. Now we need to click on the **Create a dashboard** button, which will open the following screen:

This screen shows an empty page with a message that states, **This dashboard is empty. Let's fill it up!** To fill the visualizations, we need to click on the **Add** link from the top-right corner of the page. This will open the following screen:

This screen shows the list of visualizations that we have already created. Now we can pick the visualizations by clicking on them. For example, when I click on the `log count` visualization link, it adds the data metrics visualization of the log entries count to the dashboard, as seen in the following screenshot:

The dashboard is quite empty with a single visualization, so I am going to add the other visualization, a bar chart, by clicking on another visualization. As we can see in the following screenshot, both visualizations are on the dashboard:

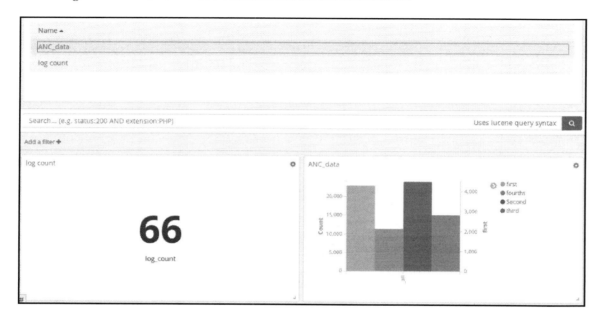

We can see that there are two visualizations in our dashboard: one is data metrics and the other is a bar chart. We have the option to add as many visualizations as we want into our dashboard, and these visualizations can be of any type. So, now, we can save the dashboard so that we can use it later on. For that, we need to click on the **Save** button on the top-right corner, which will open the following screen:

For saving the dashboard, we have two text boxes: one for the dashboard title and the other for the description. We can fill in these details, and click on the **Save** button to save the dashboard. After saving the dashboard, we can visualize it in the following screen:

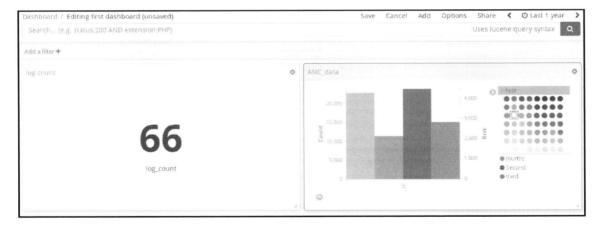

After creating the dashboard, we can search, filter, or embed it into any existing website. There are lot of things we can do using the dashboard, which I will be covering in later chapters. For now, though, let's customize the dashboard.

Customizing the dashboard

We have just created the dashboard, so now you will learn how to customize it. From the **Dashboard customization** option, we can do the following things:

- Edit the visualization
- Change the title by customizing the panel
- Move the visualization to full screen
- Delete the visualization from the dashboard
- Change the colors of the visualization
- Drag and drop the visualization to a desired location on the dashboard
- Resize the visualization as per our requirements
- Export CSV data from the visualization
- Get an Elasticsearch request, response, and statistics

Editing the visualization

For editing the visualization, we need to click on the **Edit** link on the top-right corner of the page. This provides us with the option to edit the visualization. Now, we will be able to see the settings icon on the top-right corner of each visualization. By clicking on the settings icon, we will get the following screen:

In the previous screen, we are trying to edit the data metrics visualization, so after clicking on the settings icon, we need to click on the **Edit visualization** link. This will open the edit visualization screen with data metrics. We can edit the visualization there and save it. After this, we can open the dashboard and refresh it to see the changes.

Changing the title by customizing the panel

If we want to change the title of the visualization, we can do so by clicking on the settings icon and then on **Customize panel**. This will open the following screen:

In the previous screen, we can change the title in the panel title textbox and then click anywhere outside the box to make it effective on the visualization panel. We can reset this change by clicking on the **Reset title** link under the **Customize panel** link. This will restore the old test, which we did during the creation of the visualization.

Moving the visualization to full screen

Sometimes, it is difficult to view all details of a visualization in a small box and so we want to maximize it to see the details. We can do this by clicking on the settings icon and then on the full screen icon to move it to full screen. On the live dashboard display, this can be done by clicking on the full screen icon on the top-right corner of the visualization panel.

Deleting the visualization from the dashboard

We can delete a visualization from the dashboard by clicking on the settings icon and then on **Delete** from the dashboard link. This will only delete the visualization from the dashboard. We can find the deleted visualizations under the **Visualize** tab so that we can add it to the dashboard again if we like.

Changing the colors of the visualization

When we create any graphical visualization, such as charts, it will have different colors with legends. If we want to change the legend colors, we can do so by clicking on the **Color of legend** option. For example, in the following screen, we want to change the green color. To do this, we can click on the legend. This will open the color palette so that we can choose a color:

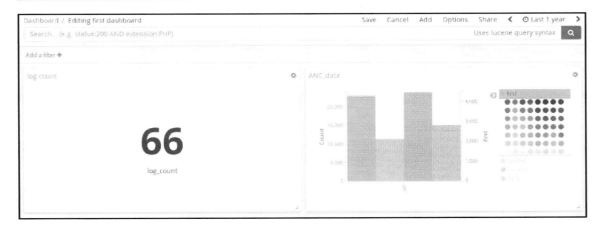

In the previous screen, we want to change the green color, so from the color palette, we can click the yellow color to change the green bar to a yellow bar:

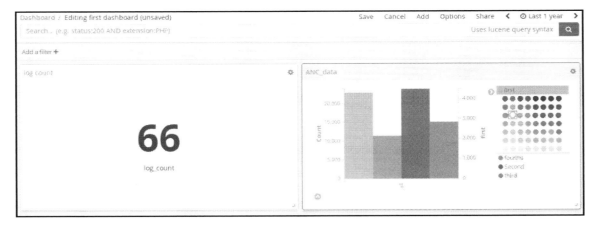

This way, we can change the colors of visualizations.

Dragging and dropping visualizations on a desired location on the dashboard

When using the dashboard, we want to show the key performance indicators at the top. To do this, we have to put the cursor on the visualization header and drag and drop it to the desired location:

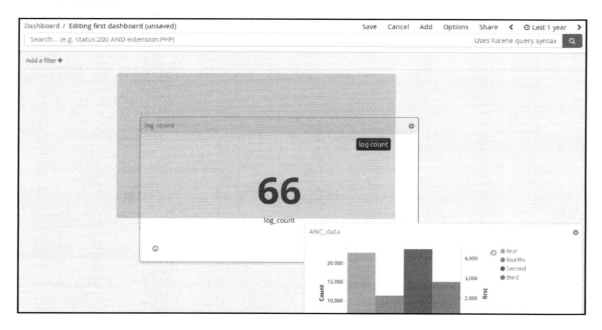

Resizing the visualization as per our requirements

We can resize the visualization by putting the cursor on the bottom-right corner of the panel and dragging and dropping it as per our requirements. This way, we can minimize the smaller visualization and maximize the bigger visualization:

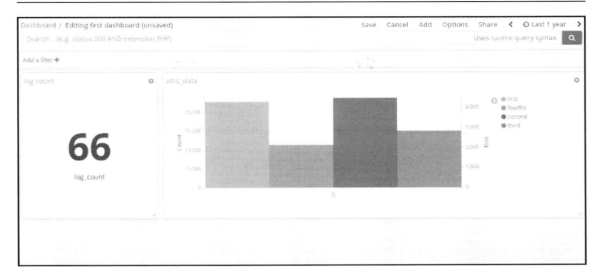

Exporting CSV data from the visualization

We can export CSV data in raw and formatted ways from each visualization. For this, we need to click on the up icon on the bottom-left corner of each visualization, which will open the following screen:

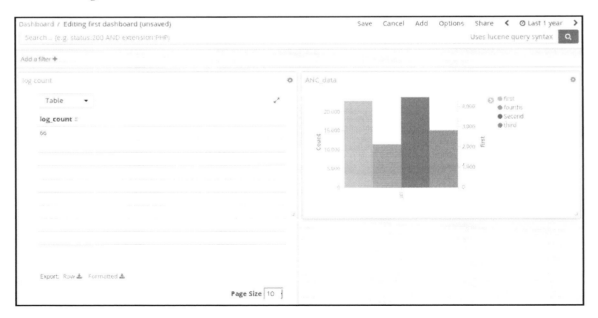

In this screen, we can click on the **Raw** or **Formatted** links, which will download the file. We can do this for any visualization. This is a very handy and useful option so that we can get tabular data from any graphical visualization.

Getting the Elasticsearch request, response, and statistics

For every visualization on the dashboard, we can get the Elasticsearch request, response, and statistics. To get these details, we need to click on the up icon on the bottom-left corner, and from the top dropdown, select **Request** to get the Elasticsearch request query:

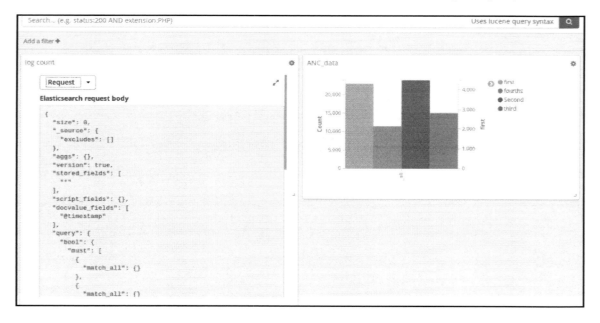

The previous screen shows us that the Elasticsearch query fired to get the visualization data. We can create all of these visualizations in the Kibana UI, but in the background, Kibana constructs the Elasticsearch query to get these results. So, from here, we can see the actual Elasticsearch request that was constructed from Kibana.

To get the Elasticsearch response, we need to select **Response** from the dropdown:

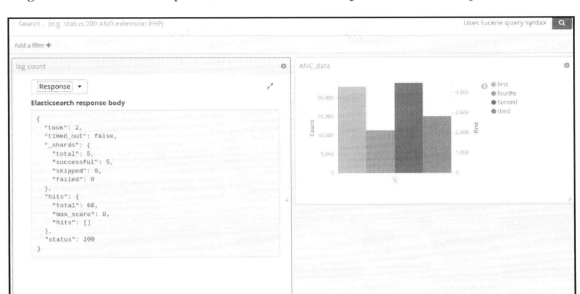

In the previous screen, we can see the response from Elasticsearch that was generated after executing the request. It shows us the status, total records, success and failure count, the total number of shards, and so on.

To get the statistics, we need to select **Statistics** from the dropdown:

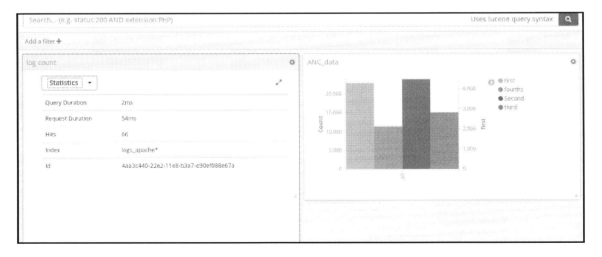

In the previous statistics screen, we can get details such as query duration, request duration, hits, and index.

Summary

In this chapter, you learned how to import Apache logs and store them in Elasticsearch by creating and executing Logstash configuration files. After moving the Apache logs into the Elasticsearch index, we verified this by listing the index using a web browser. Then, we configured Kibana to import Elasticsearch indexes and verified the same using the **Discover** tab of Kibana.

Once our log data was in place, we created a visualization using the data metrics option. Then, we created a dashboard using the visualization. After creating the dashboard, you learned to customize it using drag and drop, resizing, deleting, color options, title edit, and so on. This has given us an overall picture on how to use Kibana dashboards, which is quite superficial. You will learn more about the dashboards in the upcoming chapters.

In the next chapter, we will cover the Discover option of Kibana to explore our data. We will cover what Kibana Discover is all about and its features. We will access all documents of every index as long as they are matching with the selected index pattern. We will cover how to search, filter, and view a document's data, and how we can select the desired fields of documents. We will see the number of documents that match with a given search query. Later in the chapter, we will see how, by applying the time filter, we can get the distribution of documents over time using the histogram that is displayed on top of the page.

Exploring Your Data 3

In the last chapter, we learned how to create a dashboard from Apache log files for which we have made a complete ELK Stack. Logstash was used to take an Apache log as input and then output the log data into an Elasticsearch server. We used Elasticsearch to save that log data in an index. Finally, we used Kibana to use the Elasticsearch index in order to create a dashboard after creating visualizations. This was just a brief introduction to understanding the complete ecosystem.

In this chapter, we will deep dive to understand how we can use the Discover option of Kibana to explore our data. We can only create our visualization after exploring and understanding our data.

In this chapter, we will be covering the following topics:

- Kibana Discover and its features
- Discovering our data using Kibana Discover:
    - Configuring Packetbeat to push packet data into Elasticsearch
    - Exploring Kibana Discover to access packet data
    - Configuring Kibana to read the Elasticsearch index with packet logs

Kibana Discover

In Kibana, we have a Discover link on the left-hand side menu to discover our data. After configuring the Elasticsearch index, we can click on the **Discover** link, which will open the following screen:

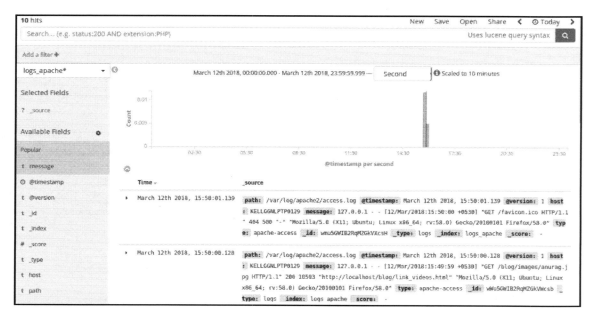

In the preceding screen, we can see our data in tabular format with **Time** and **_source**. **Time** shows the exact date and time of data insertion in Elasticsearch and **_source** shows data in JSON format. In each row of data, we have an icon in front of the date and time to expand the view. When we expand the row, it shows us the following two tabs:

- **Table**: This is used to show the data in tabular format
- **JSON**: This is used to show the data in JSON format

Apart from the tab, there are two buttons, which are as follows:

- **View surrounding documents**: By default, it shows five surrounding documents along with the selected document
- **View single document**: This button opens the selected document only

The following screenshot shows the details of a single document from the index pattern on the **Discover** page:

Apart from these tabs and buttons, we have a search box on top of the page to search any field for this data. On the left side of the page, we have a dropdown to pick the index we want to see. Following on from this is the search box, where we have a link called **Add a filter** to filter the data. If we click on the link, it will open an **Add filter** box with **Filter** and **Label** textboxes to execute the filter on the data. The following screenshot shows the filter screen from where we can apply any filter or can edit an existing filter:

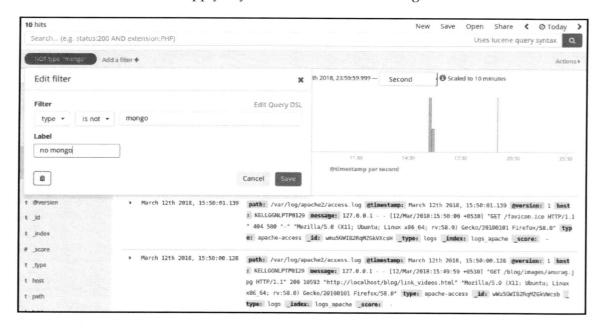

After applying the filter, the data is filtered as per the given filter option. We can also see the red box with the given filter details. We can get different links, such as select or unselect, pin or unpin, and delete filter and edit filter, by hovering over the red box with the filter details. In this box, we have a link called **Edit Query DSL** through which we can convert the filter into an Elasticsearch query and can modify it as per our requirements. The following screenshot shows the Elasticsearch query view of the applied filter:

By clicking on **the Edit Query DSL** option, we can convert the **Filter** textbox window into a Elasticsearch query text-area with the Elasticsearch query for the applied filter. Through this screen, we can modify the Elasticsearch query as per our requirements or we can paste any external query that we had already created outside Kibana.

Apart from these options, we have a histogram at the top of the screen where we can see the timing of the data input:

Through this histogram, we can find out the time when the data is inserted into the Elasticsearch index. This graph is very helpful as it gives us an insight into the data input and how much data is inserted at any given time. We can set the refresh duration of this histogram from a dropdown, which is just on top of the graph. The dropdown has different options, such as auto, milliseconds, seconds, minutes, hours, days, weeks, months, and years. Based on the selected value, this graph is refreshed and we can set this value as per our requirements. On the *x* axis, the graph shows the field with the duration of display; for example, **@timestamp per 30 minutes**. The duration of the data is displayed in front of the dropdown, which is, for example, January 1, 2018, 00:00:00.000 - December 31, 2018, 23:59:59.999. This duration can be changed by clicking on the top right-hand corner link of the duration display and then changing the value from the open box.

Discovering data using Kibana Discover

Data creation is running at a fast pace and the volume of data is increasing multifold. The story is the same in every sector as the evolution of science is providing more and more ways to gather data. Some examples of this are IOT devices, activity trackers, mobile devices, and websites; they are constantly pushing data to the servers. We need a lot of data to keep track of different aspects, such as system monitoring, fraud detection, debugging applications, and alert systems, but as the volume of data increases, it is quite difficult to search for anything.

Kibana Discover is a very useful tool for data filtering and searching. Using this, we can apply filters, write custom Elasticsearch filter queries, and search data using fields or across all fields. To explain this, I'll configure Packetbeat to push data packets into the Elasticsearch index. Later on, using that index, I will explain how we can explore this data. We can divide this into the following points:

- Configuring Packetbeat to push packet data into Elasticsearch
- Configuring Kibana to read the Elasticsearch index with packet logs
- Exploring Kibana Discover to access packet data

Configuring Packetbeat to push packet data into Elasticsearch

Beats are basically data shippers, which are grouped to do single-purpose jobs. They can be installed as agents on different servers to send data from different sources to a central Logstash or Elasticsearch cluster. Beats are written in Go, they are lightweight in design, and work on a cross-platform environment.

Packetbeat is a network packet analyzer, which reads the packets and sends the information to Logstash or Elasticsearch. We can use Packetbeat to monitor the data traveling over wires for any application. Before configuring Packetbeat, first of all, we need to install it. The process of installing Packetbeat was discussed in Chapter 1, *Revising the ELK Stack*, so you can refer to that. After installation, we can configure Packetbeat by opening the configuration file:

```
sudo vim /etc/packetbeat/packetbeat.yml
```

This opens the configuration file, as shown in the following screenshot:

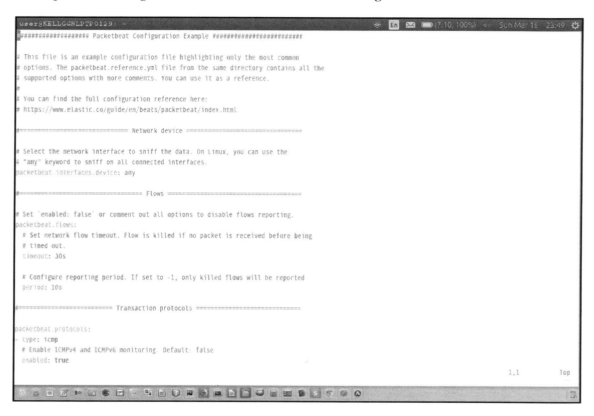

The previous screenshot shows us the Packetbeat configuration file. For configuring Packetbeat, we need to do the following:

- We need to select the network interface through which Packetbeat will capture the data. For that, we need to set the interface device. Linux supports data capture of all messages from the server on which Packetbeat is installed. Here, we can set the interface device as any in the case of Linux: `packetbeat.interfaces.device:any`. With macOS or Windows, we explicitly need to provide the interface device.
- We need to provide the username and password in the case of Elasticsearch and Kibana output if we are using a secured setup of Elastic Stack.

- In the protocol section of the Packetbeat configuration file, we need to provide the ports for each protocol that Packetbeat will use to capture the packet data. If we are using the default ports for each protocol, then Packetbeat will take data using these default ports. However, if we are using any nonstandard port for a given protocol, then we need to mention that in the Packetbeat configuration file:

- We need to set up the Elasticsearch output section by providing the IP address and port of the Elasticsearch server in case we are sending the Packetbeat output to Elasticsearch:

```
#------------------- Elasticsearch output------------------------
output.elasticsearch:
  # Array of hosts to connect to.
  hosts: ["localhost:9200"]
```

But if we are sending the Packetbeat output to Logstash, we need to set the Logstash output section by providing the IP and port of the Logstash server in the Packetbeat configuration file.

- Beats provide default dashboards for Kibana, which we can use in Kibana to customize as per our requirements. For example, if we want to create a dashboard for Apache, Beats provide us with the option to import the Apache dashboard with key visualizations, which we can customize by removing or adding more visualizations if required. So, if we want to use the Packetbeat default dashboard for Kibana, we need to set the following in the configuration file:

```
setup.kibana:
  host: "localhost:5601"
```

Configuring Kibana to read the Elasticsearch index with packet logs

After configuring Packetbeat, we can test the Elasticsearch index and verify the index with the `packetbeat` prefix. Now, once the Elasticsearch index for Packetbeat is created, we can import this index into Kibana and start playing around to create meaningful dashboards.

For creating these dashboards, we need to click on the **Management** tab on the left-hand side menu of Kibana and then click on the **Index Patterns** link:

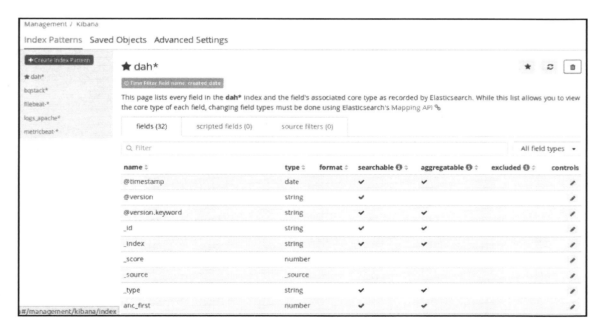

On the **Index Patterns** screen, we have a list of the previous indexes and a data type display of the default index is shown. We can select and delete any index from this screen and also mark any index as the default index. As we need to create a new index pattern, we will click on the **Create index pattern** button, which will open the following screenshot:

Here, in **Step 1 of 2: Create index pattern** and **Define index pattern**, we have the option to enter the **index pattern** that we want to add, so we will start writing the name of the index, which is `packetbeat*`. As soon as we start typing the name, Kibana will start suggesting the name of the available index. These names are coming in through the filter criteria. After filling in the name of the appropriate index pattern, we need to click on the **Next step** button, which will open the following screenshot:

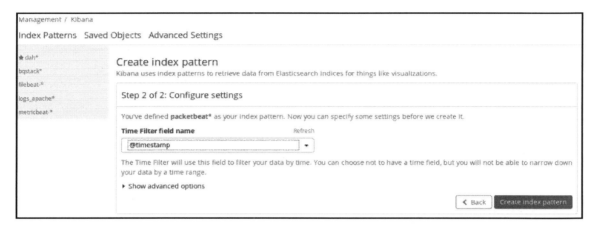

Now, we are at **Step 2 of 2: Configure settings**. Here, we need to choose the **Time Filter** field name from the dropdown, which shows all the fields that have a time and data type. Now, we need to click on the **Create index pattern** button, which will show the data types of this index. Now, the integration of the Elasticsearch index into Kibana is complete, which we can verify by clicking on the **Discover** tab on the left menu. On the **Discover** menu, we can see the index data with all the fields, which we can explore at a later date.

Exploring Kibana Discover to access packet data

We have configured the Packetbeat data in Kibana, so now we can explore it using the **Discover** tab. After clicking on the **Discover** link on the left-hand side menu, we will see the following screen:

Here, we can see that the histogram is full since there have been regular entries of packet data into the Elasticsearch index. We can explore the histogram by clicking on any of the bars, which will open a detailed bar of that duration. We can drill down by clicking on the bar on the histogram. In the following screenshot, we can see a list of documents regarding the histogram with the packet data. We can expand any document, which opens a tabular view of the data:

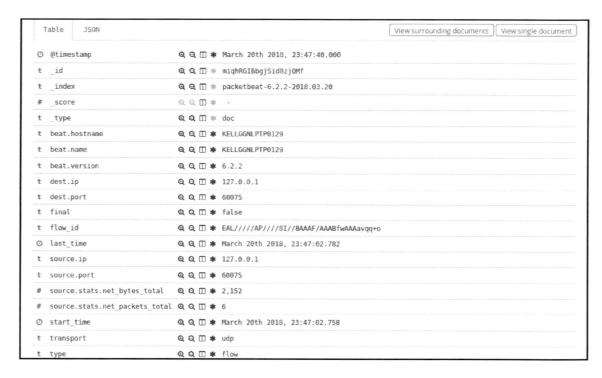

Here, we can see each field with the data in tabular form. We can directly apply the filters by clicking on icons in front of the field names. We can convert this tabular view into a JSON view by clicking on the **JSON** tab:

```
1 ▾ {
2      "_index": "packetbeat-6.2.2-2018.03.20",
3      "_type": "doc",
4      "_id": "mighRGIBbgjSid8zjOMf",
5      "_version": 1,
6      "_score": null,
7 ▾    "_source": {
8          "@timestamp": "2018-03-20T18:17:40.000Z",
9          "last_time": "2018-03-20T18:17:02.782Z",
10         "type": "flow",
11 ▾       "source": {
12             "ip": "127.0.0.1",
13             "port": 60075,
14 ▾           "stats": {
15                 "net_packets_total": 6,
16                 "net_bytes_total": 2152
17             }
18         },
19 ▾       "beat": {
20             "name": "KELLGGNLPTP0129",
21             "hostname": "KELLGGNLPTP0129",
22             "version": "6.2.2"
23         },
24 ▾       "dest": {
25             "port": 60075,
26             "ip": "127.0.0.1"
27         },
28         "start_time": "2018-03-20T18:17:02.758Z",
29         "flow_id": "EAL/////AP////8I//8AAAF/AAABfwAAAavqq+o",
30         "final": false,
31         "transport": "udp"
32     },
33 ▾   "fields": {
34 ▾       "start_time": [
35             "2018-03-20T18:17:02.758Z"
36         ],
37 ▾       "@timestamp": [
38             "2018-03-20T18:17:40.000Z"
39         ],
40 ▾       "last_time": [
41             "2018-03-20T18:17:02.782Z"
42         ]
43     },
44 ▾   "sort": [
45         1521569860000
46     ]
47 }
```

Now, the same tabular data is displayed in the form of JSON data. We can do different things in Kibana Discover, which we will cover in the upcoming subsections.

Showing the required fields

When we open **Kibana Discover**, it shows the data under the **_source** column along with the **time** column. In the _source field, we have all the fields with data being displayed, which are combined with a single space. The **_source** column shows all the fields, which makes it difficult to get the relevant information.

We can add the desired fields from the field listing area on the left section of the page. To add the fields, we need to click on the **Add** button, which appears after hovering over the field name. We can add as many fields as we want to see:

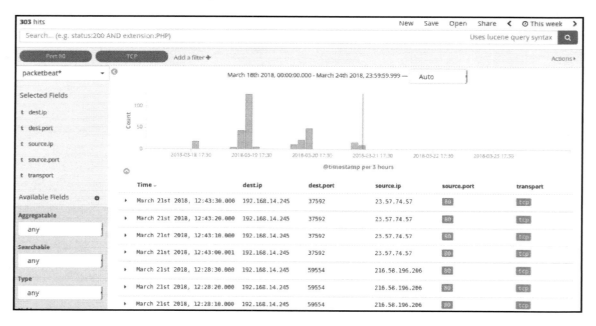

As shown in the previous screenshot, we have added the following fields through which we can easily get the required information:

- **Time**
- **dest.ip**
- **dest.port**
- **source.ip**
- **source.port**
- **transport**

Now, this list has made things quite clear and has made it quite easy to visualize the data of the fields, which is more important than the other fields.

Applying the time filter

We can restrict the search result on the basis of a time period by applying the time filter. We can only apply the time filter if our index contains a time-based event and if the field is configured as a time-based field during the Kibana index setup.

The time filter is set to 15 minutes by default and we can use the time picker to change this. Through the **Time Picker**, we can change the time filter or select a specific time interval. We can do the following to set a time filter:

1. Click on the **Time Picker** icon (**Clock** icon) on the top-right corner of the page. This will open the time selection box.
2. We have three options for time selection: **Quick**, **Relative**, and **Absolute**.
3. We can click on any shortcut link in the **Quick** filter to set the time filter:

4. In the **Relative** type, we need to provide the start time through a number of seconds, minutes, hours, days, months, or years. Now, set the end time relative to the current time, which can be past or future:

5. In the **Absolute** type, we need to select a start and end date:

6. We can also set the time interval by clicking on the histogram bar.

Elasticsearch query DSL

Kibana accepts Lucene query syntax or Elasticsearch query DSL for querying through the index. It also supports the new Kuery language, but for that we need to enable it by clicking on **Management** and then on **Advanced Settings**. On the **Advanced Settings** page, we have the following two options:

- Set **search:queryLanguage:switcher:enable** to **true**
- Set the default language to **search:queryLanguage**

Now, we have Packetbeat data in the Elasticsearch index, which we can use to get the answers for our questions. So, let's say we want to check what is happening on a certain `port` on the server. We can track it using the search box:

```
source.port:80
```

If we want to get only the records that have the source `port` as `80` and the `transport` type is `tcp`, we can modify the query and join both conditions with `AND` to filter out the result:

```
source.port:80 AND transport:tcp
```

The following screenshot shows the result of the filter option, `source.port:80`, through which we are getting the records where the source `port` number is `80`:

In the previous screenshot, we can see the search criteria as `source.port:80`, and after searching, the result has been highlighted with the search value. By combining the search criteria with AND/OR, we can get more relevant results and drill down into the data. When we submit the search request, the document table, histogram, and field lists are updated as per our search results. After searching, the total number of matching documents is shown on the top part of the page as a number of hits. We have `350` hits.

Document listing is shown in reverse chronological order, which means that the newest document is first on the listing. We can change this by clicking on the up/down arrows in front of the time column in the document display.

Filter

We can achieve the same search functionality which we have just covered under the search option using the filter option. We do this by providing the fields as `source.port`, operates as `is`, and values as `80`. We can give this filter a label, such as **Port 80 filter,** to make it more understandable for an end user, as this label tells us that we are trying to apply a filter for port `80`. In the same way, we can create other filters as well, such as for the `tcp` transport protocol. In this way, we can add filters, apply them, and further drill down by searching on top of that applied filter.

We can also apply the filter directly by clicking on the filter icon in front of any field in a tabular view. This will automatically filter the record by creating a new filter for that field. For example, we have opened the tabular view of a document, and while looking at the fields, we have found a **dest.port** field, which denotes the destination port. Now, if we want to get data for any particular port number, we can click on the plus search icon in front of this field name to apply the filter on the **dest.port** field. The filter will pick the value of that particular row against the field name, which can be modified by editing the filter value. The following screenshot shows us the filtered view with the **Edit filter** box, where we can modify the filter options:

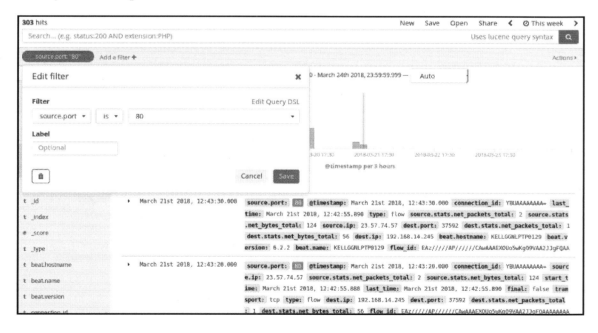

In the preceding screenshot, we are adding the filter for **source.port** using the **Add a filter** link. We can also generate the Elasticsearch Query DSL for this by clicking on the **Edit Query DSL** link in the box. A self-explanatory label can be added for the filter to make it more readable because this label will be shown on the filter and we can easily find out about the filter using its label.

Saving and opening searches

After getting the search execution result, we can save it for future use. Saving the result saves the search query string as well as the selected index pattern.

Saving the result

We need to do the following for saving the result:

1. Click on the **Save** link from the top menu option.
2. Provide the name of the search in the **Save Search** textbox and click on the **Save** button:

Opening the result

We need to do the following for opening a search result:

1. Click on the **Open** link from the top menu option.

2. Click on the search name that we want in the **Open Search** textbox:

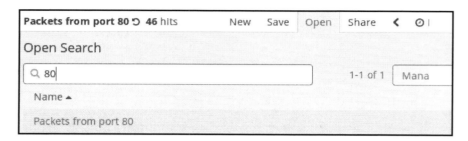

Sharing results

We can share the search results by creating and providing the URL for the search result page. We need to do the following:

1. Click on the **Share** link from the top menu option.
2. This will open the box with two options: **Share saved search** and **Share Snapshot.**
3. **Share saved search** shows the most recent saved version of this search.
4. **Share Snapshot** shows the current state of the search.
5. We can copy any of the two URLs and share them:

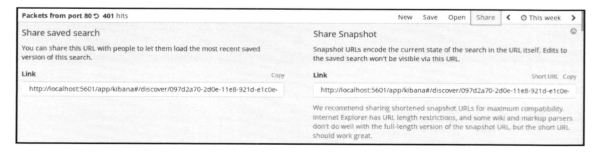

Field data statistics

We can see the field statistics by clicking on the name of the field from the left section field listing. This shows us the top five values for that field and their percentages. We can click on any field to get the statistical data:

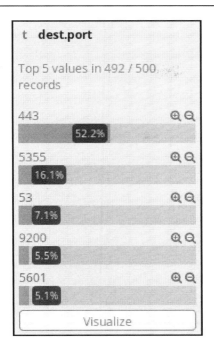

Summary

In this chapter, we saw how to explore our data using Kibana Discover. We can access all documents of every index, as long as they are matching with the selected index pattern. We can search, filter, and view a document's data, and can only select the desired fields of documents. We can see the number of documents matching a given search query. By applying the time filter, we can get the distribution of documents over time using the histogram, which is displayed on top of the page.
So, in this chapter, we have covered the Discover option, through which we can actually discover our data and make decisions by just looking at it.

In the next chapter, we will learn about different types of visualizations such as bar chart, pie chart, area chart, tag cloud, data table, and more. These visualizations give us the complete insight of data in a single view and using this we can easily take decisions. After an introduction to visualization, we will create those visualizations in Kibana using Elasticsearch index data.We will also cover how to save and share visualizations.

4
Visualizing the Data

In this chapter, we'll learn how to create a visualization of data of Elasticsearch indices. Kibana visualize provides us with a user interface, through which we can create different types of visualizations. However, in the background, it uses a series of Elasticsearch aggregations to extract the required data and processes it for visualization.

We can create this visualization using the saved search under the **Discover** tab, or we can start with a fresh search. There is a quotation that states, "*A picture is worth a thousand words*", which is quite correct for data visualization as well. When we create a visualization from a large set of data, we can make instant decisions by looking at these visualizations. It will take months if we try to make sense of that data by reading it. There are different tools available on the market to deal with this, but for dashboarding, Kibana is very popular and is growing. In this chapter, we will learn how to create different types of visualizations, such as bar charts, pie charts, data metrics, tag clouds, and histograms.

In this chapter, we will be learning about the following topics:

- **Visualizing the data**: This will cover how to create the visualization. After that, we will cover different chart types such as basic, data, maps, and time series.
- **Pie charts**: This will be covering the introduction to pie charts, metrics, and bucket aggregation, which we need for pie chart creation. After that, we will be covering the actual pie chart creation.
- **Bar charts**: This will be covering the introduction and different metrics and bucket aggregations required for bar chart creation. Then, the actual bar chart creation will be covered.

- **Area charts**: This will first cover the introduction to area charts and then the actual creation of the area chart.
- **Data metrics**: This will cover how to create this visualization.
- **Data tables:** This will explain the necessary steps to create this visualization.
- **Tag clouds**: This will discuss the details of this visualization and then you will learn how to create this type of visualization.
- **Markdown**: This will explain the steps to create this visualization.
- **Sharing visualizations**: This will cover the ways through which any visualization can be shared with users.

Creating visualizations

For creating a visualization, we need to click on the **Visualize** link on the left-hand menu, which will open a page. We will display a list of visualizations, if we have already created any; otherwise, there will be a page with a **Create a visualization** button in the middle. So, for creating a new visualization, we need to click on this button:

Now, we need to choose the visualization type from the **Select visualization type** screen. There are multiple types of visualizations, such as the ones shown in the following screenshot:

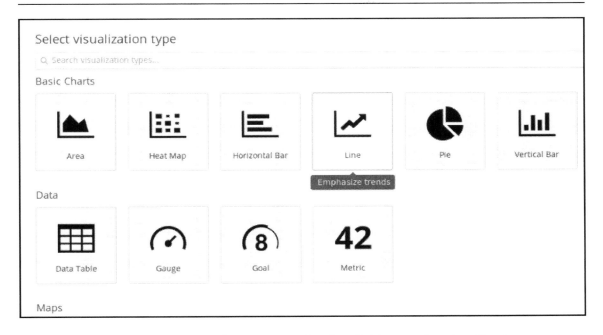

Now, we need to select the visualization type first by clicking on the visualization type box. But before selecting the right visualization type, we need to understand the data. By seeing the data, we can get the best way to depict it through visualization. For example, if we have a single dimensional data over time, we can use a histogram, but if we have related data, such as the number of votes acquired by each party in an election, we can use a pie chart. Bar charts can be used if we have two-dimensional data, such as subject name and numbers in each subject. Scatter charts can be used to scatter a point against two axes; for example, a house area and price can be easily plotted on a scatter chart. In this way, we can see our data, think, and then decide which is best suited to be displayed on the chart through visualization.

Basic charts

Basic charts are charts that are quite common in representing the data in visual form. They include line charts, area charts, bar charts, pie charts, and so on. The following is a list of the basic charts for visualization:

- **Line, area, and bar charts**: These charts are used for comparing different series in x and y axes

- **Heat maps**: These are used to shade the cells within a matrix
- **Pie charts**: These are used when all of the fields are related to each other; for example, the voting percentage for different parties in an election

Data

The following is a list of data used in visualization:

- **Data table**: This is where the data is shown in tabular form
- **Metric**: This is where a single number is displayed, which we can use to show any important metric data
- **Goal and gauge**: This is used when we want to display any progress

Maps

The following is a list of maps used in visualization:

- **Coordinate map**: This can be used for linking the aggregation of data fields with geographic locations
- **Region map**: This is a kind of thematic map where we use color intensity to show a metric's value with locations

Time series

The following is a list of time series used in visualization:

- **Timelion**: This is used to display the results from single or multiple indices by combining data from multiple time series datasets
- **Time series visual builder**: This is used to visualize time series data using data aggregations

Other

Here are some other items that are used in visualization:

- **Tag cloud**: This is where selected field values are picked for creating a cloud of words
- **Markdown widget**: This will display a form for showing information or instructions

Now, in the upcoming sections, we will cover the creation of visualization using different types.

Pie charts

Before creating a pie chart, we need to understand the different terminology that's used in Kibana for creating visualizations. So, for chart creation, in which we will discuss the pie chart for now, we need to perform Elasticsearch aggregation. There are mainly two categories of aggregation that we need to configure for creating pie charts: **metric aggregation** and **bucket aggregation**.

Metric aggregation

The total slice size of a pie chart is calculated by the metrics aggregation. In the case of a pie chart, we have the following aggregations:

- **Count**: This aggregation is the count of documents in the selected index pattern.
- **Sum**: This aggregation returns the total sum of a numeric field. After choosing this option, we can only select numeric fields.
- **Unique count**: This aggregation returns the number of unique values for a given field.

Bucket aggregation

Bucket aggregation is used to determine the type of information we are trying to get from the dataset. These are the following types of bucket aggregations for a pie chart:

- **Date histogram**: This is used to display a numeric field and organize that using the date

- **Date range**: This aggregation is used to report the values within a date range which we can specify
- **Filters**: This is used to apply filters on data
- **Histogram**: This aggregation is used for numeric fields, where we can provide the integer interval for the selected field
- **IPv4 Range**: This aggregation provides us with the option to set the range using IPv4 addresses
- **Range**: This aggregation is used to provide the range of numeric field values
- **Significant terms**: This aggregation returns interesting or unusual occurrences of terms in a set
- **Terms**: This aggregation enables us to pick the top or bottom *n* elements of the selected field

Creating a pie chart

From the **Select visualization type** screen, we need to click on the pie block. This will open the **Choose search source** screen. Here, we have the following two options:

- **From a New Search, Select Index**: This is used if we want to pick the index name
- **Or, From a Saved Search**: This is used if we want to pick from a saved search:

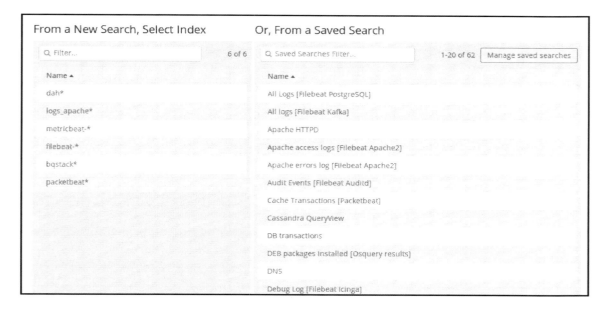

This is also a very important selection, in the sense that if we have saved any searches and want to create visualizations on the basis of the same search criteria, then we can go for the second option. This will save time in applying the search criteria again during chart creation.

If we don't want to use our saved searches, then we can go for the first option, in which we can choose any index and start creating visualizations. So, let's say we are going to create a pie chart from the metricbeat index. For that, we need to click on the **metricbeat-* index** link under **From a New Search, Select Index**. This will open the following screen:

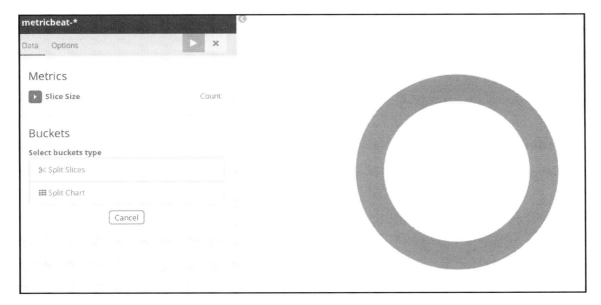

This will open the default pie chart view, which shows the count of all documents of the index metricbeat. As we are creating the pie chart using metricbeat data, the first thing we want to know is the type of system metric and their percentage in overall metric data. To create a pie chart with this information, first of all we need to know the field name through which we can get this detail, and for that we can again explore the data in the **Discover** section. So, by exploring the data in a tabular view of **Discover**, we can learn that the metricset.name field is used for storing the system metric type, such as memory and network.

Now, back to our chart creation. We need to perform Elasticsearch aggregation on the `metricset.name` field, and for that we need to do the following:

1. Click on the **Split Slices** buckets type.
2. Select **Terms** from the **Aggregation** list.
3. Under **field**, select the `metricset.name` field.
4. Under the **Custom Label** type, choose any label, such as **Metric Type.**
5. Click on the **Apply changes** button to get the visualization:

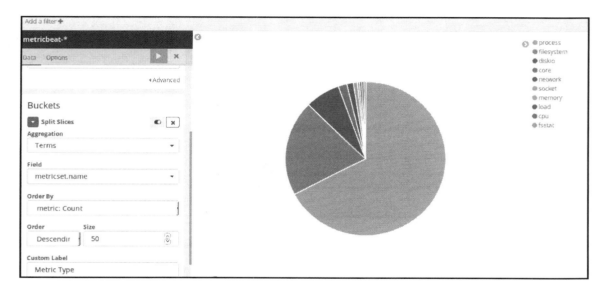

We can see that the pie chart is now on the right pane with multiple colors and a legend on the top-right corner to tell us what each of these colors represent. By looking at this pie chart, we can easily say that the maximum number of metric data belongs to the process type, and after that it is the filesystem. If we try to get the same information by reading the index data, it is going to be a very difficult task.

We have created the pie chart, but still we need to modify a lot of things to make it more meaningful and clean. To do this, we will go to the **Options** tab present next to the **Data** tab. When we click on the **Options** tab, it provides us with a lot of option to customize the chart. For example, under **Pie** settings, we have the option to make it a donut instead. We can also set the legend's position and show or hide the tooltip. Under the **Labels Settings**, we have the option to select whether we want to show or hide labels, show the top level only, or show values. To change the chart accordingly, we need to make these changes and then click on the **Apply changes** button:

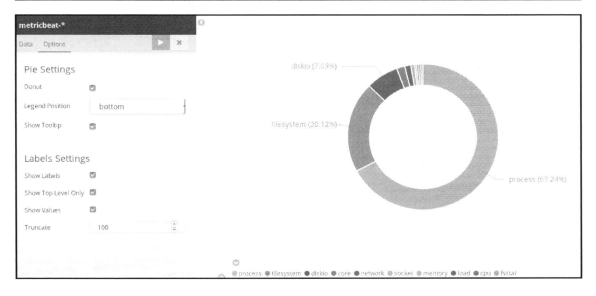

Here, we have changed the chart type to donut, changed the legend position, and added **Show Labels**. Once the chart has been created as per our requirements, we can save the pie chart by clicking on the **Save** link in the top menu. This will open a dialog box to save the visualization. We need to enter the name of the visualization and click on the **Save** button. This will save the pie chart visualization for further use.

Adding another dimension to the pie chart

In the pie chart, we can add another dimension of data. Let's say we want to check the event round trip time against each metric type. This can provide additional detail with respect to the first data point, which is the metric type in this case. Using the drill-down method, we can get granular details of this association.

To add `rtt` details with the metric type, we need to do the following:

1. Under the bucket list, click on the **Add sub-bucket** option.
2. Click on the **Split Slices** option.
3. Select **Terms**' under the **Aggregation** list.
4. Choose the **metricset.rtt** field from the field list.

5. Click on the **Apply changes** icon to refresh the pie chart:

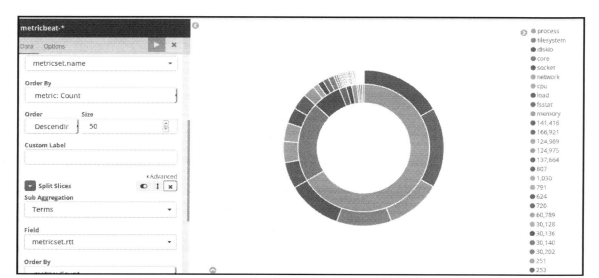

Bar charts

Bar charts are a type of visualization which are used to compare the number, frequency, or other measures for different categories of data. Bar charts are the most common type of visualization, and are easy to create and easy to interpret as well. They are used to present categorical data in the form of rectangular bars with heights/lengths proportional to the given values.

There are two categories of aggregation that we need to configure for creating bar charts: metric aggregation and bucket aggregation.

Metric aggregation

Metric aggregation computes metrics on the basis of the way the values of the documents are aggregated. The following are the types of metric aggregations:

- **Average**: This is used to calculate the average of a numeric field.
- **Max**: This is used to calculate the maximum value of a numeric field.
- **Median**: This is used to calculate the median value of a numeric field.

- **Min**: This is used to calculate the minimum value of a numeric field.
- **Percentile ranks**: This returns the percentile rankings for the values of the given numeric field.
- **Percentile**: This aggregation converts the values of the given numeric field into percentile bands.
- **Standard deviation**: This aggregation returns the standard deviation of the value in a numeric field.
- **Sum**: This aggregation returns the total sum of a numeric field. After choosing this option, we can only select numeric fields.
- **Top hit**: This aggregation returns the most relevant document being aggregated.
- **Unique count**: This aggregation returns a number of unique values for a given field.
- **Count**: This aggregation is a count of documents in the selected index pattern.

Bucket aggregation

Bucket aggregation is used to determine the type of information we are trying to get from the dataset. The following are the types of bucket aggregations for bar charts:

- **Date histogram**: This is used to display a numeric field and organize it using the date
- **Date range**: This aggregation is used to report the values within a date range which we can specify
- **Filters**: This is used to apply filters on data
- **Histogram**: This aggregation is used for numeric fields where we can provide the integer interval for the selected field
- **IPv4 range**: This aggregation provides us with the option to set the range using IPv4 addresses
- **Range**: This aggregation is used to provide the range of numeric field values
- **Significant terms**: This aggregation returns interesting or unusual occurrences of terms in a set
- **Terms**: This aggregation enables us to pick top or bottom *n* elements of the selected field

Creating a bar chart

For creating a bar chart, we need to click on the bar icon. There are two types of bar charts under the Kibana visualization type, which are the horizontal bar and the vertical bar.

Here, we'll cover the steps for creating a vertical bar, and for that we need to click on the vertical bar box, which opens the **Choose search source** page. From this page, we will once again click on **metricbeat-***, as we will follow the same index used for the pie chart:

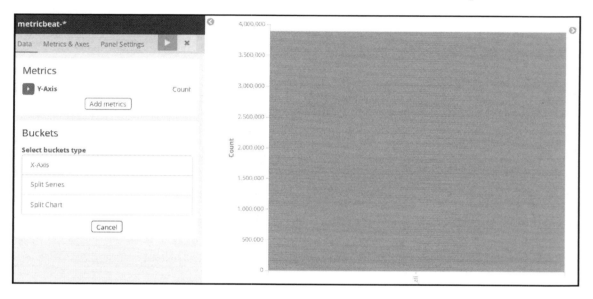

Bar chart for total count of documents

After clicking on the **metricbeat-*** index link, the screen shows a big bar, which depicts the total count of documents, since we have not defined any buckets yet. We need to do the following to create a vertical bar chart:

1. Click on the **Y-Axis** under **Metrics** and choose the appropriate option. I have chosen **Count.**
2. Also, provide the **Custom Label** if the default is not making sense.
3. Select the **X-Axis** bucket type and select **Terms** under **Aggregation.**
4. Select the `metricset.name` field name.

5. Add the custom label as **Metric Type.**

6. We can also add sub-buckets if required.

7. Click on the **Apply changes** button to refresh the bar chart on the right pane.

After applying these changes, we can see the bar chart shown in the right-hand side pane of the following screenshot:

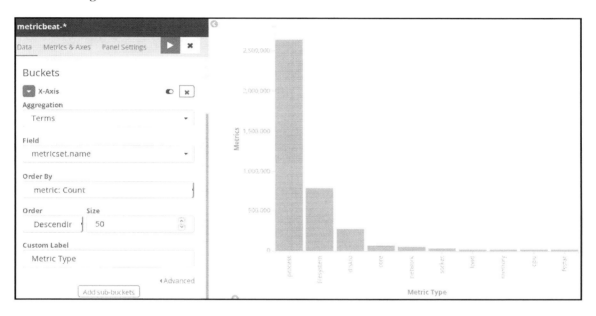

Bar chart showing metric type

The bar chart shows multiple rectangular boxes, each representing the metric type on the **X-Axis**, such as process, filesystem, diskio, and core. The counts are shown on the **Y-Axis**.

We can customize the bar using the **Metrics & Axes** and the **Panel Settings** tab in front of the **Data** tab. For example, we can change the chart type from bar to area under the **Metrics & Axes** tab. We can also change the mode from normal to stacked. The Line mode can also be set as normal, smoothed, and stepped. Under the **Y-Axis**, we can change the **title**, **mode**, **position**, and **scale type**. Under **Panel Settings**, we can change the legend position and show or hide tooltips:

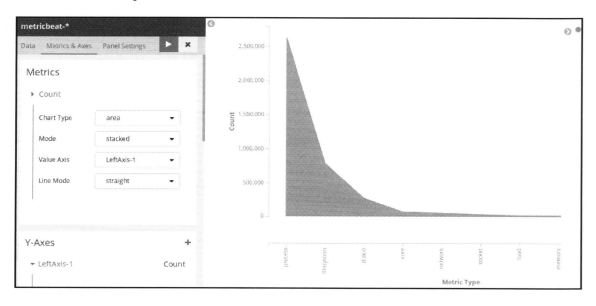

I have explained some changes which we can do, but there are many options available, and we can play around to see their effects on the chart.

Once we are done with the chart, we can save the bar chart by clicking on the **Save** link on the top menu, which opens a textbox that says **Save visualization**. We need to enter the name of the visualization and click on the **Save** button. This will save the bar chart visualization for further use.

Area charts

An area chart is used to display graphically quantitative data. It is a kind of line chart where the area between axes and lines are emphasized with colors or textures.

Creating an area chart

From the **Select visualization type** screen, we need to click on the **Area block**. This will open the **Choose search source** screen. Here, we have the following two options:

- **From a New Search, Select Index**: This is used if we want to pick the index name
- **Or, From a Saved Search**: This is used if we want to pick from a saved search

If we don't want to use our saved searches, then we can go for the first option, in which case we can choose any index and start creating visualizations. So, let's say we need to create an area chart from the metricbeat index. For that, we need to click on the **metricbeat-* index** link under **From a New Search, Select Index**.

Now, for the area chart creation, we need to perform Elasticsearch aggregation on the `metricset.name` field, and for that we need to do the following:

1. Click on the **X-Axis** under buckets type.
2. Select **Terms** from the **Aggregation** list.
3. Under **field**, select the **metricset.name** field.
4. Under the **Custom Label** type, add any label such as **Metric Type.**
5. Click on the **Apply changes** button to get the visualization:

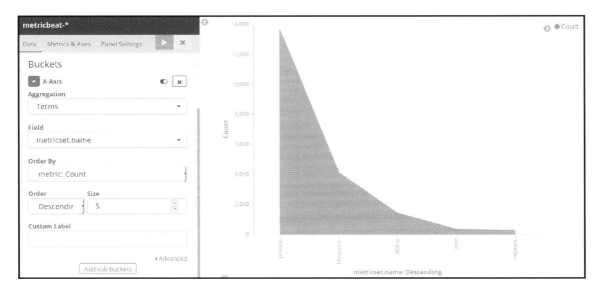

Once we are done with the chart, we can save the bar chart by clicking on the **Save** link on the top menu, which opens a textbox save visualization. We need to enter the name of the visualization and click on the Save button. This will save the area chart visualization for further use.

We have covered pie charts, bar charts, and area charts, which are all under the basic chart type. Similarly, we can create other basic charts, such as line charts, horizontal bar charts, area charts, and heat maps.

Data metrics

We have covered the basic charts in the previous sections, so now we'll cover the metric visualization under data. Metric visualization is just a single number which displays any count or calculation.

Creating a data metric

To create the metric visualization, we need to click on the metric box on the **Select visualization type** page. Now, we need to click on the index named **metricbeat-*** on the **Choose search source** page, which will open the default page with a metric number displayed, along with a count of all the documents. If we don't want the default single count with the all document count, then we can configure it to show metrics for values of any field, which we have selected. For this, we need to do the following:

1. Click on **Split Group** under the **Buckets** option.
2. Select **Terms** under the **Aggregation** option.
3. Under the **Field** option, select the field's name for which we want the metrics. I am using the same field as before, `metricset.name`.
4. Click on the **Apply changes** button to refresh the data metric:

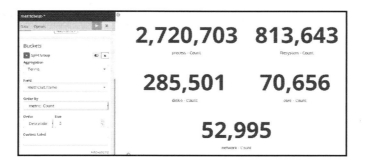

We can save this data metric by clicking on the **Save** link on the top menu, which opens a textbox save visualization. We need to enter the name of the visualization and click on the save button. This will save the data metric visualization for further use.

Data tables

The data table is a tabular form of data display in which we can add columns as per our requirements. The data table is quite helpful as it gives us a tabular display of data, and by using the filter, we can drill down and get details of the different fields that we have added using the table.

Creating the data table

To create the data table, we need to click on the data table box on the chart type selection page. Now, we need to click on the index named **metricbeat-*** on the **Choose search source** page, which will open the default page with a count of all the documents on the tabular view. To create the data table, we need to do the following:

1. Click on **Split Rows** under the **Buckets** option.
2. Select **Terms** under the **Aggregation** option.
3. Select `metricset.name` under the **Field** option.
4. Now, click on the **Add sub-bucket** button on the bottom of the page, which will open another split rows block.
5. Repeat steps 1 to 3 for the other fields.

6. Click on the **Apply changes** button to refresh the data table:

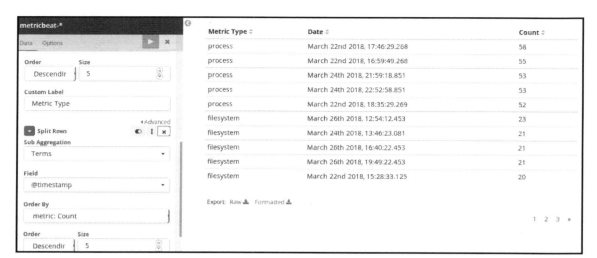

Here, we have added two columns called metric type and date, showing when the document was added. We have the export option to export this data into CSV format. We can save this data table in the same way as we saved the previous graphs.

Tag clouds

A tag cloud is basically words that are uniquely picked from the selected field of the document. A field value with more occurrences is shown in a prominent way to make it more visible than the field value with less occurrences. For example, if I pick the Metricbeat field, **metricset.name,** the tag cloud type graph will pick unique values of the field such as network, process, filesystem, and more, and, based on their occurrence in the document, the text will be displayed in the chart.

Creating a tag cloud

To create the tag cloud visualization, we need to click on the **Tag cloud** box on the **Select visualization type** page. After that, we need to click on the index named **metricbeat-*** on the **Choose search source** page, which will open the default blank page:

On the left-hand side of the page, we can see only one link under buckets, which is **Tags**. We need to do the following for creating the tag cloud:

1. Click on the **Tags** link under the **Buckets** option.
2. Select **Terms** under the **Aggregation** option.
3. Under the **Field** option, select the `metricset.name` field, which we are using for all our chart examples.
4. Change **Custom Label** to **Metric Type.**
5. Click on the **Apply changes** button to show the tag cloud:

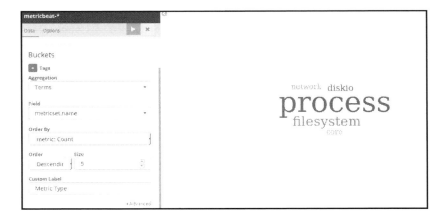

We can see that the tag cloud is created for the `metricset.name` field with five values. Because `Size` is set to 5 in the textbox, we can increase this as per our requirements. We have the **Options** tab to change some settings of the tag cloud, such as text scale, orientation, font size, and show or hide label. We can play around with these options to get the desired result:

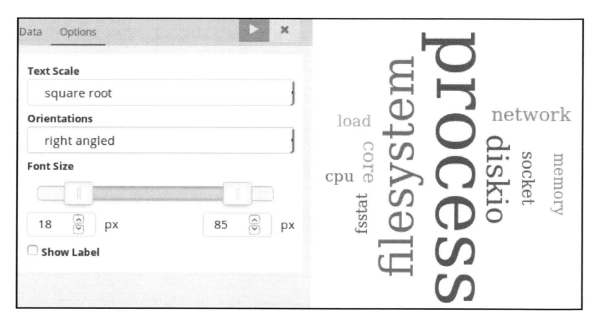

Once we are done with our changes, we can save the tag cloud in the same way we did for the other charts.

Markdown

Markdown is the simplest visualization in Kibana, and comes under the **other** category. Markdown provides us with the option to create visualizations by providing any text message. We can create the text message and put it into the dashboard.

Creating a markdown visualization

To create the markdown visualization, we need to click on the **Markdown** box on the **Select visualization type** page. After that, we need to do the following:

1. Add the text content in the given text-area under the font size controller.
2. Increase or decrease the font using the **Font Size** controller.
3. Click on the **Apply changes** button to show the markdown:

This will create the text markdown chart, which we can add to a dashboard as per our requirements. We can save this visualization in the same way as we did with the earlier charts.

Sharing visualizations

We have created various types of visualizations and saved them, so now it's time to share them with others.

We can share our visualizations in the following two ways:

- **Share saved visualization**: We can use this type to share the most recently saved version of visualization with people.
- **Share Snapshot**: This option provides us with the snapshot URLs, through which we can share the current state of visualization. If we change anything in the visualization after extracting this URL, nothing will change in the shared version.

The following screenshot represents both options of sharing the visualization.

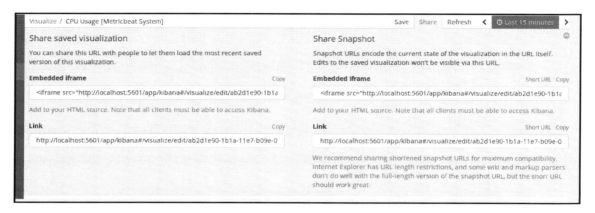

Summary

At the beginning of this chapter, we discussed different types of visualizations, such as pie charts, bar charts, area charts, data metrics, data tables, tag clouds, and markdown. Then, we covered them in detail, alongside the type of aggregations they support for metrics and buckets, and then we covered how to create these charts one by one by setting the aggregation and selecting the data field.

By creating different types of visualization, we can integrate them into a dashboard and then we can do many things, such as search, filter, and drill-down, using simple clicks on the charts. This helps us to explore our data by visualizing it in an integrated way, since filters on dashboards work on all visualizations of an Elasticsearch index.It also provides us with the option to download the reports from the visualization directly by clicking on the down arrow and then on the export link. So, here, we have covered the topics related to Kibana visualization.

In the next chapter, we will cover everything related to Kibana's dashboard creation, including beautification and its usage by searching and filtering. The main objective of any dashboard is to provide a way through which decision makers can view the complete overview and make decisions easily.

5
Dashboarding to Showcase Key Performance Indicators

In this chapter, we'll learn about dashboarding and how this will help in data analytics. Data analytics is used to perform analysis on data and get information out of raw data. In any organization, we have decision makers who rely on data for making decisions on certain points and for them, these dashboards are boons since they provide them with data with filter, search, and drill-down capabilities, and through that they can easily identify any outliers and drill down to get to the root cause of any anomaly in data.

In Kibana, we have the option to integrate different visualizations in a single place to create a dashboard, which we learned about in the previous chapter. I will be taking the same visualizations that we created in the previous chapter and explain how we can create an integrated dashboard and make it look presentable by placing the visualizations in the right order and by resizing them accordingly. Before creating a dashboard, the first question which comes to mind is, *what is the purpose of the dashboard and what types of visualizations are we going to add to make it more meaningful and more helpful for decision makers?* For example, if we want to monitor the system's performance using the Kibana dashboard, there are different visualizations that are very important, such as memory consumption, CPU usage, disk usage, memory usage versus total metrics, network traffic, and the number of processes. In this way, we'll only integrate the visualization that we have already created, and are going to create, to make the dashboard.

In this chapter, we will be covering the following topics:

- Creating the dashboard
- Arranging visualizations:
    - Moving visualization
    - Resizing visualizations
    - Removing visualizations
    - Showing in full screen
    - Showing visualization data
    - Modifying the visualizations
    - Saving the dashboard
    - Sharing the dashboard
    - Cloning the dashboard
- Exploring the dashboards:
    - Search query
    - Adding a filter
    - Applying a time filter
    - Clicking on a visualization

Creating the dashboard

We created the visualization for showing metric data in the previous chapter and saved it under the **Visualize** tab of Kibana. Now, by using these visualizations, we'll design a new dashboard. To create the dashboard, click on the **Dashboard** link on the left-hand side menu in Kibana:

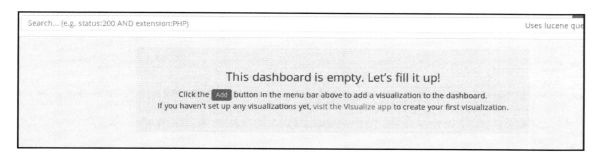

We will get a empty screen with a message **This dashboard is empty. Let's fill it up!** We need to do the following to create a dashboard:

1. Click on the **Add** button on the page or **Add link** on the top menu.
2. On the **Add Panel** screen, we have two options: **Visualization** and **Saved Search.**
3. Under **Visualization**, add the visualization that we created and saved earlier:

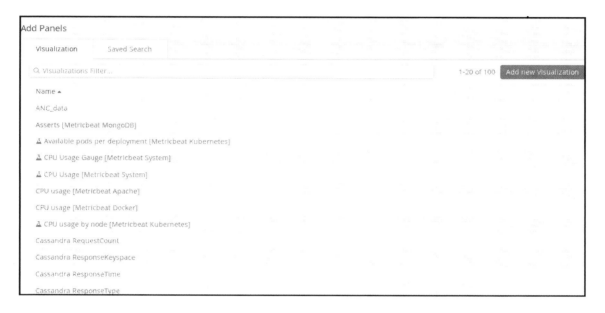

4. Under **Saved Search**, add the saved search under Kibana Discover.
5. After adding all the required visualizations, click on the up arrow in the top-right corner.
6. This will show all visualizations one after another, which we have just added into the dashboard:

After these steps, our dashboard is ready with visualizations. Now, we need to save it by giving it a meaningful name. Our raw dashboard is ready with visualizations, so now we need to arrange and resize them to design the dashboard properly.

Arranging visualizations

For arranging the dashboard properly, first we need to edit the dashboard by clicking on the **Edit** link on the top menu. There are different things that we can perform to arrange the dashboard.

Moving visualizations

We want to show the key performance indicators on the top of the page to make the dashboard effective and more meaningful. For this, we need to move the visualizations and rearrange them as per the order of their importance. So, to rearrange the visualizations, we need to do the following:

1. Click on the **Edit** link on the top menu and hover over the visualization title bar.
2. Click and hold the mouse to drag and drop it.
3. Drag the visualization and drop it into a new, desired location.
4. Release the mouse button.
5. Click on the **Save** link on the top menu and save the dashboard:

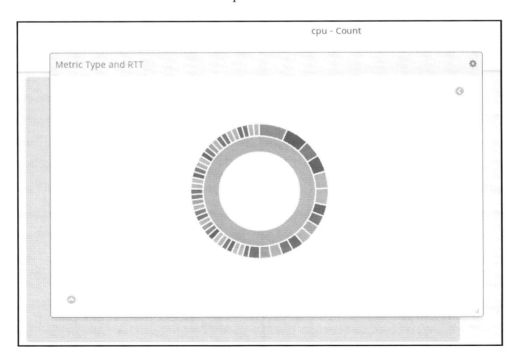

Resizing visualizations

Sometimes, one type of visualization takes more space and others take less space, and it looks weird if we show them in the same size box. For example, if we want to show the data table and a data metric, then the data metric can be shown in much less space in comparison to a data table, since a data table has multiple columns with multiple rows, which requires more space than a data metric, which only requires a single line with less width required. To handle these issues, we have the option to resize the visualization. To resize a Kibana visualization, we need to perform the following steps:

1. Click on the **Edit** link on the top menu.
2. Hover over the bottom-right resize icon to convert the mouse cursor to the resize tool.
3. Drag the mouse by clicking the left button to change the dimension of the visualization container.
4. Release the mouse button to freeze the size.
5. Click on the **Save** link to save the dashboard:

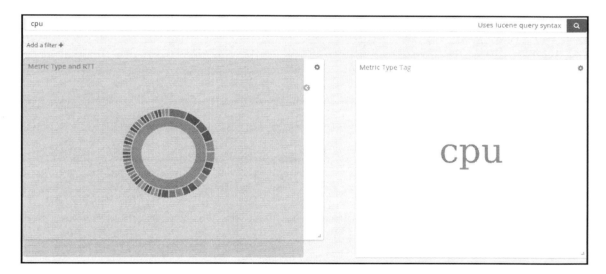

Removing visualizations

We can remove any visualization from the dashboard if it is added, as it is not required for dashboard display. Removing a visualization from the dashboard will only remove it from the dashboard, and it will still be available under **Visualization**. We can add this again from the visualization. To remove a visualization from the dashboard, we need to do the following:

1. Click on the **Edit** link on the top menu.
2. Click on the **Settings** button in the top-right corner of the visualization box.
3. Click on the **Delete from dashboard** link on the pop-up screen. This will remove the visualization from the dashboard.
4. Click on the **Save** link to save the dashboard:

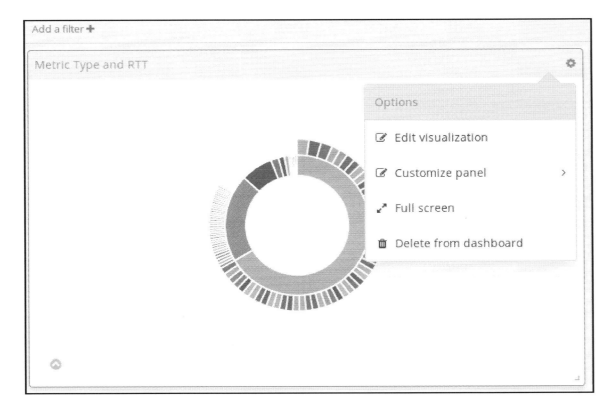

Showing in full screen

We have the option to show the dashboard in full screen and for that we need to do the following:

1. Click on the **Full screen** link on the top-right link.
2. This will open the dashboard in full screen:

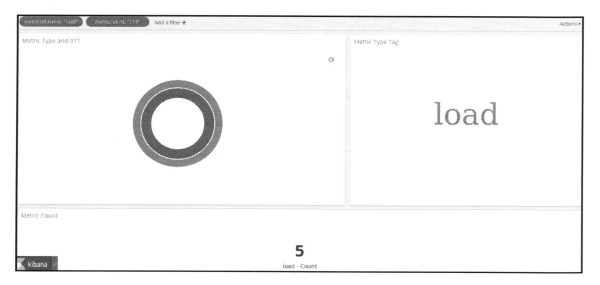

3. To close the full screen display, we have the button on the bottom-left corner of the page. We can restore the normal view by clicking on this button.
4. Apart from the full screen display, we can also collapse the left menu by clicking on the **Collapse** link in the same menu, which is located on the bottom-left corner of the page:

Showing visualization data

Visualization is always good for decision makers as it gives us a way of getting a complete idea of the data, but sometimes it is required to view the data behind the visualization. Luckily, Kibana provides us with the option to view the data behind the visualization. To display the raw data, we need to do the following:

1. Hover over the visualization box to display the container controls.
2. Click on the up arrow icon on the bottom-left part of the visualization box.
3. This will open the tabular data display for the visualization:

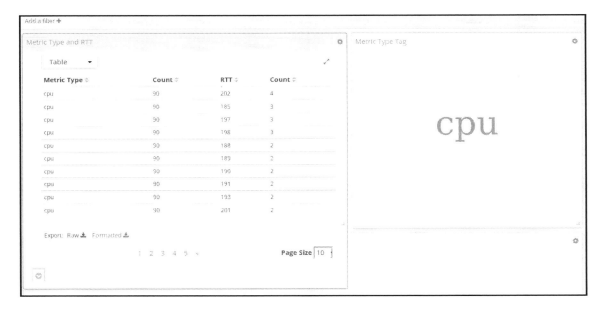

4. There is a dropdown on top of the data display through which we can convert the tabular display.
5. We can convert the tabular display to raw Elasticsearch JSON request, response, and request statistics for the visualization:

Metric Type and RTT

Request ▾

Elasticsearch request body

```
{
  "size": 0,
  "_source": {
    "excludes": []
  },
  "aggs": {
    "2": {
      "terms": {
        "field": "metricset.name",
        "size": 50,
        "order": {
          "_count": "desc"
        }
      },
      "aggs": {
        "3": {
          "terms": {
```

6. These statistics show query duration, request duration, total number of matching records through hits, and the index that was used to search the records:

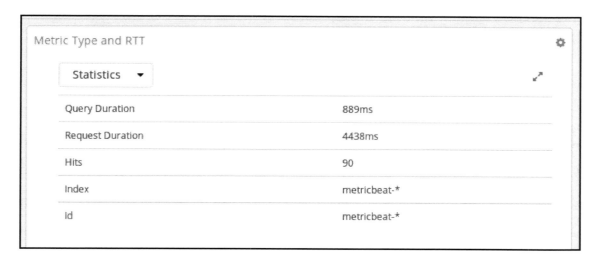

Metric Type and RTT	
Statistics ▾	
Query Duration	889ms
Request Duration	4438ms
Hits	90
Index	metricbeat-*
Id	metricbeat-*

7. We can export the tabular data by clicking on `Raw` or the **Formatted** link in front of **Export** below the tabular data. **displayRaw** is used to export the raw data as it is stored in Elasticsearch.

8. Formatted is used to export the results using Kibana field formatters.

9. To return back to normal visualization from the data display, click on the **Collapse** button on the bottom-left corner of the container.

Modifying the visualization

Sometimes, we want to make changes to the visualization, and for that we need to do the following:

1. Click on the **Edit** link on the top menu.
2. Click on the **Settings** button in the top-right corner of the visualization box.
3. Click on the **Edit visualization** link on the pop-up screen.
4. This will open the dashboard visualization into edit mode under the **Visualize** tab.
5. We can edit the visualization and save it.
    1. Open the dashboard again to see the changes in the visualization on the dashboard:

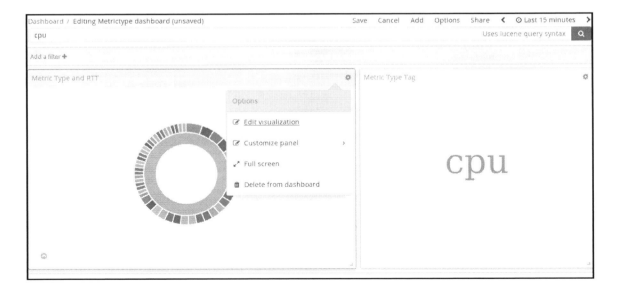

Saving the dashboard

After doing all of the required changes on the dashboard, we can save it for further use. For saving the dashboard, we need to do the following:

1. Click on the **Save** link on the top menu.
2. This will open the **Save dashboard** box.
3. Enter the dashboard's title and description in the given textboxes.
4. If you want to save this dashboard as a new dashboard, then tick the checkbox that says **Save as a new dashboard.**
5. If you want to store the time with the dashboard, then tick the checkbox that says **Store time with dashboard.**
6. Click on the **Save** button. This will save the dashboard. You will get the success message on the top bar:

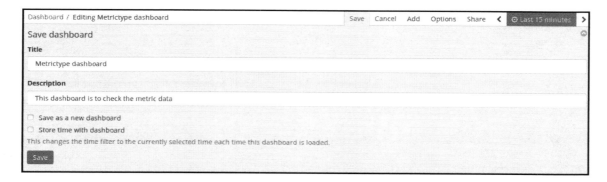

Sharing the dashboard

We have created various types of visualizations and integrated them to create the dashboard. After saving it, we can share it with others. We can share our dashboard in two ways.

Sharing the saved dashboard

If we want to share the most recently saved version of the dashboard with other people, we do this. All updates after sharing the link will be visible to users.

Sharing the snapshot

This option provides us with the snapshot URLs through which we can share the current state of the dashboard. If we change anything in the dashboard after extracting this URL, nothing will change in the shared version:

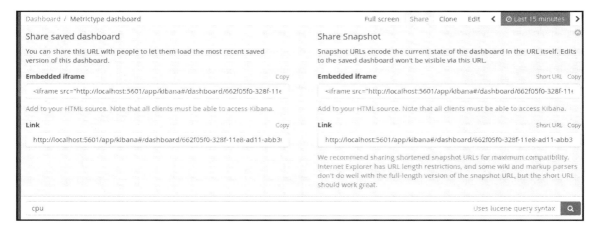

Cloning the dashboard

We can clone the dashboard for creating an exact copy of the original dashboard, and for that we need to do the following:

1. Click on the **Clone** link in top menu. This will open a box for cloning the dashboard:

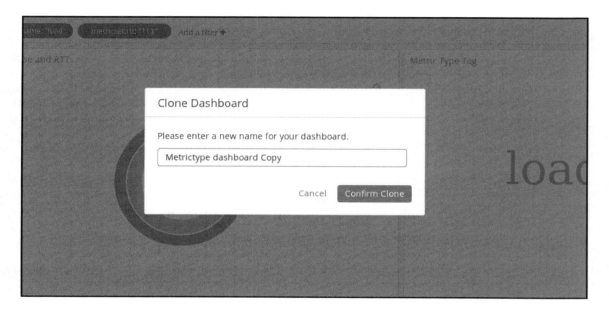

2. Enter the name of the newly cloned dashboard and click on the **Confirm Clone** button.
3. The newly cloned dashboard will be created and loaded.

In this way, we can clone the actual dashboard and work on the copy of the main dashboard. We can use this feature if we are going to change any settings which may break the dashboard, so rather than doing it on the main dashboard, we can first test it on the cloned dashboard. If everything works properly, the same changes can be applied to the main dashboard as well.

Exploring the dashboard

The main reason for any dashboard creation is to have a better understanding of the data we have. It could be any data, such as system metrics, log data, application data, or transactional data. But just by looking at the data, we will not get any insight because if it is too small, only we will be able to get any information out of it, which means that it is going to be a really tough task to make any decisions using that data. To make life easier and to understand the data we used to create the dashboard, we use the top management and decision makers to understand the data and make quick decisions. As we have created and saved the dashboard, we are now going to explore it in different ways. The dashboard shows the graphical representation of key performance indicators for our data and in order to get these details, we have the option to drill down further in Kibana. We have different ways to drill down further, and some of them will be covered in the upcoming subsections.

The search query

Here, I will take the same example of the metric-type dashboard. This shows us different visualizations for metric types, such as process, filesystem, memory, CPU, load, and network, and in all of the visualizations we are getting details for all these types. Now, if I want to get more details about how the CPU is performing and what the CPU metrics are in different visualizations, the best way to achieve this is by adding the text CPU in the search box and hitting *Enter*. This will exclude all other types from the dashboard and would only show CPU-related metrics:

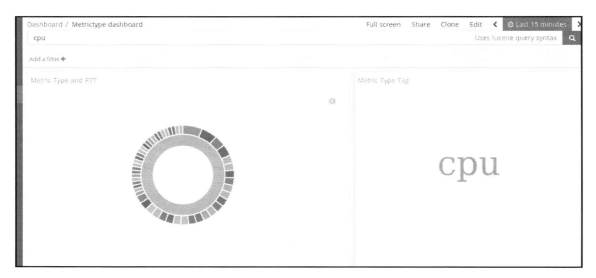

We can use Lucene queries to apply more than one search and add them using conditions to get more customized results:

```
metricset.name:cpu && metricset.rtt:200
```

In the previous search criteria, we are trying to drill down to those documents, where the metric name is CPU and whose `rtt` is `200`:

```
metricset.name:cpu || metricset.name:memory
```

In the previous search criteria, we are fetching those documents whose name is either CPU or memory. In this way, we can apply different search criteria to drill down further and get the appropriate results in the form of dashboard visualizations. There are basically two ways to search: the first is to provide the string and hit *Enter*, and the other is to mention the field name, and then use a colon and insert the value of that field. In the first way, it searches through all the fields to get the result while in the other way, we use this to provide the field name to search for the value:

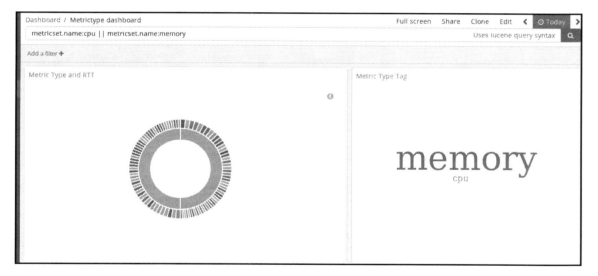

Search, in the Kibana dashboard is a very interesting feature as it gives us the option to apply filters on data and show the filtered dashboard visualization.

Adding filters

We can also drill down using the filter, as we have done in searching. For example, if we want to filter on any particular field value, we need to add the filter and for that we need to do the following:

1. Click on the **Add a filter** link on the top bar below the search textbox:

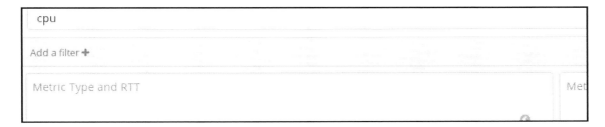

2. This will open up the **Add filter** pop-up box:

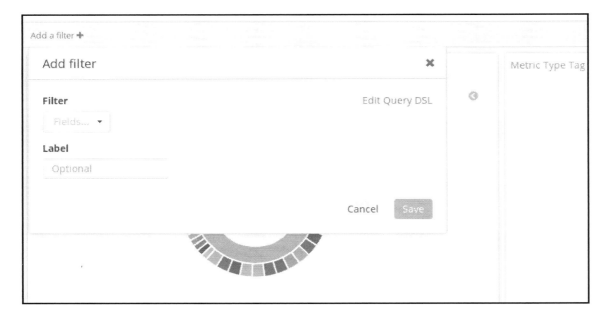

3. Select the field name from the **Filter** dropdown.
4. This will show an additional textbox for operators:

5. Select the operators, such as is, is not, is one of, is not one of, exists, or does not exist.
6. This will further generate the text box for values:

7. Select the value from the dropdown.
8. We can provide the label by entering the text for the label of the filter.
9. Now, click on the **Save** button. This will apply the filter on the dashboard.

This way, we can apply the filter on the dashboard and repeat the same process again to apply multiple filters. In the same way, we can add as many filters as required. In this way, we are able to create filters using the Kibana UI, but we also have the option to write custom Elasticsearch queries to create a filter on the dashboard:

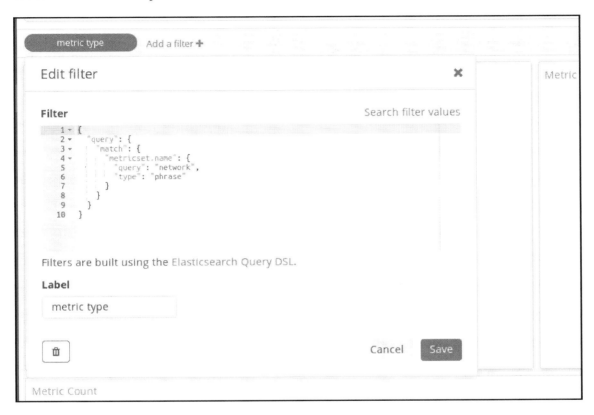

This is quite helpful. Since we know the Elasticsearch query language, we can write more effective queries to achieve the filter. For doing that, we have the link **Edit Query DSL** and we can open the query editor by clicking on it. Now we can rewrite the query here as per our requirements. We have a delete icon on the bottom-left of the panel to delete the filter.

So, here, we'll create another filter for `RTT` by adding a filter for `.rtt` between `100` to `200`:

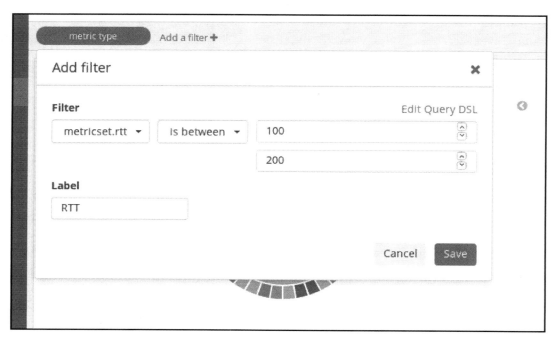

We can see that after applying the filter, the visualization further drills down with `RTT` between `100` and `200`. Now we can see the Elasticsearch query DSL for this applied filter by clicking on the **Edit Query DSL** link:

```
{
  "range": {
    "metricset.rtt": {
      "gte": 100,
      "lt": 200
    }
  }
}
```

Here, we can see that the Elasticsearch query is using the range filter for getting the results of `RTT` between `100` and `200`. We can change the range or add additional conditions by editing this query.

I have given the label as `RTT` and clicked on **Save** to apply this filter as well:

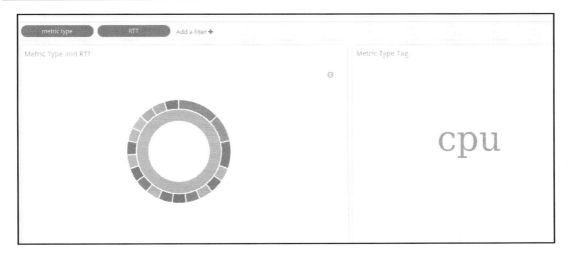

In the previous screenshot, we can see that there are two filters that are applied, and because we have provided the labels to the filters, we can easily identify that the first filter is for the metric type while the other is for `rtt`. We can easily identify the graphics changes after applying these filters as it further drills down the visualization. We can verify the filter result by hovering over the visualization to get the metric data display. In the same manner, we can apply other filters as well.

Applying the time filter

Apart from the search and filter options, we have the option to apply the time filter, as sometimes we are interested to know about time-related data, for example, if we want to know what happened yesterday or want to know the metrics between the last 15 days or the last month. The time filter gives us the luxury to drill down through the date time filter. There can be different use cases for using the time filter; for example, if there was an application failure on a certain interval, then it is important to check the dashboard for that particular time span instead of exploring the dashboard of a complete month. This provides us with the targeted dashboard through which we can easily diagnose the problem of an application. To apply the time filter, we need to do the following:

1. Click on the time picker from the top-right corner of the page:

2. We will get the time filter box with the **Quick**, **Relative**, and **Absolute** options.

3. By default, we can see that when the **Quick** option is selected, we have different options, such as **Today**, **This week/This month/This year**, **Yesterday**, **Day before yesterday**, **This day last week**, **Previous week/Previous month/Previous year**, and **Last 15 minutes/Last 30 minutes**:

4. Under the **Relative** tab, we have the option to set the start time and end time with respect to the start time. The relative time can be in the future or the past:

5. Under the **Absolute** tab, we have the option to set the start date time and end date time, where we need to use the date-time picker to choose this:

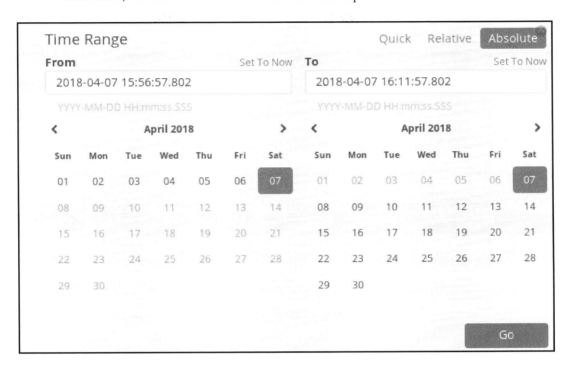

6. We can also use the left and right navigation icon along with the time picker to move forward or backwards in time.

We can apply the time filter, and then on that filtered dashboard, we can search or apply further different filters. This way, Kibana provides us with the option to apply all filters to get the most relevant result through which we can easily make any decision.

Clicking on visualizations

The easiest and most convenient way to filter the dashboard is by clicking on the visualization to filter. For example, in the metric type pie chart, we can click on any part to drill down on that level:

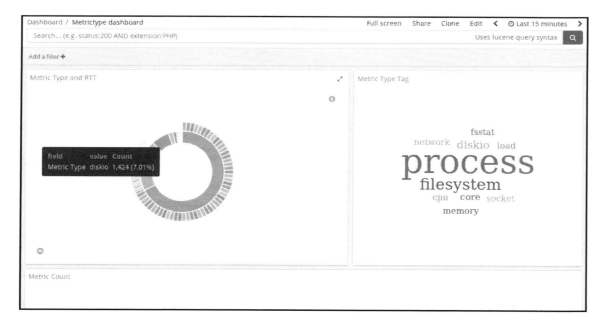

For example, in the previous screen, I have clicked on the green section, which is showing the metric type as **diskio**. After clicking on this section, we can see the filter that has been applied as **diskio**. We can see the result in the following screenshot:

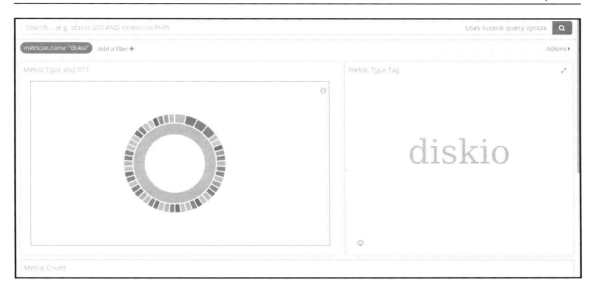

So, here we can see that we have applied the filter on the metric type as **diskio** and the complete dashboard is now filtered on that. In the same way, we can apply filters on anything just by clicking on that section. Similarly, in the next visualization, which is the tag cloud, we can click on any word to filter it:

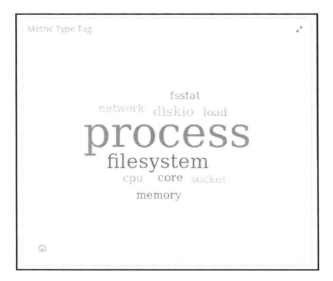

For example, if I click on the **load** metric type from the tag cloud, it will filter out on the basis of that and result in the following screenshot:

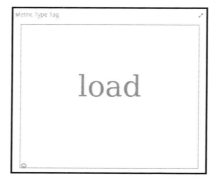

In this way, we can play around and apply as many filters as are possible. This type of filter is a shortcut for applying filters through the given link and is quite convenient for handling top-level management, as this does not require any understanding of using filters. You just need to click on the section of interest and Kibana will drill down to that level.

Now, I will show you how we can see the filter code that is generated in the background:

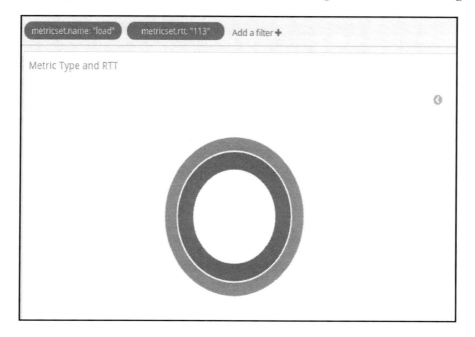

In the previous screenshot, I have filtered by clicking on the section with an RTT value of 113, which is available for the metric type as load. The red part is showing the metric type as load and the blue part is showing an RTT value of 113. After getting this result of the visualization, we can see the filter tab with the following filter text display:

```
metric.rtt:'113'
```

After clicking on the **Edit** button on the filter menu after hovering over it, we will get the following screenshot:

Here, we can see that in the filter edit box, the condition for rtt is 113 is applied. We can also get the Elasticsearch query DSL for the same and in this way, just by clicking, we can get the Elasticsearch query that can be modified and applied by clicking on the **Save** button in the filter box.

Summary

In this chapter, we have covered the process of creating the dashboard after creating and integrating the visualization, and then we looked at how we can apply a filter on it. We have seen four different ways of filtering; for example, searching the required field or searching across all the fields to drill down through dashboard visualizations. Then, we covered how to apply filters using the **add a filter** link on the top menu. The filter option not only provides us with the box to do all kinds of filtering, but also provides us with a way to convert the filter that we have created using Kibana UI in an Elasticsearch query DSL.

We have also covered how we can save the dashboard for further use and share it with others by sharing the static dashboard or most recent dashboard that reflects all the new changes. We can edit this to do things, such as reorder the visualizations to move the key performance indicators on top or resize the visualizations to show them as per their size or area required.

In the next chapter, we will learn about Timelion, which is a time series based data visualization of Kibana. In Timelion, we can write simple expressions to play with time series data, perform different calculations, and can visualize the result. It provides us with the option to apply different methods using chaining and consolidate the result into a single chart. There are different styling functions available in Timelion, which can be used to make the graphs more effective and meaningful. Also, there are mathematical functions to apply mathematical calculations.

6
Handling Time Series Data with Timelion

In this chapter, we will learn about Kibana Timelion, which works on time series data of Elasticsearch. It provides a totally different interface, through which we can chain queries, do transformations, and do visualization in a single place. Timelion provides us with a way through which we can integrate multiple data source (indices) into a single visualization. It also provides a wide range of mathematical functions that can be used on data such as sum, cumulative sum, division, derivatives, and many more.

This chapter will be very interesting. If you learn Timelion's way to interact with data, it is quite easy to deal with many available functions and apply them to create visualizations such as plotting a graph with a series on the current time against which we can draw the plot for the same data series in any other time duration such as yesterday, a week ago, a month ago, or a year ago. It is difficult to get started as there is no UI option available on the Kibana Timelion page. However, once you are familiar with it by using the different functions that are available, it is easy to create visualizations using Timelion.

Timelion was introduced with Kibana 5.0 and we need not do any installation for it as it comes in-built with Kibana. There is another visualization tool, Grafana, that was compared many times with Kibana. Grafana and Kibana both have their own pros and cons, but Kibana was lacking mainly on handling time series data but after introducing Timelion they have filled that gap and now we can play around with any timeseries data from Elasticsearch.

Thus, we can say that Timelion is an important feature of Kibana and can we use it to create rather useful graphs, which can be included in the dashboard. It has different data sources such as Elasticsearch, and World Bank data, through which we can get the data directly into the Timelion graphs. Through function chaining, we can achieve multiple operations/features on a single graph. Apart from functions, it has different function parameters that are very handy, such as offset.

Timelion interface

On Kibana, we have a link **Timelion** on the left menu and by clicking on it we can open the Timelion interface:

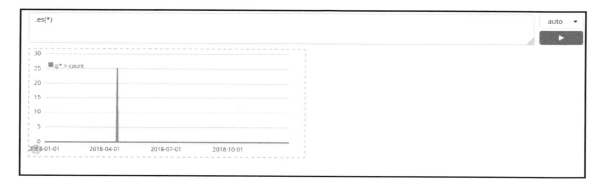

On the Timelion screen, we can see a textbox with the **.es(*)** expression, which denotes that currently we are getting data from all the indices. The .es function counts the number of documents in Elasticsearch and creates the default graph showing the amount of documents created over a selected time span. It shows the default query, which fetches everything from Elasticsearch and draws it over time. In front of the expression box, we have a dropdown to set the refresh duration and below that dropdown we have an execute button, which is used to run the query written inside the expression box.

We have a visualization below the expression box, which shows the timeseries graph. Timelion provides with us hints such as, if we put a dot after .es(*), then Kibana will show us the list of functions available in a dropdown:

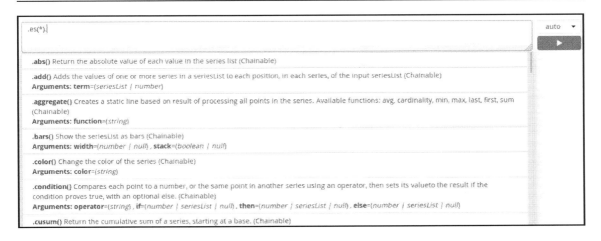

We can see the functions in the dropdown in ascending order of name, that is, .abs(), .add(), .bars(), .color, .condition(), and so on. Timelion has its own language expression for defining the functions. It provides us with the chaining feature through which we can link the functions together. Each expression starts with a dot symbol and uses a dot to link with the other functions. It provides the autofill feature after typing the dot.

We can add multiple graphs on a Timelion sheet and to add a new graph we need to click on the **Add link** from the top menu bar. There is a **New** link, which creates a fresh new sheet for Timelion. Using the **Save** button, we can save the Timelion sheet or currently focused visualization. By saving the Timelion, we can use it later for the dashboard. We can change the date range using the date-time picker in the upper right corner.

Timeline expression

When we open the Timeline window for the first time, it shows the expression .es(*), which means it shows all the indexes of Elasticsearch and combines them. If we want to fetch any specific Elasticsearch index, then we need to provide the name of the index inside the .es() method, as shown in the following command:

```
.es(index=metricbeat-*)
```

In this way, we are specifying the name of the index as `metricbeat-*`. It helps us to get the details from any specific index:

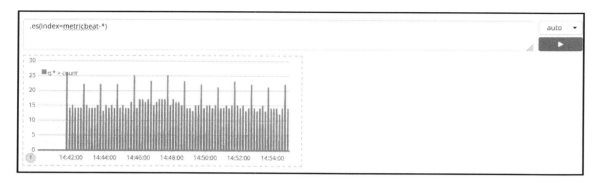

The Timelion expression starts with a dot. After that, we provide the function name and then the parentheses, in which we provide all the parameters that we can apply. By default, an asterisk is shown inside the parentheses to fetch all the available index data.

.es function parameters

The `.es` function is used to pull the data from the Elasticsearch instance. The `.es` function can have multiple parameters and each parameter has a name that can be set inside the parentheses to set the value of that property. The parameter also has an order and we must follow the order to run the expression. If we skip the name of the parameter, Timelion will automatically assign the name as per the chosen order for the values. Now, let's speak about the parameters:

- The first parameter is q, which is used in queries and is used to filter the data based on the given value:

  ```
  .es(q=*)
  .es(q=country:de)
  ```

- The second parameter is `index`, which can be used to specify the name of the Elasticsearch index on which we will perform the operations. In this way, we can apply the query on a single index instead of multiple indices:

  ```
  .es(index=metricbeat-*)
  .es(q='some query', index=logstash-*)
  ```

- Another parameter is `metric` in which we can specify the type of metric we want to apply on the index such as `agg`, `avg`, `sum`, `min`, and `max` followed by the field name:

  ```
  .es(metric=min:system.process.name)
  ```

- We can use the `split` parameter for splitting the series by a limit, for example, `hostname:5` to fetch the top five hostnames:

  ```
  .es(split=country:4, metric=sum:bytes)
  ```

- Another parameter is `offset`, which can be used to offset the data by giving a time range:

  ```
  .es(offset=-1w)
  ```

- We also have the time-field parameter, which can be used to set any field of type date for the *x* axis. We have two options to set the time field: setting `timelion:es.timefield` from the **Advanced Setting** link of Kibana or by using this time-field parameter of the `.es` function. The **Advanced Setting** option applies the time field globally while the parameter option sets it for individual series.

Chainable methods

There are various methods in Kibana Timelion that can be used as chainable method, which means we can add them to any method by placing a dot and then the method name. Many of them are used for different calculations, which we can perform on Elasticsearch index data. We can perform different calculations such as sum, average, min, and max using Timelion and it is very useful for applying them to create the visualization. Using the data of the Elasticsearch index, we can do the calculations and transform the data to create different visualizations. Next, we will discuss the available chainable methods.

.sum()

We can use the `.sum()` method in a scenario where we want to combine certain metrics such as to calculate the total amount of memory usage for the server using the `metric` argument:

```
.es(metric='sum:system.memory.used.bytes')
```

Here, we are combining the system memory used in bytes metric:

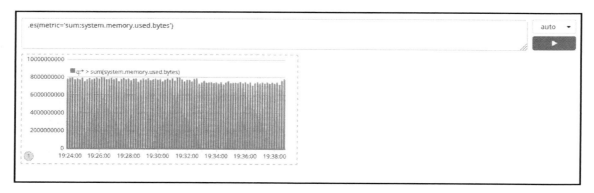

The sum function can be useful for all these types of scenarios where we are trying to consolidate a metric over time.

.avg()

We use this `.avg()` function for getting the average of a numeric field in Elasticsearch index data. For explaining this function here, we can use the `.avg()` function on the same field to get the average metric:

```
.es(metric='avg:system.memory.used.bytes')
```

Using the preceding expression, we can fetch the average for system memory consumed in bytes. The following screen shows the result of the expression; we can see the graph depicting the average of system memory consumed in bytes:

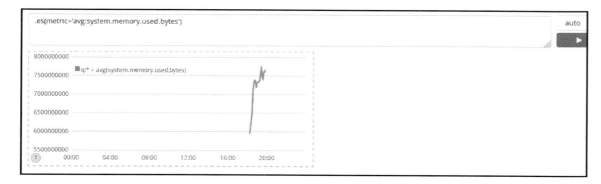

.min()

The `.min()` function returns minimum values of one or more series in each position. It sets a point to the lowest value:

```
.es(metric='min:system.memory.used.bytes')
```

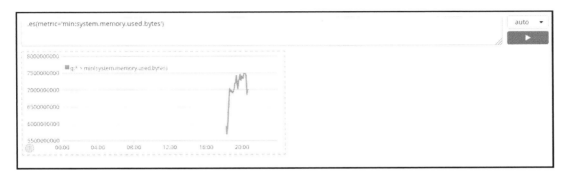

.max()

Similar to the `.min()` function, we have the `.max()` function, which returns the maximum values of one or more series in each position and sets a point to the highest value:

```
.es(metric='max:system.memory.used.bytes')
```

Now, if we can compare the image of the `.max()` function with the image of the `.min()` function, we can see the same type of trend but one is on a lower range than the other. By applying these functions, we can get the insight of the data and can easily know the data range with their trends.:

.log()

The `.log()` function takes each value in the series list and returns the logarithm for that value. We can use the `.log()` function for calculating the logarithm of all values and also specify the logarithmic base optionally:

```
.static(1500).log()
```

In this way, by passing any static value, we can get the logarithm of that value.

.abs()

The `.abs()` function returns the absolute values for each value in the series. We can use this function if we are getting non-absolute values for the *y* axis on the graph and to plot the graph properly we need to convert them into absolute values:

```
.static(-5).abs()
```

Here, we can convert the static value −5 into the absolute value 5:

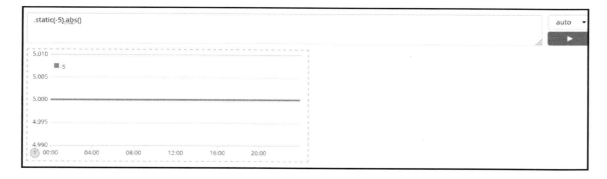

.divide()

The `.divide()` function is used to divide the values of one or more series. For example, we can use this function to convert a series from bytes to megabytes by dividing it by `1048576`:

```
.es(metric=max:system.network.in.bytes).divide(1048576)
```

.multiply()

The .multiply() function multiplies the series by a given number. We can use the .multiply() method to convert all outbound traffic to a negative value by multiplying it by −1:

```
.es(metric=max:system.network.out.bytes).multiply(-1)
```

.derivative()

It is very important to plot the rate of changes for network traffic, as without that we will not be able to track the rate at which the values are changing. The derivative() function is used to ensure that we are plotting the rate of change. We only need to append the derivative() function and there is no parameter in this function:

```
.es(metric=max:system.network.out.bytes).derivative().multiply(-1)
```

We can see the previous graph and now after seeing this graph we can easily compare the plotted values:

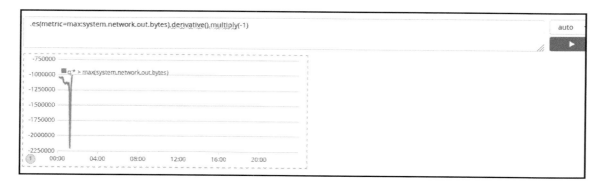

.bars()

The .bars() function is used to show the data series in the form of bars:

```
.es(*).bars()
```

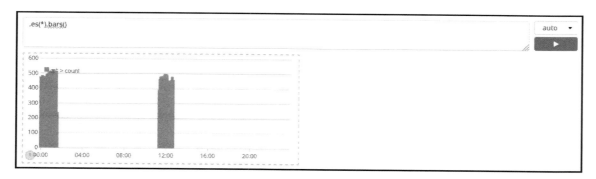

By default, the visualization shows a line graph, but we can change it to a bar chart using the .bar() function.

.color()

The `.color()` function is used to change the color of the series. It is very important when we are showing multiple metrics on a graph and in that case we can differentiate them using different colors:

```
.es(metric='max:system.memory.used.bytes').color('blue')
.es(metric='min:system.memory.used.bytes').color('green')
```

Here, we are showing the min and max plots with two different colors, blue and green, for `system.memory.used.bytes`.

.label()

The `.label()` method is used to change the label of the series. In the previous example, we can see long labels such as `.es(metric='max:system.memory.used.bytes').color('blue')` and `.es(metric='min:system.memory.used.bytes').color('green')`. They have taken a lot of space on the graph and are also quite difficult to read. Here, we can apply the `.label()` function to make it more meaningful and clean:

```
.es(metric='max:system.memory.used.bytes').color('blue').label('max memory usage')
.es(metric='min:system.memory.used.bytes').color('green').label('min memory usage')
```

So, here, we have applied the label function after the `color` function to change the label:

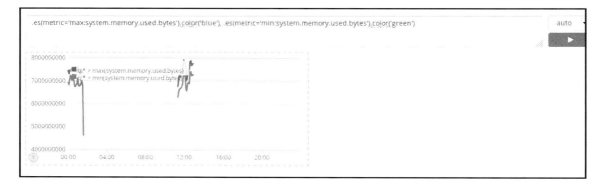

.legend()

The .legend() function is used to set the position and style of the legends:

```
.es(metric='max:system.memory.used.bytes').label('max memory
usage').legend(ne,1) .es(metric='min:system.memory.used.bytes').label('min
memory usage').legend(ne,1)
```

Here, we have used the .legend() function with the first parameter, which is showing the location, while the second parameter is showing the number of columns. As well as these two parameters, we also have two more parameters to show the time value in legend on graph hovering and other to set the time format. Kibana provides us with the type hint, so at any time we can check and modify the function's parameters:

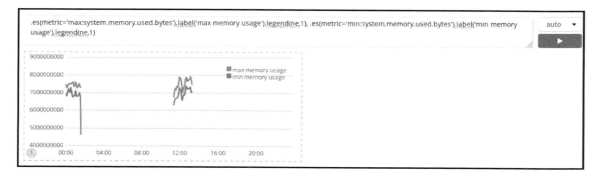

.movingaverage()

The .movingaverage() function is used to calculate the moving average for a given time window. We can use the short form of the function as .mvavg(). It is used to smooth the series by applying a moving average to the series values:

```
.es().color(blue), .es().mvavg(5h).color(green)
```

Here, we have taken a normal series plot and an other with a moving average. We have applied the color green to the moving average plot so that it can be easily distinguished by seeing the plot:

Here, you can see that the normal metric plot has a lot of curves while the moving average plot is quite smooth.

.trend()

The `.trend()` function uses the regression algorithm and draws a trend line using that. We can use the `.trend()` chaining function on any series for drawing a trend line instead of the normal plot:

```
.es().color(blue).trend(),   .es().color(red)
```

In the previous example, we are plotting two graphs, that is, one normal series value plot and the other using the regression trend, that is, the `.trend()` function:

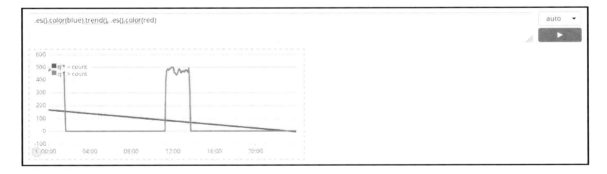

.range()

We can use the `.range()` function to change the max and min of a series and re-plot the graph according to the given values. The `.range()` function limits the series to a new range of values by rewriting the minimum and maximum value for the series. We can use this function when we are more concerned about any specific data range rather than the complete range:

```
.es().color(blue).trend(), .es().color(red).range(150,50)
```

Here, we have set the range for the red plot while the blue plot will be shown in the same way:

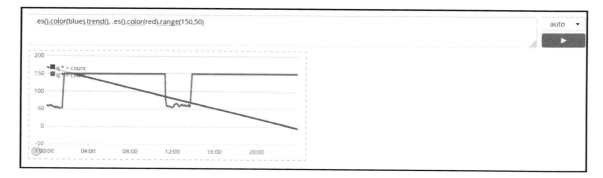

.precision()

The `.precision()` function is used to round the decimal number as the number of values of the decimal portion:

```
.static(1.456786).precision(1)
```

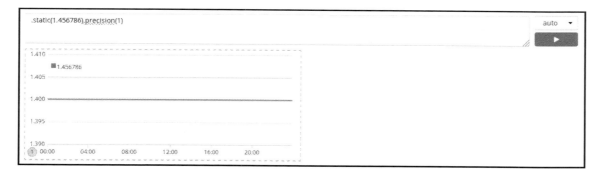

If we put 0 in the precision parameter, we will get the following:

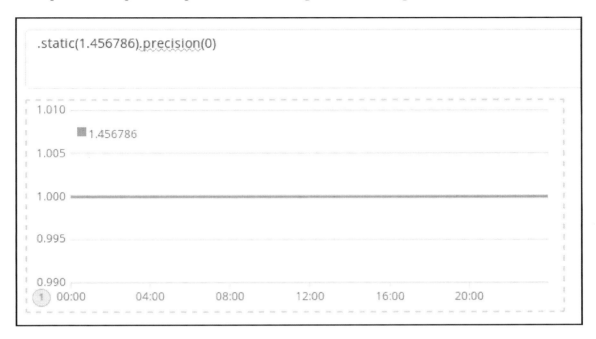

In this way, the `.precision()` function converts the decimal part of a number as per the given parameter.

Data source functions

Kibana Timelion provides us with the option to load the data into the graph. We have already discussed one data source, `function.es()`, which loads data from Elasticsearch. Apart from `.es()`, Timelion also provides us with some more data sources from whuch we can load the data.

Some of them are World Bank and Quandl. We will now discuss the sources one by one.

Elasticsearch

The first data source is Elasticsearch and it is applied by default when we open the Timelion interface on Kibana. It is denoted with the `.es()` function and provides a lot of functionalities through which we can play around on the Elasticsearch index data.

The `.es()` function has different parameters, which we have already discussed such as `split`, which splits the series plot by the value of a specific field and the `metric` parameter to control the calculation of the y axis value. We can specify additional metrics aggregation, for example, `avg`, `min`, or `max`:

```
.es(metric='max:system.memory.used.bytes').label('max memory
usage').legend(ne,1).lines().movingaverage(),
.es(metric='min:system.memory.used.bytes').label('min memory
usage').legend(ne,1).lines().movingaverage()
```

In above block I have written two expressions to fetch the moving average where in first expression the max value of memory consumption is extracted and in second expression min value of memory consumption is extracted. After extracting the values I have given the label, applied the legend location, set the graph type as line and applied movingaverage function to get the moving average of the value.

Static/value

We can use `.static()` or its alias `.value()` to draw a plain horizontal line for a given value. This is quite useful for setting a threshold plot or any critical line display on the graph:

```
.es(), .static(250, label='Normal level')
```

Here, we have created the normal level line display through which it is quite easy for us to distinguish above the normal line and below the normal line on the plotted graph:

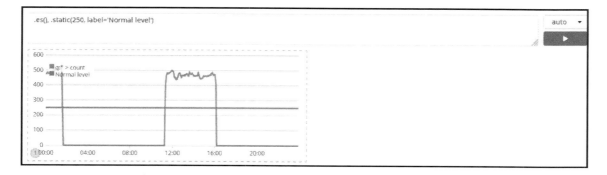

World bank

Kibana Timelion offers us functions to load the World Bank data directly into Timelion graphs. The World Bank data sources a lot of statistical data from throughout the world such as population and GDP. We can use the `.wbi()` or `.worldbank_indicators()` function to get the World Bank data into our graph. The function accepts the following two parameters:

- **Country**: This is the ISO code for the specific country.
- **Indicator**: This is a valid World Bank Indicator. We can get the details of these indicators on Work Bank's data portal. For example, **NY.GDP.MKTP.CD** is used for the GDP of a country, and **SP.POP.0014.TO.ZS** is used for population ages 0 to 14 in percentage.

To plot the GDP of India and Pakistan, we can use the `.wbi()` function as follows:

```
.wbi(country=in, indicator=NY.GDP.MKTP.CD), .wbi(country=pk,
indicator=NY.GDP.MKTP.CD)
```

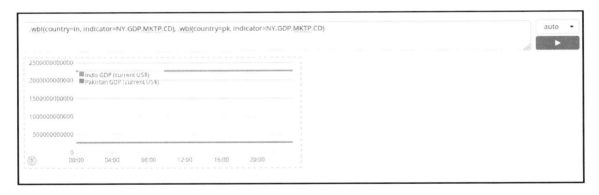

Along with the `.wbi()` function, we also have the `.wb()` function in which we can pass the path of the World Bank API request as the code parameter. We can use the `.wb()` function if we are using different URLs of the World Bank data portal.

Now, if we want to see what has been happening with the world GDP since the five years ago, first we need to select **Last 5 years** from the **Quick** option of the date time picker in the upper right corner of the page.

After that, we need to provide the following expression:

```
.wbi(indicator=NY.GDP.MKTP.CD).trend().label('Trend of world GDP'),
.wbi(indicator=NY.GDP.MKTP.CD).color(blue)
```

Here, we are plotting two things: first, the trend of the world's GDP flow using regression and, second, the actual plot of the world's GDP data. This will plot the following graph:

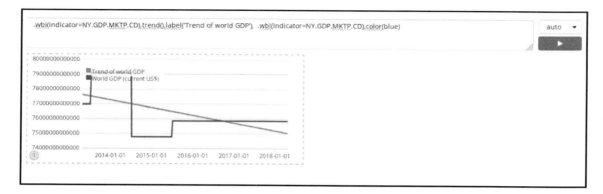

In the preceding graph, the blue plot is showing the actual flow of the world's GDP data and the green plot is showing the trend of GDP. So, after looking at this graph, we can say that the world's GDP has been decreasing over a period of 5 years.

After checking the span of 5 years, now let's check the last 2 years. For that, we need to again set the time as **Last 2 years** from the date time picker in the upper right corner and click on **Apply**:

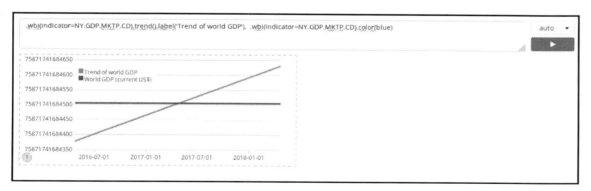

Now, in this chart of the world's GDP for the last 2 years, we can see that the blue plot is showing the actual GDP data and the green plot is showing the GDP trend for the last 2 years. Now, in the following chart, we can see that the GDP is increasing:

Setting the offset for data sources

All of the data source functions have a common parameter known as offset. We can use this function to fetch the data by a specific time range. It is quite an interesting feature as we can use it to compare the data from different time ranges. We can pass positive or negative values by adding the unit. Units can be denoted as follows:

```
s:  seconds
m:  minutes
h:  hours
d:  days
w:  weeks
M for months
y:  years
```

We can do the following to draw the current data series against the last hour data series:

```
.es().label(current), .es(offset=-1h).label('prev hour')
```

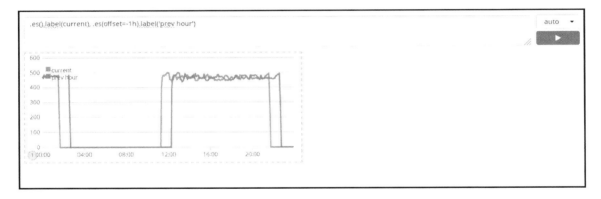

The offset parameter for data source is very important as these kinds of graphs cannot be created in Kibana visualizations. In Timelion, we can draw graphs through multiple time ranges using custom labels such as the "current date", "last week", or "last month" and when we plot these types of graphs, it provides us with a clear insight as to what is going on, that is, whether the trend is going in a positive direction, or negative direction, or there is no change.

Now, let's take another example. We will plot the graph using offset and try to analyze the trend. I'll plot a graph by comparing the current data with yesterday's data:

```
.es().label("Original"),.es(offset=-1d).label("yesterday's offset"),
.es().subtract(.es(offset=-1d)).label("Difference").lines(steps=1,fill=2,wi
dth=0)
```

In the preceding example, I have done two things: first, plotted the current data and yesterday's data in a normal linear form, and second, subtracted yesterday's data from the current data and plotted a filled line graph on top of that.

In this way, the generated graph is showing the difference in a more clear way, which we can easily understand. Refer to the following screenshot:

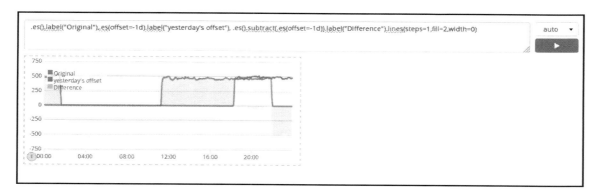

So what we have done so far is created a time range difference graph using the offset parameter and then applied some formatting on top of it to make it more appealing and clear to understand for the end user.

Saving Timelion graph

After creating the required graph in Timelion, it is important to save it for future use and for that we need to click on the **Save** link in the upper right menu of Kibana, which will open the following screen:

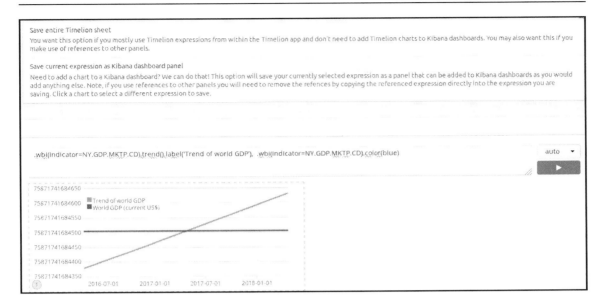

Here, we have the following two options:

- **Save entire Timelion sheet**: We can use this option if we want this Timelion expression to be used in the Timelion section only and do not want to include the graphs in Kibana dashboards.
- **Save current expression as Kibana dashboard panel**: We can use this option if we want to add the Timelion graph into the Kibana dashboard. This option will save the panel of the currently selected expression and after saving that, we can add this to the Kibana dashboard in the same way as we add other visualizations.

Now, let's save it in the first way by clicking on the first section:

In the preceding screenshot, we need to provide the name of the sheet and click on the **Save** button. This will save the Timelion sheet. Now, we can open this sheet anytime from Timelion the screen. Just click on the **Open** link from the upper right menu, which will open the following screen:

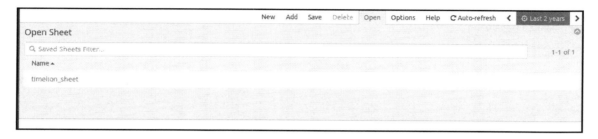

In the **Open Sheet** screen, we can see all the saved Timelion sheets. Now, we can click on **Save Sheet** to open it.

In this way, we can save and open the Timelion sheet and use the saved expressions whenever required. Now, let's use the second method to save the current selected graph only, for that we need to click on the **Save current expression as Kibana dashboard panel** box.

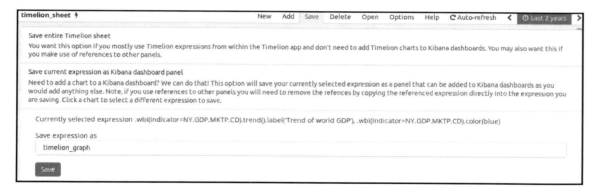

In the preceding screenshot, fill the name of the Timelion graph and click on the **Save** button, which will save the Timelion graph.

Now, we will add this Timelion graph to the Kibana dashboard and, for that, we need to click on the **Dashboard** link from the left-hand menu:

Now, from the dashboard screen, click on the **Add** button to add the Timelion graph into the dashboard:

On dashboard **Add Panels** screen, we can search the name of the Timelion graph and click on the name to add it into that dashboard area:

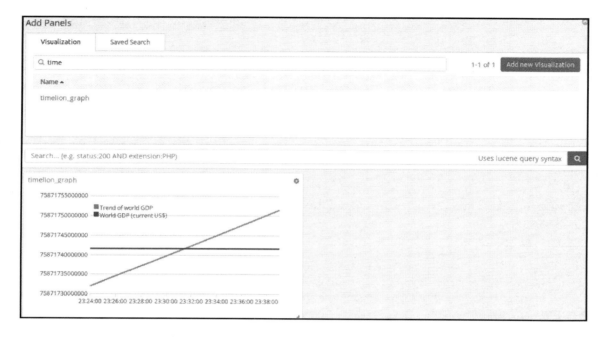

In this way, we can add the Timelion visualization on the Kibana dashboard along with other visualizations.

Timelion sheet option

Through sheet options, we can set a number of columns which must be divided evenly into 12 and the number of rows each graph should take. We can set these values to change the graph areas as per the requirement:

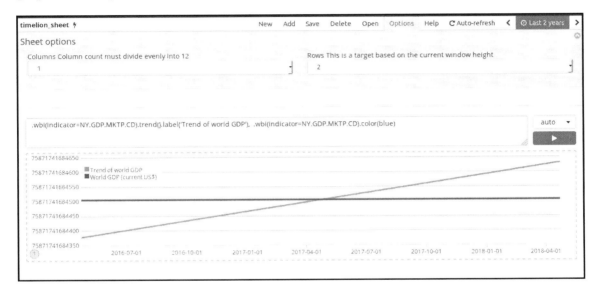

Deleting Timelion sheet

We can delete a Timelion sheet and for that we need to click on the **Delete** link on the upper right menu of Kibana:

We will get a confirmation pop-up screen with a message that says **You can't recover deleted sheets**. Now, click on the **Delete** button on the popup to delete the current Timelion sheet.

Timelion help

We have a **Help** link on the upper right menu of Kibana. We can get the help screen with function reference and keyboard tips options by clicking on the **Help** link.

Function reference

Under **Function reference**, we can get help for all the available functions:

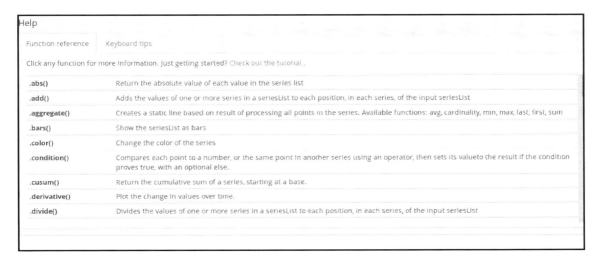

Here, we can get the list of Timelion functions. We can scroll down to get more functions and by clicking on any function, we can get more details about that function. This is quite helpful as we can take the function reference from here in order to use it in the Timelion expressions.

Keyboard tips

Under **Keyboard tips**, we can get keyboard shortcuts, which we can use during Timelion graph creation:

The preceding screen shows the **Keyboard tips** tab, where we can see keyboard shortcuts and their description. These shortcuts are quite handy as they increase the productivity.

Timelion auto-refresh

The Timelion autorefresh option is quite handy. This is because, in order to check changes in the data, we need to click on the **Submit** button, but using the autorefresh option, we can set the page refresh rate. For example, if we set autorefresh to 5 seconds, the page will refresh automatically after every 5 seconds and we can easily see the changes without clicking on the **Submit** button every time:

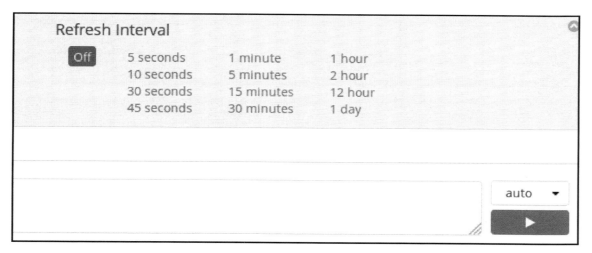

In the preceding screenshot, we have multiple options from 5 seconds to 1 day for setting the autorefresh interval.

Summary

In this chapter, we covered Kibana Timelion features and expressions, through which we can create graphs. There were different styling functions, which can be applied to make graphs more effective and meaningful, such as .color() and .label(). Apart from styling functions, we also discussed other mathematical functions, which can be used to perform various mathematical operations on series data.

Furthermore, we covered various data sources such as Elasticsearch, static, and the World Bank and how we can use them for creating graphs. These data sources provide us the functions through which we can directly use their data into our graphs.

We also covered how to use the `offset` parameter to plot time difference graphs for getting instant information about how data has evolved over time and through which the management can take decisions. We also explained the GDP trend through offset parameter by taking the World Bank data source.

Then, we covered various options that we can use in Timelion such as to save them in the form of sheets for later use or save it as a graph in order to utilize the graph in the Kibana dashboard. Then, we have explained the help option of Timelion through which we can take the function reference and keyboard tips. So, in this chapter, we have covered all the aspects of Timelion and their importance.

In the next chapter, we will cover Kibana Dev Tools and look at different ways through which we can interact with Elasticsearch. Dev Tools has a console to run Elasticsearch queries directly from Kibana. We will also cover the options to profile the queries and aggregations using the query profile and aggregation profile options of Dev Tools. This provides us with a tool through which we can monitor the query and aggregation execution. Finally, we will cover the Grok debugger through which we can test our grok syntax and apply that on test data to validate the syntax.

7
Interact with Your Data Using Dev Tools

Kibana depends on Elasticsearch in order to read the indices and generate visualizations and dashboards. Very often, we need to interact with the Elasticsearch cluster to get some details, fetch data, and delete records or indices for which we have to do the curl request either from the Elasticsearch client or console. Kibana provides a console from where we can directly interact with Elasticsearch APIs. It not only provides the editor but also many other features that are quite useful, as follows:

- Syntax completion
- Formatting of expressions
- Copying the `curl` command to execute from Terminal

It also provides an output window in which we can see the Elasticsearch response. Therefore, on a single window, we have an input window for the Elasticsearch expression and an output window to get the results of the expression that we are going to execute.

Dev Tools also provides us the **History** tab through which we can see the queries that we had executed earlier and want to use again. We can also customize the font size and text wrapping and enable or disable auto-complete.

In Kibana Dev Tools, we have a dedicated help section from where we can see different documentation options such as a format of query. It also provides the keyboard shortcuts that we can use to perform many operations under the Kibana Dev Tool page.

In this way, Kibana Dev Tools is very important for interacting with Elasticsearch directly from Kibana, and we can perform every operations on the Elasticsearch cluster. It also provides **Search Profiler** and **Grok Debugger** if we are using X-Pack with Kibana.

Console

Kibana Dev Tools is a development tool that can be used to interact with the Elasticsearch index. In Dev Tools, we have a screen with a console plugin. Console plugin has UI through which we can interact with Elasticsearch using REST API. Console UI has the following two blocks:

- **Editor**: We can request the Elasticsearch cluster through statements or queries using the REST API
- **Response pane**: This shows the response of the Elasticsearch request:

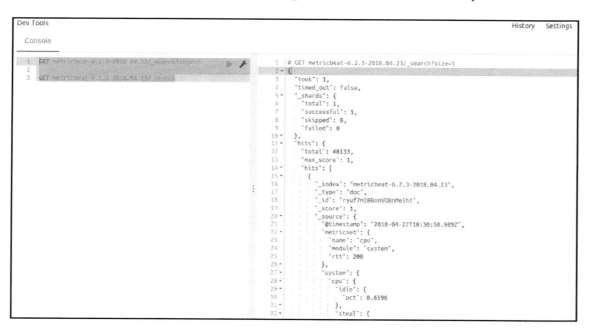

In the previous screen, we can see the left and right block. The left block is a request editor where we can write the Elasticsearch queries, and the right block is a response pane on which we can get the response from Elasticsearch.

The request editor provides the feature of syntax completion, as seen in the following screen:

As shown in the preceding screenshot, when we started typing _sea, the suggestion box opened with different options. From these options, we can pick the value we want to use for the Elasticsearch query. Auto-suggest is a very important feature in Kibana Dev Tools, as during query syntax creation these suggestions are very useful because it saves time and iterations to debug the issue in query. Auto-suggest feature suggests keywords when we start typing, and from these suggested keywords we can pick the one as per our requirement.

On the following screen, we can see the settings icon:

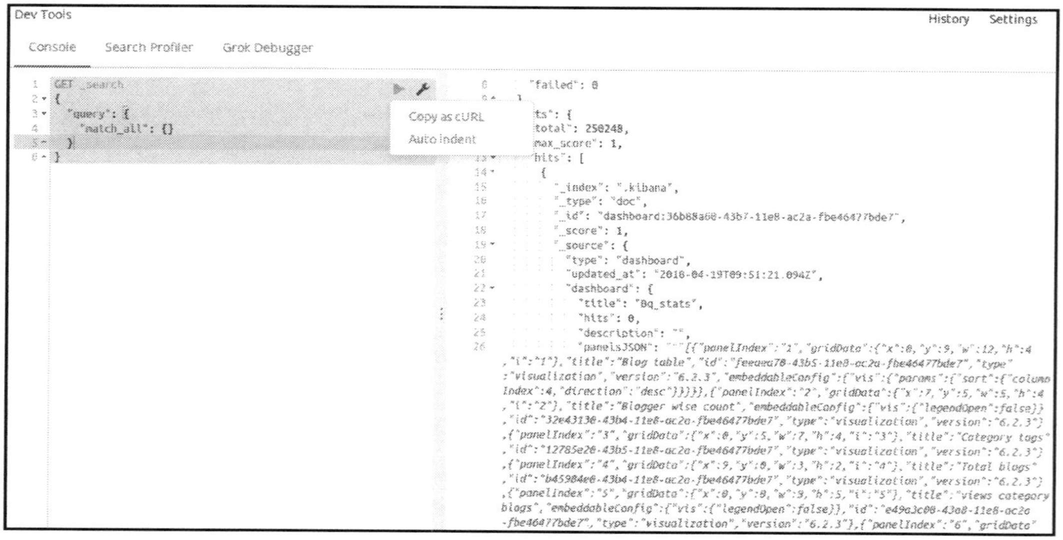

The settings icon has the following two options, which appear after clicking on the icon:

- **Copy as cURL**
- **Auto indent**

Copy as cURL

The **Copy as cURL** option copies the code in the form of the `curl` syntax, which we can directly paste on Terminal to run it and get the result back from Elasticsearch.

For example, we have the following code on a console query pane:

```
GET _search
{
  "query": {
    "match_all": {}
  }
}
```

Now if we copy this code using the **Copy as cURL** option and then paste it, we will get the following `curl` code:

```
curl -XGET "http://localhost:9200/_search" -H 'Content-Type:
```

```
application/json' -d'
{
  "query": {
    "match_all": {}
  }
}'
```

Now we can directly paste this code on a Terminal and hit *Enter* to send the request on Elasticsearch, and then will get the response back from Elasticsearch.

Auto indent

Using the **Auto indent** link, we can indent the queries in different ways. Take the example of an unformatted query. See the following screenshot:

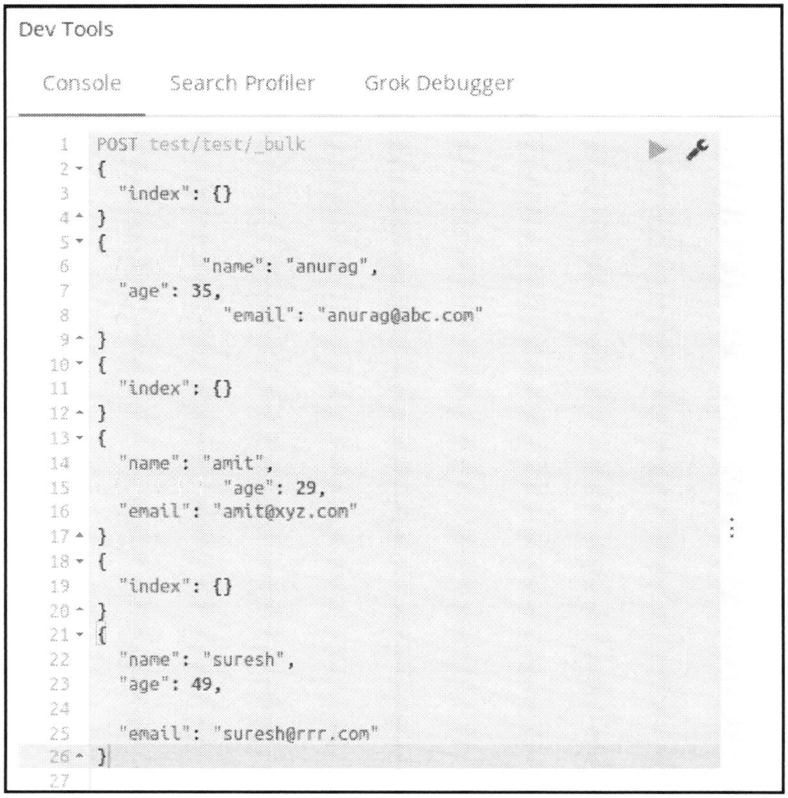

In the previous screenshot, a query is not formatted properly, and when we click on **Auto indent**, it will format it properly in a single line. See the following screenshot:

```
Dev Tools

Console      Search Profiler      Grok Debugger

1  POST test/test/_bulk                                           ▶  🔧
2  {"index":{}}
3  {"name":"anurag","age":35,"email":"anurag@abc.com"}
4  {"index":{}}
5  {"name":"amit","age":29,"email":"amit@xyz.com"}
6  {"index":{}}
7  {"name":"suresh","age":49,"email":"suresh@rrr.com"}
8
```

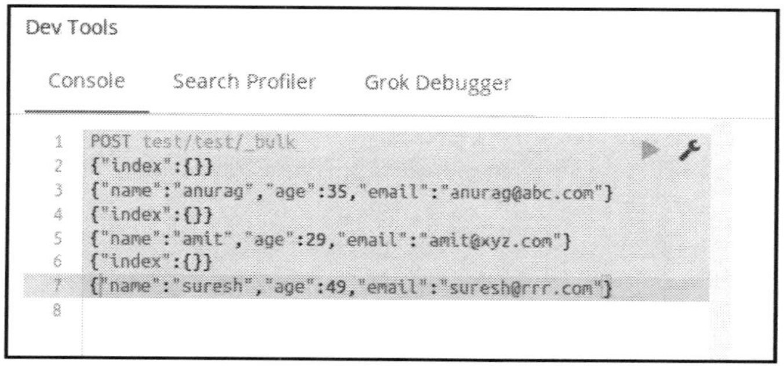

In the preceding screenshot, the query is indented in a single line. Now, if we again click on the **Auto indent** link, it will format the query in an expanded way. See the following screenshot:

```
Dev Tools

Console      Search Profiler      Grok Debugger

 1  POST test/test/_bulk
 2▼ {
 3      "index": {}
 4▲ }
 5▼ {
 6      "name": "anurag",
 7      "age": 35,                                                ▶  🔧
 8      "email": "anurag@abc.com"
 9▲ }
10▼ {
11      "index": {}
12▲ }
13▼ {
14      "name": "amit",
15      "age": 29,
16      "email": "amit@xyz.com"
17▲ }                                                              ⋮
18▼ {
19      "index": {}
20▲ }
21▼ {
22      "name": "suresh",
23      "age": 49,
24      "email": "suresh@rrr.com"
25▲ }
26
```

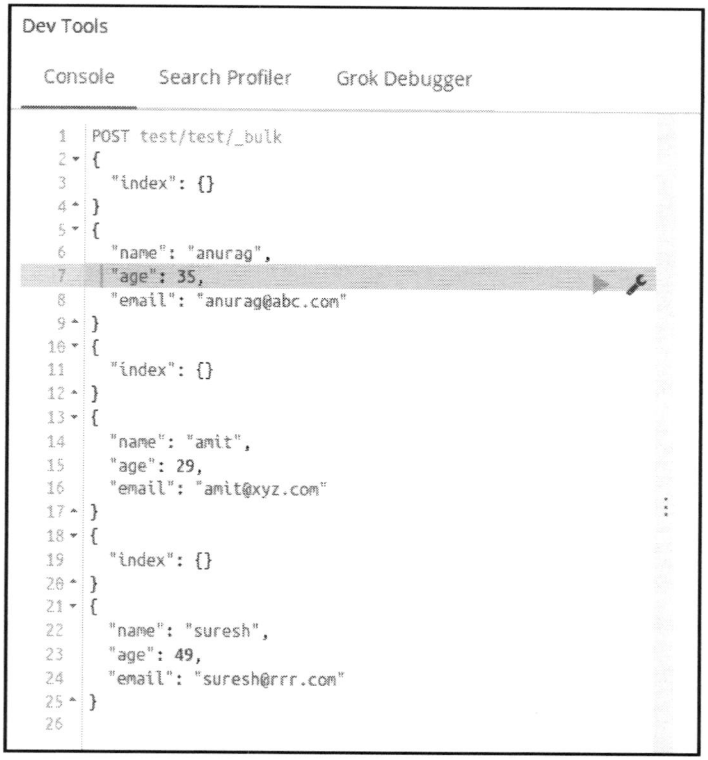

In the previous screenshot, we can see that the query is formatted in an expanded way. After this, the **Auto indent** link works as a toggle link, and on every click, it converts the format into a single line format, and expanded format and vice versa.

We also have a button name, that is, **click to send request**, which we can see in the following screenshot:

This button is used to run the code of request pane and get the response on the right pane. Whenever we write something or change something on the left pane, we need to click on this button to get the updated result on the right pane.

Multiple requests in console

In the Dev Tools console editor, we can write multiple requests one after another. See the following code:

```
POST test/test/_bulk
{"index":{}}
{"name":"anurag","age":35,"email":"anurag@abc.com"}
{"index":{}}
{"name":"amit","age":29,"email":"amit@xyz.com"}
{"index":{}}
```

```
{"name":"suresh","age":49,"email":"suresh@rrr.com"}
{"index":{}}
{"name":"mahesh","age":21,"email":"mahesh@ggg.com"}
{"index":{}}
{"name":"atul","age":32,"email":"atul@ee.com"}

GET test

DELETE test
```

Here are three different operations:

- Create test index with five documents
- Get the index data
- Delete the test index

Now to run them in one go, we need to select all and then click on the **Execute** button. After the query execution, we should get the following response:

```
# POST test/test/_bulk
{
  "took": 4873,
  "errors": false,
  "items": [
    {
      "index": {
        "_index": "test",
        "_type": "test",
        "_id": "ICl_B2MBTOSncJz8RPug",
        "_version": 1,
        "result": "created",
        "_shards": {
          "total": 2,
          "successful": 1,
          "failed": 0
        },
        "_seq_no": 0,
        "_primary_term": 1,
        "status": 201
      }
    },
    {
      "index": {
        "_index": "test",
        "_type": "test",
        "_id": "ISl_B2MBTOSncJz8RPug",
        "_version": 1,
```

```
      "result": "created",
      "_shards": {
        "total": 2,
        "successful": 1,
        "failed": 0
      },
      "_seq_no": 0,
      "_primary_term": 1,
      "status": 201
    }
  },
  {
    "index": {
      "_index": "test",
      "_type": "test",
      "_id": "Iil_B2MBTOSncJz8RPug",
      "_version": 1,
      "result": "created",
      "_shards": {
        "total": 2,
        "successful": 1,
        "failed": 0
      },
      "_seq_no": 0,
      "_primary_term": 1,
      "status": 201
    }
  },
  {
    "index": {
      "_index": "test",
      "_type": "test",
      "_id": "Iyl_B2MBTOSncJz8RPug",
      "_version": 1,
      "result": "created",
      "_shards": {
        "total": 2,
        "successful": 1,
        "failed": 0
      },
      "_seq_no": 1,
      "_primary_term": 1,
      "status": 201
    }
  },
  {
    "index": {
      "_index": "test",
```

```
            "_type": "test",
            "_id": "JCl_B2MBTOSncJz8RPug",
            "_version": 1,
            "result": "created",
            "_shards": {
              "total": 2,
              "successful": 1,
              "failed": 0
            },
            "_seq_no": 0,
            "_primary_term": 1,
            "status": 201
          }
        }
      ]
    }

    # GET test
    {
      "test": {
        "aliases": {},
        "mappings": {
          "test": {
            "properties": {
              "age": {
                "type": "long"
              },
              "email": {
                "type": "text",
                "fields": {
                  "keyword": {
                    "type": "keyword",
                    "ignore_above": 256
                  }
                }
              },
              "name": {
                "type": "text",
                "fields": {
                  "keyword": {
                    "type": "keyword",
                    "ignore_above": 256
                  }
                }
              }
            }
          }
        },
```

```
      "settings": {
        "index": {
          "creation_date": "1524839167262",
          "number_of_shards": "5",
          "number_of_replicas": "1",
          "uuid": "fcNQImaMTFCD89NYZkBN9A",
          "version": {
            "created": "6020399"
          },
          "provided_name": "test"
        }
      }
    }
}

# DELETE test
{
  "acknowledged": true
}
```

In this way, we can write multiple Elasticsearch queries and execute all of them in one go.
See the following screenshot:

The console sends the queries one by one to Elasticsearch and displays the response on the
right pane. This gives us a nice way through which we can execute and debug queries.

Profiling queries

Elasticsearch has a profiler API through which we can inspect and analyze the search queries, but it has a very large JSON output, which is quite difficult to analyze manually. Kibana Dev Tools with X-Pack provides a simple way to inspect and analyze the Elasticsearch profiler result. Dev Tools transforms the Elasticsearch JSON output into query profile's visualization, through which we can easily inspect what is happening and analyze it, and in this way, we can diagnose poorly performing queries and fix them thereafter.

For profiling the Elasticsearch query, we need to click on the **Search Profiler** link after the console link. This will open the following screen:

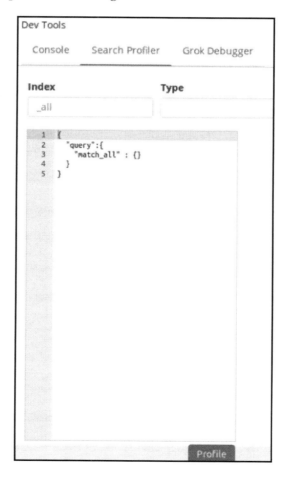

By default, the _all index is autopopulated under the **Index** field, which we can change to any specific Elasticsearch index. Now click on the **Profile** button, which will open the following screen:

On this screen, we can see the right pane with two tabs, **Query Profile** and **Aggregation Profile**.

Query profile

It is showing us the listing on index with the shard name and cumulative query execution time. By default, the shard name is collapsed, which we can expand by clicking on the greater than symbol before shard name. The following screenshot shows the expanded view:

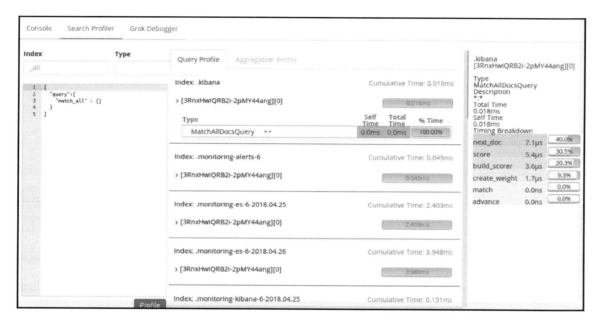

In the preceding screen, we can see the type of shard with **Self Time**, **Total Time**, and **% Time**. If we hover on the type name, a right pane data appears with timing breakdown upto Lucene method-level details of the query. **Search Profiler** shows the name of searched indices, below them the shards in each index and then the query execution time.

In the previous example, it is showing the query type as `MatchAllDocsQuery`, and that is why the **Self Time** and **Total Time** is the same.

Now I am going to explain it by creating a fresh index:

```
POST profiletest/test/_bulk
{"index":{}}
{"name":"anurag","age":35,"email":"anurag@abc.com"}
{"index":{}}
{"name":"amit","age":29,"email":"amit@xyz.com"}
{"index":{}}
{"name":"suresh","age":49,"email":"suresh@rrr.com"}
```

```
{"index":{}}
{"name":"mahesh","age":21,"email":"mahesh@ggg.com"}
{"index":{}}
{"name":"atul","age":32,"email":"atul@ee.com"}
```

After creating this index, we can go to the **Query Profile** screen and change the _all index to the profiletest index. Now to do the little complex query, I am going to change a match_all query and search as follows:

```
{
 "query": {
 "bool": {
 "should": [
 {
 "match": {
 "name": "anurag"
 }
 },
 {
 "terms": {
 "name": [
 "mahesh",
 "atul"
 ]
 }
 }
 ]
 }
 },
 "aggs": {
 "stats": {
 "stats": {
 "field": "email"
 }
 }
 }
}
```

In the preceding query, I am doing a query with two subquery components—one for search and another for simple aggregation. Now on clicking the **Profile** button, we would get the following screen:

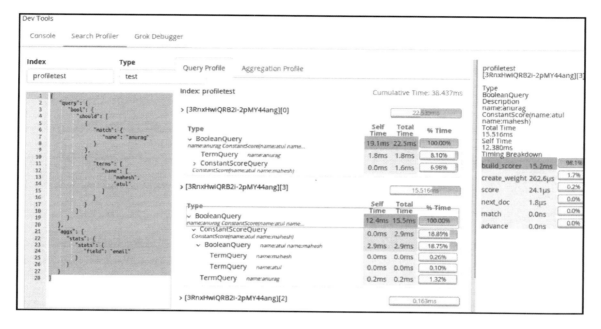

In the preceding screenshot, we can see the query details. As in the previous case, we were getting all `MatchAllDocsQuery` queries because we were just matching all the documents, but here, we are doing `BooleanQuery` that is divided into `TermQuery` for each criteria. Here, we can see the difference between **Self Time** and **Total Time** of query. **Self Time** shows the duration that the query component took to execute. Total time shows the time that the query component and its children took to execute.

Aggregation profile

In the previous query, we have performed a aggregation as well. For aggregation profiling, we need to click on the **Aggregation Profile** tab next to **Query Profile**. This tab will be disabled by default and will only be enabled when we have the aggregation in the query:

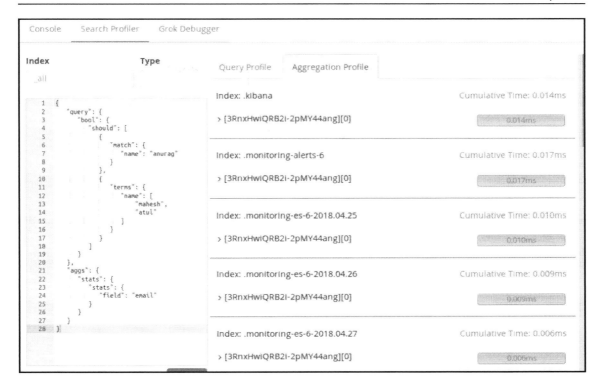

In the previous screenshot, we can see the aggregation profile result for the given query. To get the aggregation detail, we need to click on the expand button in front of the shard name:

If we want to view the timing break down, we have to click on the aggregation row. See the following screen:

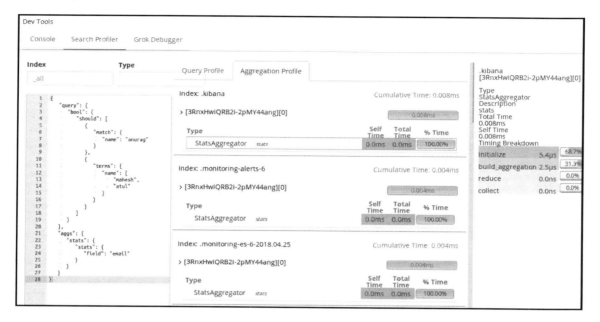

On the right pane, we can see the Lucene method-level breakup of the query through which we can get more insights into the query execution. In this way, we can do the profiling of aggregation queries.

Grok debugger

Grok is basically used for pattern matching, and we can structure an arbitrary text by parsing it through grok expressions. Grok patterns can be used for the grok processor in Dev Tools and in the Logstash grok filter. There are more than 120 grok patterns that Elastic Stack supports.

There are different data sources from where we can get arbitrary data such as syslog logs, Apache logs, MySQL logs, or any other type of log. Now, these types of data are not labeled with a field name, and without that, we cannot process it in Elasticsearch or Kibana. To overcome this issue, we need to parse the log data with grok expression. For that, we need to map the log values with field names in the grok expression and then simulate it to get the values in the field. Once this is done, we can use that expression into Logstash grok filter to filtering this log data.

To create the grok expression, we need to click on the **Grok Debugger** link after **Search Profiler**, which will open the following screen:

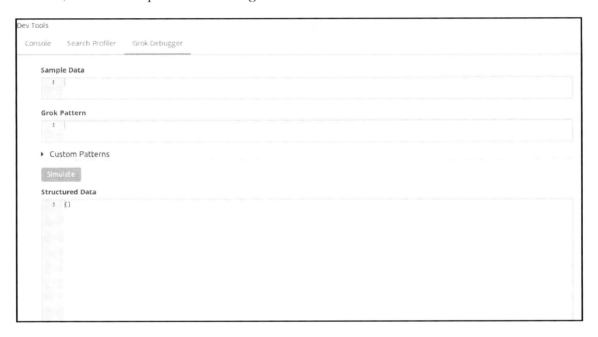

Now, we need to fill in the **Sample Data** for the data that we want to parse using grok. For example, we can add the following data:

```
127.0.0.1 GET /index.html 10124 0.021
```

Now, under the **Grok Pattern**, we can add the following pattern to parse the sample data:

```
%{IP:client} %{WORD:method} %{URIPATHPARAM:request} %{NUMBER:bytes}
%{NUMBER:duration}
```

See the following screenshot we have added the **Sample Data** and **Grok Pattern**:

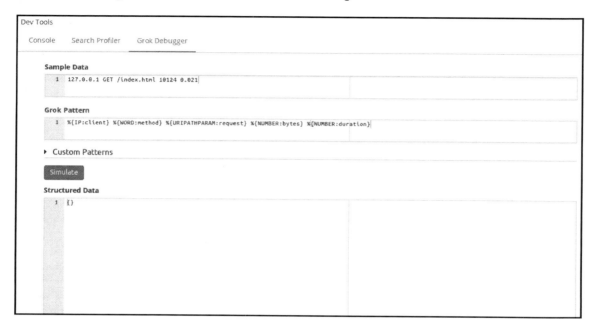

If we are not using the **Grok Pattern** provided by Elastic Stack, we can write our own custom pattern, and for that, it has to be added in the **Custom Patterns** section:

▼ Custom Patterns

ℹ **Enter one custom pattern per line. For example:**

POSTFIX_QUEUEID [0-9A-F]{10,11}
MSG message-id=<%{GREEDYDATA}>

After adding these values, we need to click on the **Simulate** button, which will return the following output under **Structured Data**:

```
{
  "duration": "0.021",
  "request": "/index.html",
  "method": "GET",
  "bytes": "10124",
  "client": "127.0.0.1"
}
```

See the following screenshot the **Structured Data** result after simulation:

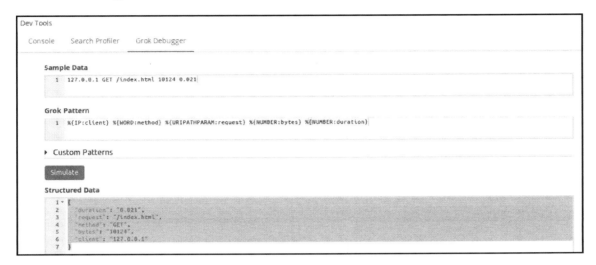

In this way, by providing **Sample Data**, we can get **Structured Data** by applying the **Grok Pattern** and clicking on the **Simulate** button.

Summary

In this chapter, we covered Kibana Dev Tools and the ways in which we can interact to Elasticsearch. It has a console to run Elasticsearch queries directly from Kibana. In a console, we can write multiple queries and can execute them all by simply selecting them all and clicking on the execute button. Dev Tools sends all queries to Elasticsearch one by one and then shows the results on the right pane as soon as it receives the response from Elasticsearch.

Console has other options as well, such as query formatting, through which we can properly format the Elasticsearch query from an unformatted query to a formatted syntax. If we click on the same link, it will convert the formatted query to a compact single-line formatted view and vice versa. Another option is to copy the Elasticsearch query from it console in `curl` format. After copying the query in the curl format, we can directly paste on terminal to execute it. This option is quite handy, as we don't need to remember the curl format and can just paste it to execute the query in the Terminal.

We also covered the ways to profile the queries and aggregations using query profile and aggregation profile options. This gives us a handy tool through which we can monitor the query and aggregation execution and can tweak it accordingly. At last, we have covered **Grok Debugger**, through which we can test our grok syntax and apply that on test data to validate the syntax. After this validation, we can apply that grok syntax on a dataset. Using the grok syntax, we can convert the unlabeled data to a labeled data and can use it in Elasticsearch or Kibana.

In the next chapter, we will cover Kibana Management, using which we can tweak the Kibana behavior. To demonstrate Management, we will create an index pattern in Kibana using server-metrics index of Elasticsearch. Then, we will use Management's the "set as default index pattern" feature to mark it as the default one. Then, we will see how we can configure the index field through Management and can transform the values as per the field type. Also, we will see the advanced settings option through which we can tweak the Kibana's behavior, such as the date format. Then, we will see security, where we can create users and roles and assign roles to the users.

8
Tweaking Your Configuration with Kibana Management

Kibana management is there for tweaking the behavior of Kibana and to change the configuration at runtime. Using management, we can create the index pattern and configure it as well. By default, Kibana Management comes with a few options that can be extended after installing X-Pack, which adds many other capabilities to Kibana management.

So, there are different things that we can perform using Kibana management, such as index patterns to access the Elasticsearch index in Kibana, saved object to access already created dashboards, visualizations, or searches. It also gives us the feature to import or export these saved objects. We can also delete any saved object from the Kibana management screen.

If we have installed X-Pack, an additional feature of reporting would be added to Kibana management. Using this feature, we can download any generated report directly from the list it shows. Under Kibana, we have the last option as advanced settings; using this option, we can change different types of runtime configurations such as `dateFormat:dow`, using which we can set the first day of the week. It shows Sunday by default, which we can change by editing this setting value.

Apart from these Kibana options, we have some other options as well if we have installed X-Pack; for example, under security, we have the users and roles option, using which we can create different roles, and users can assign the roles to the users. Under Elasticsearch, license management is shown, using which we can manage the license and such, and watcher to see the status of different watch and to create new watch as well. Under Logstash, we have pipeline, using which we can create the Logstash configuration and can deploy them. So, in this chapter, we will cover the following topics:

- **Index pattern**: Here, we will cover the details of the index pattern and then the following things:
  - Creating the index pattern
  - Setting the default index pattern
  - Refreshing the index pattern fields
  - Deleting an index pattern
  - Managing fields
- **Saved objects**: Under saved objects, we can get all saved objects that we have saved, such as the dashboards, visualizations, and all those searches that were saved.
  - Dashboards
  - Searches
  - Visualizations
- **Advanced settings**: We can use the advanced settings feature to edit the settings that control the behavior of Kibana.
- **Reporting**: Under reporting, we can get all reports generated using the X-Pack feature of reporting.
- **Security**: Under security, we have two options: users and roles. We can create roles and users and can assign the roles to the users.
- **Watcher**: It can be used to perform some actions based on certain conditions that we apply.

Index pattern

To add the Elasticsearch index to Kibana, we need to configure the index pattern. This is the first step to work with Elasticsearch data.

Creating the index pattern

To create a new index pattern, we need to do the following:

1. Click on the **Management** link on the left menu.
2. Click on the **Index Patterns** link on the **Management** page. This will open the following screen:

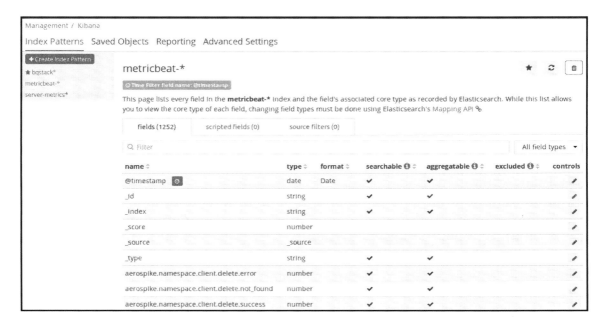

The preceding screenshot shows us the **metricbeat** index pattern fields, their data types, and additional details, as this index pattern was already created.

3. Now, click on the **Create index pattern** button in the top-left to create a new index pattern. This will open the following screen:

The preceding screenshot shows step 1 of 2 for index creating an pattern.

4. On this screen, we need to provide the keyword for index name in the search box. Below the search box, it shows different Elasticsearch index names.

5. Now if you want to add the **server-metrics** index of Elasticsearch, you need to add this name in the search box, which will give the success message, as shown in the following screenshot:

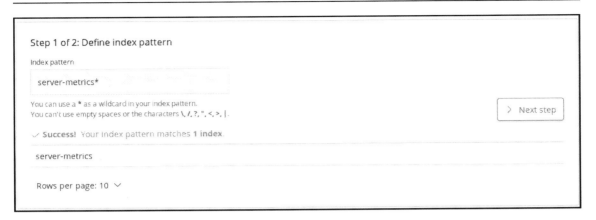

6. Click on the **Next step** button to move to the next step. The given screenshot shows the next screen:

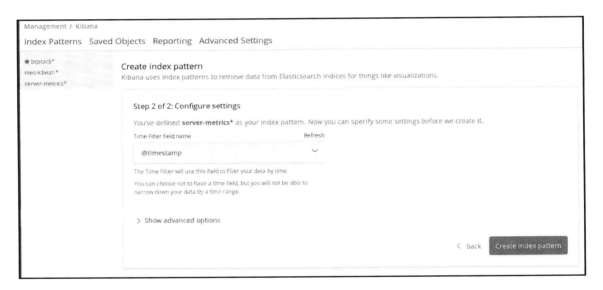

The preceding screen is step 2 of 2, where we need to configure settings.

7. Now pick the time filter field name and click on **Create index pattern**. This will open the following screen:

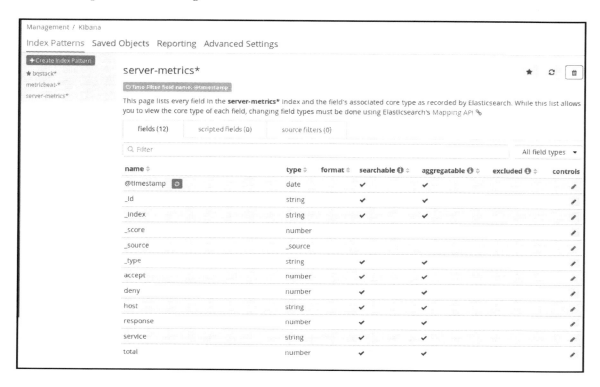

The preceding screenshot shows the field names and data types with additional attributes.

8. Now we can check the index pattern data using Kibana **Discover**. So click on **Discover** on left menu and choose the **server-metrics** index pattern. This will show the index data.

So, this way, we can create a new index pattern, and we can see the Elasticsearch index data in Kibana.

Setting the default index pattern

The default index pattern is shown on every option of Kibana by default, and we need not bother to change the index pattern on the discover, visualize, timelion, or dashboard page. On the index pattern page a star mark is shown just before the name of the index.

For setting the default index pattern, we need to click on the index pattern name and then click on the star symbol link on top-right side of the page. This will convert the index pattern to the default one:

In the preceding screenshot, I have set **server-metrics** as a default index pattern by clicking on star (**Set as default index**) icon.

Refreshing index pattern fields

All fields of the Elasticsearch index are mapped in Kibana when we add the index pattern, as the Kibana index pattern scans all fields of the Elasticsearch index. However, whenever any new field is added to the Elasticsearch index, it will not be shown automatically, and for these cases, we need to refresh the Kibana index fields.

To refresh the fields, we need to click on the index pattern name and then on the refresh link in the top-right of the index pattern page:

The preceding screenshot shows that when we click on refresh link, it shows a pop-up box with a message **This action resets the popularity counter of each field**. It also shows two buttons: **Cancel** and **Refresh**. Clicking on the **Refresh** button refreshes the fields.

Deleting an index pattern

If we want to delete an index pattern from Kibana, we can do that by clicking on the delete icon in the top-right corner of the index pattern page. It asks for confirmation before deleting and deletes the pattern after confirmation. The following screenshot shows the delete operation:

This delete will only delete the index from Kibana, and there will be no impact on the Elasticsearch index.

Managing fields

Under index pattern, we can get the tabular view of all the index fields. We can sort the values by clicking on the table header. We have the filter option, through which we can filter the field name by typing it. After filter textbox, we have a dropdown to filter the fields according to field type; it has the following options:

- **date**
- **string**
- **number**
- **_source**

Under the **controls** column, against each row, we have the pencil symbol, using which we can edit the field's properties. The given screenshot shows us the field listing of the index pattern:

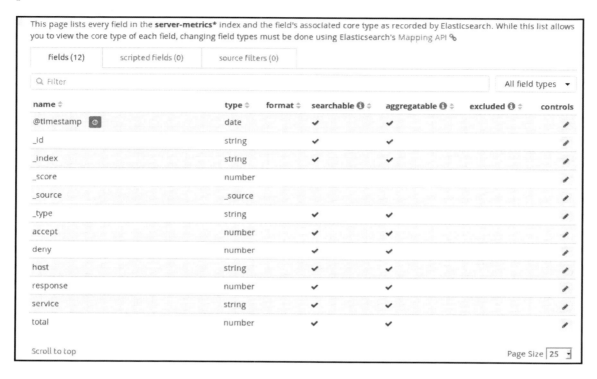

After clicking on the edit control for any field, we can manually set the format for that field using the format selection dropdown. For every type of data, we have different set of formats that we can change after editing the field.

On the edit screen, we can set the field popularity using the popularity textbox. After making all these changes, we can save it by clicking on the **Update field** button. We can cancel those changes by clicking on the **Cancel** button.

Under Kibana's **Management** option, we have a field formatter for the following types of fields:

- **String**
- **Dates**

- **Geographic point fields**
- **Numbers**

At the bottom of the page, we have a link **scroll to top**, which scrolls the page up.

String

String fields have support for two formatters: String and URL. In the **String** field formatter, we can apply the following transformations to the content of the field:

- **Lower Case**
- **Upper Case**
- **Title Case**
- **Short Dots**
- **Base64 Decode**

This screenshot shows the string type format and the transform options:

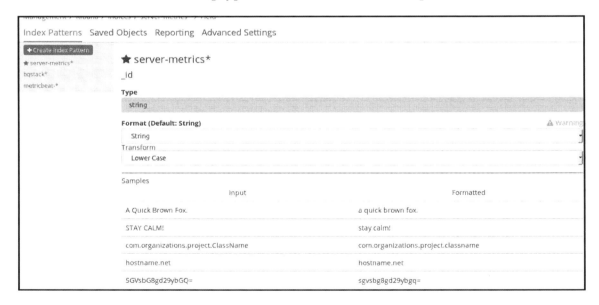

In the URL field formatter, we can apply the following transformations to the content of the field:

- **Link**
- **Image**

Dates

The date field has a support for **date**, **string**, and **URL** formatters. For the **string** and the **URL** type formatter, we have already discussed in previous string type.

The following screen shows the date type field with an option to change the format and popularity of the field:

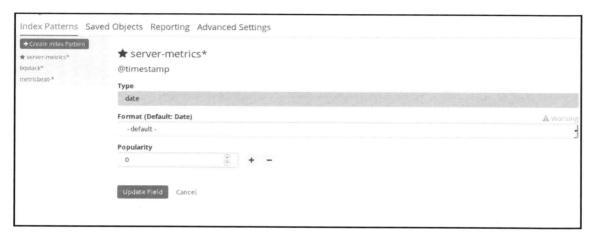

The date formatter enables us to use the display format of the date stamps, using the moment.js standard definition for date time.

Geographic point field

The geographic point field supports the same string field formatter:

- **Lower Case**
- **Upper Case**
- **Title Case**
- **Short Dots**
- **Base64 Decode**

Numbers

Number fields support the URL, Bytes, Duration, Number, Percentage, String, and Color formatters. In our previous formatters, we already learned about URL and String.
The next screenshot shows the number type field, with the option to set the format and the popularity of the field:

The duration field formatter displays the numeric value of a field in the following increments:

- **Picoseconds**
- **Nanoseconds**
- **Microseconds**
- **Milliseconds**
- **Seconds**
- **Minutes**
- **Hours**
- **Days**
- **Weeks**
- **Months**
- **Years**

The color field formatter enable us to pick colors with specific ranges of numeric values. We can select the Color field formatter that displays the Range, Font Color, Background Color, and Example fields, after which we can pick the color.

Number, Bytes, and Percentage formatters enables us to pick the display formats of numbers using the `numeral.js` standard format definitions.

Saved objects

Under saved objects, we can get all objects that we have saved, such as the dashboards, visualizations, and all those searches that were saved. We can export everything like saved dashboards, visualizations, and searches by clicking on the **Export everything** button. We can also import these by clicking on the **Import** button if we have a exported JSON file. The following screenshot shows the **Export** everything and the **Import** button in the top-right corner:

The preceding screenshot shows the saved object page with a tabular view for dashboard, searches, and visualizations. The **Dashboards** tab is opened by default, which shows a list of saved dashboards.

Dashboards

It shows the count of the dashboard, along with the dashboards title on the tab. Thde following is the dashboard heading. We have a search box to search the dashboard and then a list of saved **Dashboards**:

If we hover on the name of a dashboard, it shows an eye icon. We can click on this eye icon to open the dashboard. We can select single or multiple dashboards for performing operations. After selecting the dashboards, we can export or delete them and for that, we need to click on the **Export** or the **Delete** button. Clicking on the **Export** button exports a JSON file that we can use to import later.

Searches

Searches shows the count, along with the title on the tab. We have a search box to search the saved searches and, below that, we have a list of saved searches:

If we hover over the name of a saved search, it shows an eye icon. We can click on this eye icon to open the search page. We can select single or multiple saved searches for performing delete or export operations. We can export or delete them by clicking on the **Export** or **Delete** button. Clicking on the **Export** button exports a JSON file that we can use to import later.

Visualizations

The **Visualizations** tab shows the list of saved visualizations. It shows the count of saved visualizations next to the visualizations heading. Below that, we have a search box to search the saved visualizations and and then a list of saved visualizations:

If we hover over the name of a saved visualization, it shows an eye icon. We can click on this eye icon to open the visualization edit page from where we can edit the visualization. We can select single or multiple saved visualizations for performing delete or export operations. We can export or delete them by clicking on the **Export** or **Delete** button. Clicking on the **Export** button exports a JSON file that we can use to import later.

Advanced settings

Using the advances settings feature, we can edit the settings that control the behavior of Kibana. We can change the default format of the date, the default index for timelion, can set the precision for decimal values, or it can set the default query language:

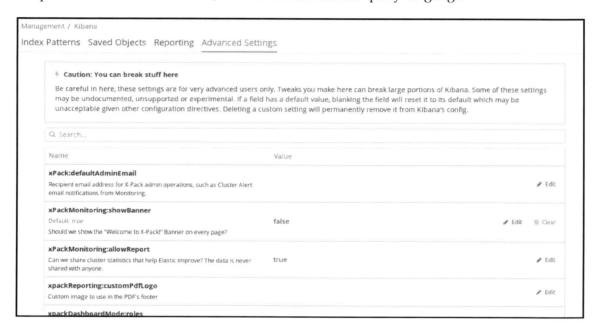

 We should avoid changing anything unless we are very sure about the change we will perform.

To set any advanced option, we need to do the following:

1. Click on the **Advanced Settings** link on the **Management** page
2. We have a search box, through which we can search the option to modify
3. Click on the **Edit** link in front of the option that you want to change
4. Modify the value as per the requirement
5. Click on the **Save** button to save the changes

These are very sensitive changes that can cause performance issues in Kibana, and if anything breaks, it is quite difficult to diagnose.

There are many options available under advanced settings, and we can tweak all those under this option. In this chapter, I will explain some of them.

xPack:defaultAdminEmail

This option will be available only if we have installed X-Pack. Here, we can provide the admin email ID for getting cluster alerts notifications:

The preceding screenshot shows us the option in edit mode. Here, we can enter the email ID and save it by clicking on the **Save** button.

search:queryLanguage

By default, the search language is Lucene. By using this option, we can modify the query language used by the query bar. We can set **lucene** query syntax or **kuery**, which is an experimental new language created specifically for Kibana:

In the preceding screenshot, we can see the edit mode of **search:queryLanguage**. Here, we have a dropdown with the **lucene** and **kuery** options.

search:queryLanguage:switcher:enable

This option is there to show or hide the query language switcher on query execution bar. It is set to false by default, which we can change by clicking on the edit link. This is handy if we want to use lucene as well as kuery language during query creation and execution.

dateFormat

The `dateFormat` is used to format the date in a pretty format. It follows the date formats mentioned in the `moments.js` file. We can use any format as per our requirements; consider this example:

```
MMMM Do YYYY, HH:mm:ss.SSS
```

dateFormat:tz

The `dateFormat:tz` option gives us the option to set which timezone to use. It has different timezones along with the **Browser** option. This **Browser** option enables us to automatically detect the timezone using the browser. Some options of this advanced settings are as follows:

```
Browser
Africa/Abidjan
Africa/Freetown
Africa/Maseru
America/Grand_Turk
America/Indiana/Winamac
America/Indianapolis
America/Santa_Isabel
Asia/Anadyr
Asia/Jayapura
Asia/Katmandu
Asia/Kuala_Lumpur
Asia/Singapore
Asia/Thimbu
Atlantic/Azores
Atlantic/Cape_Verde
Australia/Adelaide
Australia/Lord_Howe
Canada/Central
Canada/Pacific
Chile/Continental
Hongkong
Iceland
Pacific/Truk
```

These names are only a few options in the dropdown, as the actual list is quite long.

dateFormat:dow

`dateFormat:dow` defines the day that starts the week. By default, it is set to `Sunday`, which we can change to any day as per our requirement. It has the following options:

```
Sunday
Monday
Tuesday
Wednesday
Thursday
Friday
Saturday
```

defaultIndex

By default, this property is set to **null**. We can add the kibana index ID here to make that index a `defaultindex`:

The preceding screenshot shows the **defaultIndex** setting section, where we can add the index ID and save it. The same operation can be performed from the Kibana index pattern page by clicking on the star button. This feature is useful when we have to work mainly on any single index; then, we can make that index pattern a default one using this setting.

In the same way, there are various other settings that can change from this screen.

Reporting

Under reporting, we can get all reports that were generated using the X-Pack feature of reporting. Using X-Pack, we can generate the reports for any visualization or dashboard:

The preceding screenshot shows us the list of generated reports using X-Pack. In the last column, we have a download icon, through which we can download the `.pdf` report anytime it is required.

Security

We will get the security option under **Management** if X-Pack is installed. Under security, we have two options: users and roles. We can create roles and users and can assign the roles to the users.

By default, there is no user management in Elastic stack, so anyone can open the interface directly. By installing X-Pack, default security is enabled, and we have the option to extend it using the users and roles option.

Roles

Using the roles option of security, we can create new roles and edit the existing, not reserved roles. You will be confused about reserver roles, so let me explain to you that reserved roles are the roles that X-Pack creates itself by default, and we cannot make any changes in these roles:

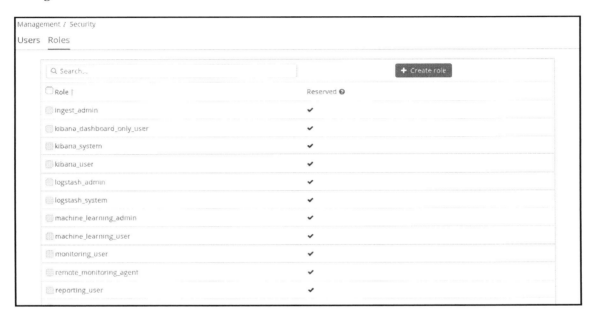

The preceding screenshot shows us the list of roles with a tick mark for reserved or not reserved. There is a **Create role** button, using which we can create a new role. I will cover the role creation and edit part in Chapter 9, *Understanding X-Pack features* chapter.

Users

We can create new users and edit the existing not-reserved users, using the users option of security. We can assign different roles to the users. Reserved users are the users that X-Pack creates itself by default, and we cannot change the attributes of these users:

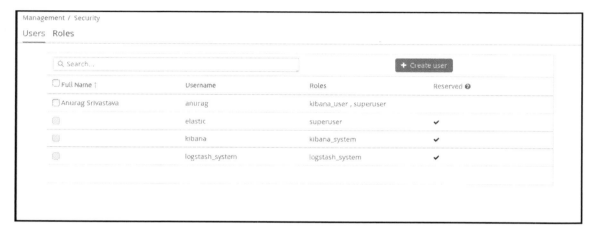

The preceding screenshot shows us the list of users with full name, username, roles, and a tick mark for reserved or not reserved. There is a **Create user** button, using which we can create a new user. I will cover the user creation and edit part in Chapter 9, *Understanding X-Pack features* chapter.

Watcher

We use watcher to perform some actions based on certain conditions that we apply. Conditions are based on the index data that we send to the watch. This loaded data is known as **Watch Payload**, and it can be loaded from different sources, such as from Elasticsearch or from external HTTP service.

On the **Management** screen, we have the option of Watcher. Watcher does not come by default with Elastic stack and enables when we install X-Pack into Kibana and Elasticsearch:

The preceding screenshot displays a list of **Watches** that are running.

Watches have the following possible states:

- **Firing**: Watch is triggered and actively performing the actions
- **Error**: There is an error state and watch is not working properly
- **Ok**: Watch is working properly but not firing right now
- **Disabled**: Watch is disabled and not able to fire

Creating the watch

To create a watch, we need to click on the **Create new watch** button, which opens a dropdown with two values:

- **Threshold alert**: It is used to send the alerts on a specific condition
- **Advanced watch**: In the advanced watch, we have the option to edit the raw JSON and add schedule, input, condition, and actions

Threshold alert

Here, we will create the threshold alert and for that we need to click on **Threshold Alert**, which will open the following screen:

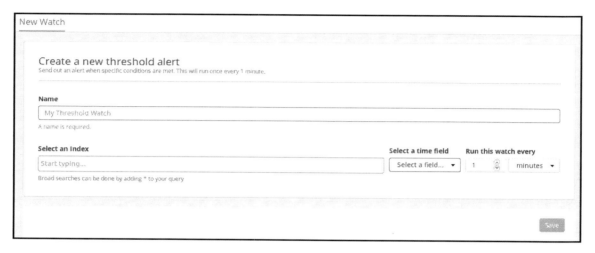

We need to type a name for the watch and then select the index by typing the name. Once index is selected, we need to provide the time field from the index and set the time interval to run the watch. After doing these changes, the screen expands and opens as the following screen:

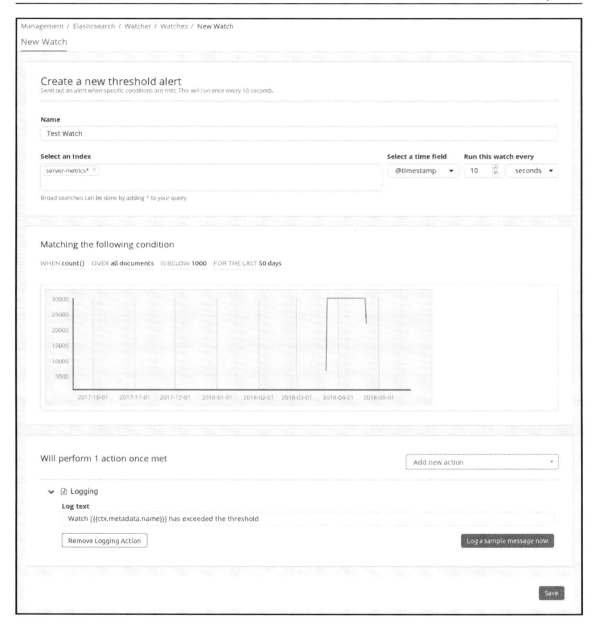

In the preceding screenshot, we need to set the matching condition. I have added the condition as follows:

```
WHEN count() OVER all documents IS BELOW 1000 FOR THE LAST 50 days
```

This condition is configurable, and we can change it by clicking on these values and changing them as per our requirement. Once the matching part is done, we need to set the action. For that, we need to click on the **Add new action** dropdown and pick the required action. I have picked the logging option that will add the log entry once the condition is met. Except for logging, we can also pick the email option to send the email to the admin user or use slack to send message to the slack user or channel. This way, we can create the watch using the **Threshold Alert** option.

Advanced watch

Advanced watch is there for those people who are more familiar with Elasticsearch queries, as it provides us with the option to add schedule, input, condition, and action in the form of Elasticsearch query that is in the JSON format. Threshold alert option is totally based on UI where user can pick the dropdowns and create the watch.

In the case of advanced watch, we need to click on **Create new watch** and then pick **Advanced Watch** from the dropdown. This will open the following screen:

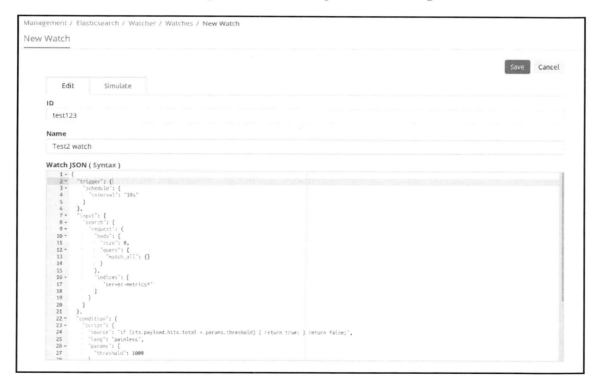

In the preceding screenshot, we have the option to add ID, name, and watch JSON. Under watch JSON text area, the JSON is already given, and we need to modify the JSON code to add schedule, input, condition, and action. I have used the same condition that I have mentioned for threshold alert, and here's the JSON watch code for the same:

```
{
  "trigger": {
    "schedule": {
      "interval": "10s"
    }
  },
  "input": {
    "search": {
      "request": {
        "body": {
          "size": 0,
          "query": {
            "match_all": {}
          }
        },
        "indices": [
          "server-metrics*"
        ]
      }
    }
  },
  "condition": {
    "script": {
      "source": "if (ctx.payload.hits.total &lt; params.threshold) { return
true; } return false;",
      "lang": "painless",
      "params": {
        "threshold": 1000
      }
    }
  },
  "actions": {
    "my-logging-action": {
      "logging": {
        "text": "There are {{ctx.payload.hits.total}} documents in your
index. Threshold is 10."
      }
    }
  }
}
```

In the preceding code, you can see the schedule, input, condition, and action blocks, and the values that I have given for them. After adding ID, name, and watch JSON code, we need to click on the **Save** button to save the watch.

Once the watch is created, we can see them from the list page and click on the ID to get the details of the watch:

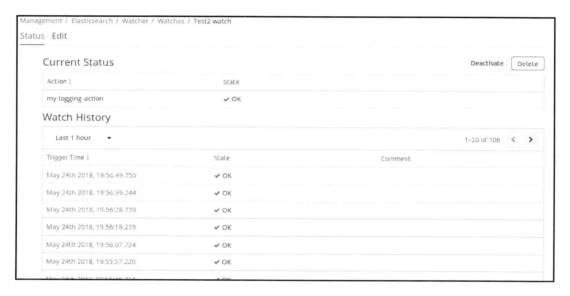

In the preceding screenshot, we can see the detail page where we have the current status and watch history. By clicking on the trigger time under watch history, we can get the details like execution status and execution output.

Deleting the watch

We need to do as follows if we want to delete a watch:

1. Go to the watch list page by clicking on the **Watcher** link under **Management**.
2. Click on the checkbox before the name of the watch.
3. Click on the **Delete** button.
4. It will show a popup with a **This will permanently delete 1 Watch. Are you sure?** message.
5. Click on the **Delete 1 Watch** button. This will delete the watch.

Summary

This chapter covered the Kibana management, through which we can tweak the behavior of Kibana. Then, we covered the index pattern where first we created the index pattern by taking the server-metrics index of Elasticsearch.

After creating an index pattern, we covered the set as the default index pattern feature of Management, through which we can set any index pattern as a default. This is quite helpful. As for discover, visualize, and dashboard, we need not worry about the index pattern selection in case we want to work on any particular index.

Then, we went through the refresh index field, through which we can update any change in Elasticsearch index into the Kibana index pattern. After refreshing, we looked at the delete index pattern, through which we can delete any index from Kibana.

We can configure the index fields by setting it through managing fields. Here, we can set the format and transform the values as per the field type. The saved objects option of management is there, through which we can get saved dashboards, searches, and visualizations. We can view them, and we can also delete from this page.

The advanced settings option can control the behavior of Kibana; we can change the format of the date and more using this feature. Using reporting, we can download the saved reports. Security can be used to create roles and can give the roles to the users. Through watcher, we can perform some actions based on the conditions that we can apply.

In the next chapter, we will cover some important features of Kibana. There are some features on which we will focus; the first is handling time series data and applying conditional formatting on that. After that, we will see how we can create a trend by plotting through moving average on data. Then, we will cover visual builder, through which we can perform Timelion operations, using the normal Kibana UI, rather than typing Timelion expressions. Lastly, we will cover GeoIP for Elastic Stack and look at how to plot the data on a map, using IP address fields.

9
Understanding X-Pack Features

The default Elastic Stack comes with Elasticsearch, Kibana, Logstash, and Beats. We can extend the Elastic Stack setup by installing X-Pack. It has different features, such as providing security, monitoring, reporting, alerting, and graph and machine learning capabilities in an easy-to-install package.

By default, there is no security in Elastic Stack, and through X-Pack, we can enable authentication and define roles and permissions. It monitors the Elastic Stack and provides us with the feature to monitor the application's health seamlessly. Also, we can easily generate PDF reports, using Kibana visualization, after installing X-Pack.

We can seamlessly integrate X-Pack in a running Elastic Stack setup by a simple installation process. The X-Pack security feature provides us with the option to secure Elastic Stack. Using it, we can set password protection, add authentication, filter on IP, or encrypt communications.

In this chapter, we will cover the following topics:

- **Installing X-Pack**: Here, we will cover the steps to install X-Pack on Elastic Stack. It will include the following steps:
    - Installing X-Pack into Elasticsearch
    - Installing X-Pack into Kibana
- **Features of X-Pack**: Under this topic, we will cover the main features of X-Pack, as follows:
    - **Monitoring**: Under monitoring, we will cover Elasticsearch and Kibana monitoring
    - **Security**: With X-Pack, we have the option to secure our data and manage users with roles

- **Machine learning**: Machine learning is basically the use of algorithms and methods on data to get the data-driven predictions, decision making, and modeling
- **Application Performance Monitoring** (**APM**): This is built on top of Elastic Stack to monitor the performance of external applications
- **Logging**: We can use the logging feature of X-Pack to ingest logs from different data sources
- **Metrics**: Through metrics, we can fetch metrics data from the operating system and running services on the server

Installing X-Pack

In this section, we will take a look at the steps to install X-Pack for Elasticsearch and Kibana. It provides various features, as we have already discussed. It also changes the different views, such as adding the **Reporting** tab under **Visualization** and the **Query Profile** under **Dev Tools**. Similarly, there are many additions, which we may notice after installing X-Pack. Now let's take a look at how to install X-Pack.

Installing X-Pack into Elasticsearch

To install X-Pack to our Elasticsearch setup, we will need to perform following steps:

1. First, we need to stop Elasticsearch.
2. Move to the Elasticsearch setup directory and then enter the following command:

```
bin/elasticsearch-plugin install x-pack
```

3. After successfully running the command, start Elasticsearch.
   1. Generate default passwords, as follows:

```
bin/x-pack/setup-passwords auto
```

The preceding command will create the passwords automatically, which we will need to copy to log into the system.

Installing X-Pack into Kibana

To install X-Pack into our Kibana setup, we need to perform the following steps:

1. First, we need to stop Kibana. To stop Kibana on Ubuntu, run the following command:

   ```
   sudo service kibana stop
   ```

2. Move to the Kibana installation directory and then enter the following command:

   ```
   bin/kibana-plugin install x-pack
   ```

3. We will need to add the following credentials to the `kibana.yml` file:

   ```
   elasticsearch.username: "kibana"
   elasticsearch.password:  "<pwd>
   ```

4. Start Kibana, after successfully installing X-Pack for Kibana. To start Kibana on Ubuntu, run the following command:

   ```
   sudo service kibana start
   ```

5. After that, we will need to navigate to Kibana by entering the following URL on our browser:

   ```
   http://localhost:5601
   ```

6. Now, we will need to **Log in** through the `elastic` user, with the created password:

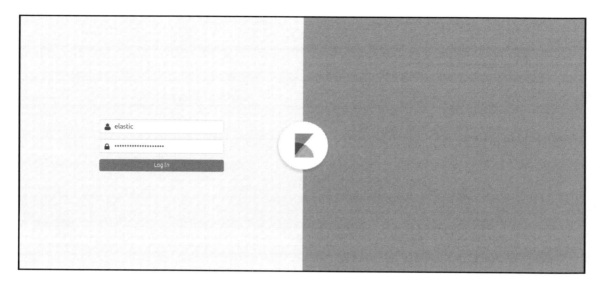

The preceding screenshot shows us the login page on Kibana after installing X-Pack. Here, we can log in with the created credentials, during X-Pack installation. The username is elastic and is the admin user, with which we can access all features on X-Pack.

Features of X-Pack

In this section, we will discuss the main features of X-Pack. The main feature, which we will discuss first, is monitoring (from the introduction section), where we will discuss how to monitor Elasticsearch and Kibana. Then, we will discuss the security feature of X-Pack using which we can create users and roles, and based on the assigned roles, a user can access different sections of Kibana. Machine learning is a very prominent feature of X-Pack, which was introduced in Version 5.4 of Kibana. Machine learning in Kibana uses algorithms and methods on data to get the data-driven predictions, decision making, and modeling. We will also discuss APM, which is built on top of Elastic Stack, to monitor the performance of external applications. The next important feature is logging, which is used to ingest logs from different data sources. Metrics is another important feature, using which we can fetch metrics data from the operating system and run services on the server. So, let's take a look at each of these features in detail.

Monitoring

On the main dashboard page, we have the link for monitoring under **Manage and Administer the Elastic Stack**:

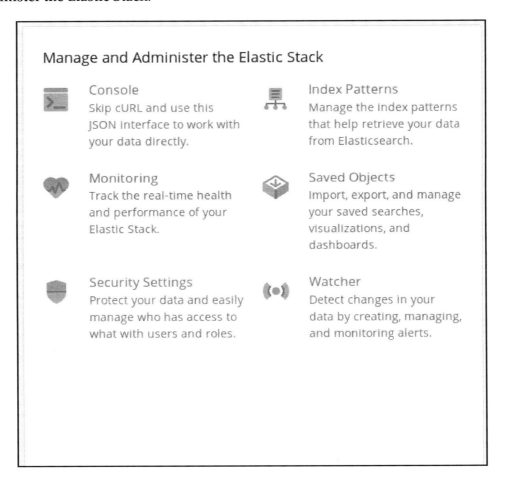

Through monitoring, we can track the health and performance of our Elastic Stack in real time. It is quite helpful, as we can monitor our Elastic Stack from a single page.

By clicking on the **Monitoring** link, we can open the monitoring page of Kibana:

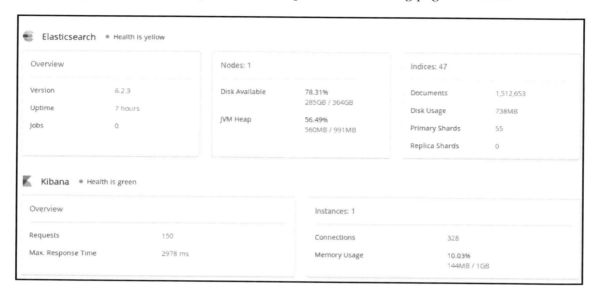

In the preceding screenshot, we can see the following two sections: **Elasticsearch** and **Kibana**.

Elasticsearch monitoring

We have three boxes for Elasticsearch monitoring—next to the title it shows the **Health** as **Yellow**, **Green**, or **Red** and it has the following sections:

The **Overview** block shows us the Elasticsearch version, uptime, and running jobs. We can click on the title **Overview** to open the detail page of **Overview**:

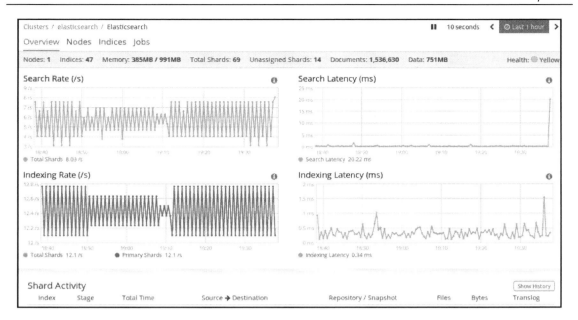

This screenshot shows the detail view for **Overview**. Here, we have different graphs for **Search Rate**, **Search Latency**, **Indexing Rate**, **Indexing Latency**, and **Shard Activity**. It also shows nodes count, indices count, memory consumption, total number of shards, unassigned shards, number of documents, and data size, along with health.
Nodes shows the count of nodes after the title, disk availability in percentage and numbers, and JVM heap availability in percentage and numbers. We can click on the title **Nodes** to open the detail page of **Nodes**:

The preceding screenshot shows the detail view of **Nodes**. Here, we have the node **Name**, **Status**, **CPU Usage** with **max** and **min** indicators, **Load Average** with **max** and **min** indicators, **JVM Memory** percentage with **max** and **min** indicators, **Disk Free Space** with **max** and **min** indicators, and the number of **Shards** in the node.

By clicking on the node name, we can open the detail page of the node:

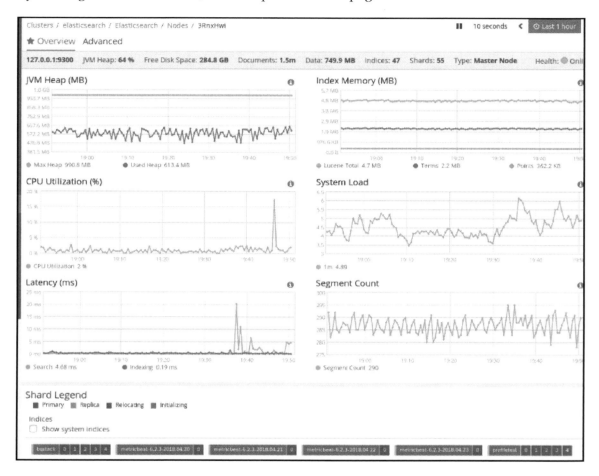

The preceding screenshot shows different graphs, such as **JVM Heap**, **Index Memory**, **CPU Utilization**, **System Load**, **Latency**, **Segment Count**, and **Shard Legend**. It also shows the IP address of Elasticsearch, the JVM heap percentage, free disk space, document count, data size, the number of indices, the number of shards, and the type of node and its health.

By default, the **Overview** tab opens, but we can click on the **Advanced** link to open the advanced view, where we have more details, such as the garbage collection count, index memory Lucene graphs, request rate, and indexing time:

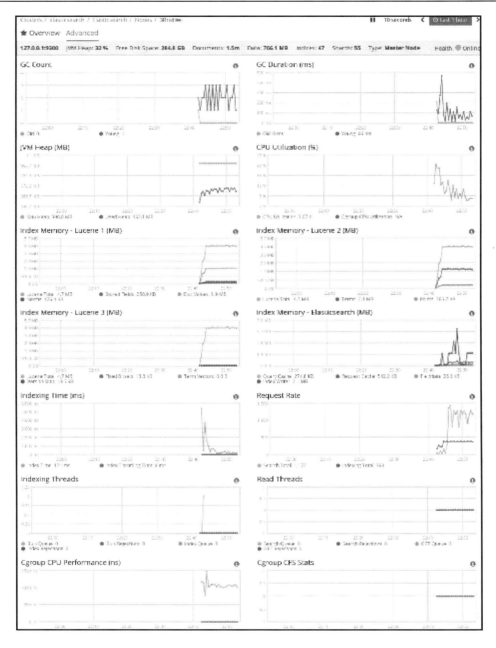

The preceding screenshot shows the advanced view of the node details.

Indices shows the number of indices in front of the title, the number of documents, disk usage in MB, the count of primary shards, and the count of replica shards. We can click on the title **Indices** to open the detail page of **Overview**:

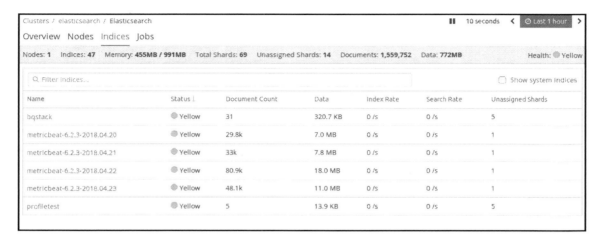

In the screenshot, we can see the index listing with **Status**, **Document Count**, **Data**, **Index Rate**, **Search Rate**, and **Unassigned Shards**. This page also provides the metrics, such as the node count, the index count, memory consumption, total shards, unassigned shards, and total documents and total data size.

We can click on the index name to open the detailed **Overview** page:

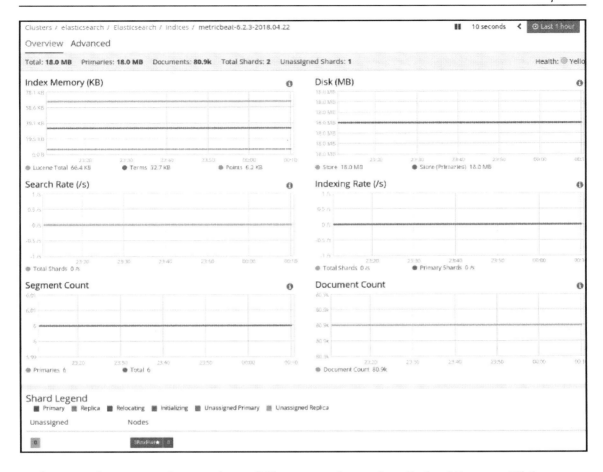

In the preceding screenshot, we have different graphs, such as **Index Memory**, **Disk**, **Search Rate**, **Indexing Rate**, **Segment Count**, and **Document Count**.

Kibana monitoring

In **Kibana** monitoring, we have two sections, **Overview** and **Instances**. The text and color next to the title shows the **Kibana Health** as **Yellow**, **Green**, or **Red**:

As you would notice from the preceding screenshot, it has the following sections: **Overview** shows the number of requests and the maximum response time in milliseconds. We can click on the **Overview** link to open the detail page:

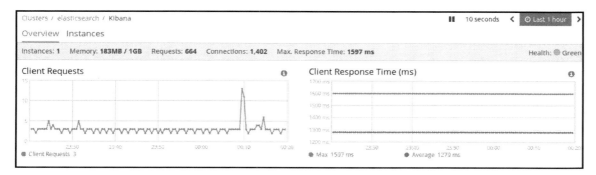

The preceding screenshot shows two graphs; the first shows **Client Requests** and the second shows **Client Response Time** in milliseconds, with maximum and average response time along, with the **Health** indicator. It also shows us the metrics such as the instance count, memory consumptions, the request count, the number of connections, and the maximum response time in milliseconds.

Instances shows the instance count next to the title, the number of connections, and memory usage in percentage and numbers. We can click on the **Instances** title to open the detail **Overview** page:

The preceding screenshot shows the instance **Name**, **Status**, **Load Average**, **Memory Size**, **Requests**, **Response Times**, and so on. It also shows metrics such as instance count, memory consumptions, request count, the number of connections, and the maximum response time in milliseconds, along with the health indicator.

We can click on the instance name to open the **Instances** detail page:

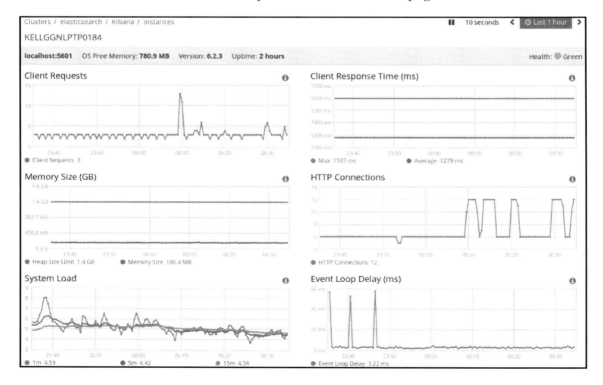

The preceding screenshot shows us the graphs for **Client Requests, Client Response Time, Memory Size, HTTP Connections, System Load, Event Loop Delay**, and so on. It also shows some metrics such as IP address/host name, OS free memory size, version, and the up-time duration, along with the health indicator.

Security settings

With X-Pack, we have the option to secure our data and to manage users with roles. We can customize the roles as per the requirement and assign them to the user. On the dashboard, we have the option of **Security Settings**:

By clicking on the **Security Settings** link, we can open the **Management** page with various options such as **Security, Elasticsearch, Kibana**, and **Logstash. Security** has two options, that is, **Users** and **Roles**:

In the preceding screenshot, we can see the **Users** and **Roles** option under **Security**. Now we will discuss more about both of them.

Users

Under **Users**, we can see the list of existing users with the option to add new users:

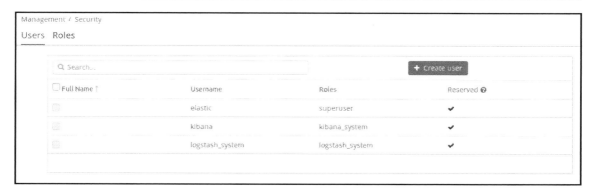

The preceding screenshot shows the list of default users, which were created during X-Pack installation. The user list shows **Full Name**, **Username**, **Roles**, and **Reserved** options along with a **Search** box to search the users. We can create new users by clicking on the **Create user** button.

The following screenshot shows the **Create user** form. In this form, we have the option to add **Username**, **Password**, **Password Again, Please**, **Full Name**, and **Roles**. By adding these details, we can create a new user:

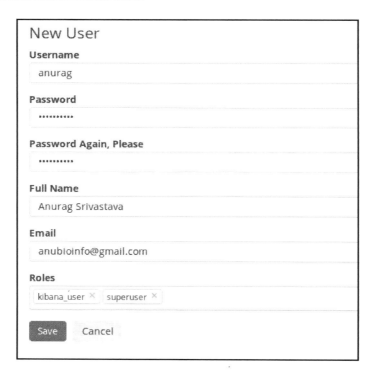

In the preceding screenshot, I have filled in the new user details and assigned it the role of a **superuser**. After saving this form, we can get the listing page with this new user:

In this screenshot, note that the new user has been added to the list, but there is no check box against the **Reserved** column. That is because this user has been created by the admin and not by X-Pack, so we can perform the delete operation on this user or any other user that the admin can create. When we select the user by clicking on the check box, the **add user** button changes to the **delete user** button, using which we can delete the user.

Roles

Along with users, we have different roles as per the functionality the a user can perform. So when we click on the **Roles** link of **Security** settings, it opens the role listing page:

In this screenshot, we can see that there are different roles, such as **ingest_admin** and **kibana_system**. All of these roles are reserved roles, and we cannot edit or delete these roles. We have a button called **Create role** to add a new role as per our requirement:

In this preceding screenshot, we can see the **New Role** form, where we have different options such as **Name** of the role, **Cluster Privileges**, **Run As Privileges**, and **Index Privileges**. After filling in these details, we can save the form to create a new role.

So, now, I would like to show you the screen with role creation:

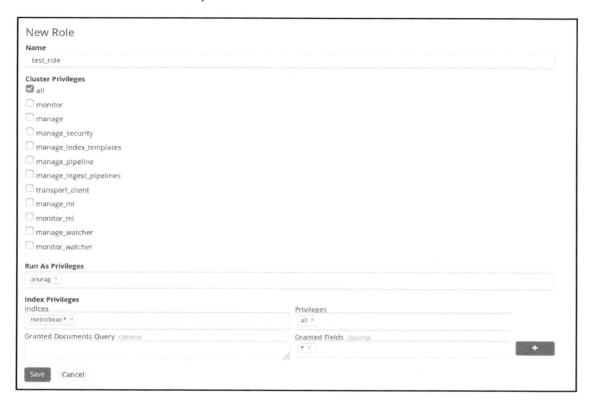

So, I am creating a role named **test_role**; after saving this form, the role will be created and listed in the role page:

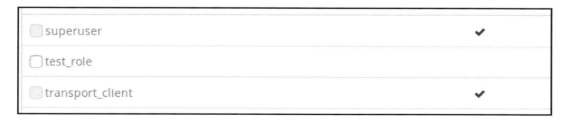

This role is also created by admin; hence, it is not reserved, and we can modify or delete it. If we want to edit the role, we will need to click on the name of the role that will open the edit form. For delete, we will need to select the role by clicking on the checkbox in front of the role name and click on the **Delete** button on the top-right corner of the listing.

Machine learning

Machine learning is also a very powerful feature of X-Pack. Machine learning is basically the use of algorithms and methods on data to get the data-driven predictions, decision making, and modeling. In Elastic Stack, we can use machine learning to solve different problems, such as detecting the anomaly in data or keeping a check on any suspicious login activity or sudden changes in data. We can use it for predictive analysis for future behavior, and then can take decisions based on the analysis. In the next chapter, we will discuss machine learning in detail.

Other options of X-Pack

Apart from all the previous features, X-Pack provides various enhancements in each Kibana options such as **Dev Tools**, **Management**, and **Timelion**, which we have covered in respective chapters. There are some additions into the dashboard after installing X-Pack, which we will discuss here. After logging in, we can get the following dashboard screen with different features:

In this screenshot, we have different shortcuts and some important features that we can use by clicking on them. For example, on the top-right corner, we have a button named **Set up index patterns**.

We can click on this button if we have the data in Elasticsearch and want to configure it in Kibana. This button click will open the Kibana management screen with the **Create index pattern** page. From this page, we can configure the Elasticsearch index to create the index pattern, which Kibana uses to read the Elasticsearch index data.

The following screenshot shows us the **Create index pattern** page:

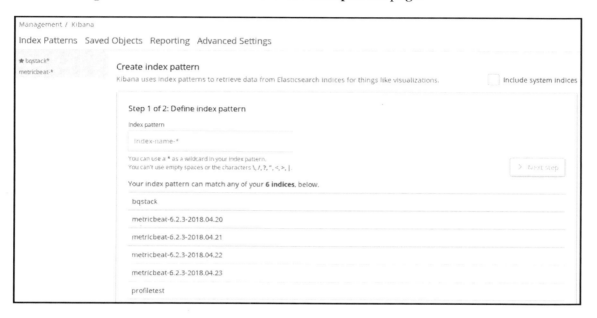

In this way, we can create the index pattern by selecting the Elasticsearch index after searching and selecting the index.

On the main screen, after logging in, we have different boxes for performing various actions. We will discuss each of them here. The first box is APM.

Application Performance Monitoring

APM is built on top of Elastic Stack to monitor the performance of external applications. APM stores the data in Elasticsearch, and using Kibana, we can monitor the performance:

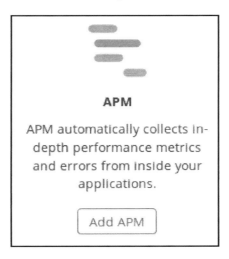

We can perform minor changes in our application to collect the detailed performance information from the application, using APM.

There are three components of APM, as follows:

- **APM Agents**: These are the libraries that runs inside the application process
- **APM Server**: This receives the data from the agent, processes them, and stores them inside Elasticsearch
- **APM UI**: UI is a preconfigured dashboard to monitor the application; X-Pack basic is required for APM

Currently, we have APM agents for Node.js and Python, which we can configure to get an insight of our application build on Node.js or Python. We will not cover complete installation and the workings of APM here, as it is outside the scope of this book.

Logging

We can use the logging feature of X-Pack to ingest logs from different data sources. These logs can then be visualized using preconfigured dashboards:

This preceding screenshot is the second box, and by clicking on the **Add log data** button, we can open the following screen:

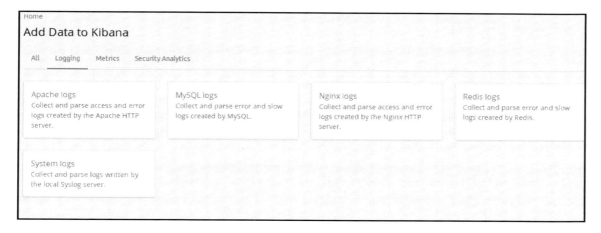

In this screenshot, we have different options to ingest the logs:

- **Apache logs**: Using the **Apache logs** option, we can collect and parse the data from log files `error.log` and `access.log`, which is created through the Apache HTTP Server
- **MySQL logs**: Using the **MySQL logs** option, we can collect and parse data from MySQL log files, that is, **Error** and **Slow** logs, which is created through the MySQL server
- **Nginx logs**: Using the **Nginx logs** option, we can collect the access and error logs, which is created through the Nginx HTTP Server and parse them
- **Redis logs**: Using the **Redis logs** option, we can collect and parse data from Redis log files, that is, error and slow logs, which is created through the Redis server
- **System logs**: Using the **System logs** option, we can collect and parse the logs, which are created through the local Syslog server

Apache logs

We need to do the following to set up the Apache logs:

1. Install `geoip` and the user agent plugins of Elasticsearch. These plugins are not installed by default, so we need to install them using the following commands under the Elasticsearch installation folder:

    ```
    bin/elasticsearch-plugin install ingest-geoip
    bin/elasticsearch-plugin install ingest-user-agent
    ```

2. Install Filebeat. You can refer to the steps that I have already explained to install Filebeat in the preceding chapter. In case of Debian-based systems, we can run the following commands:

    ```
    curl -L -O
    https://artifacts.elastic.co/downloads/beats/filebeat/filebeat-
    6.2.3-amd64.deb
    sudo dpkg -i filebeat-6.2.3-amd64.deb
    ```

3. Edit the Filebeat configuration. We need to edit the `/etc/filebeat/filebeat.yml` file to set the following connection information:

    ```
    output.elasticsearch:
      hosts: ["<Elasticsearch url>"]
      username: "elastic"
    ```

```
        password: "<password of elastic user>"
    setup.kibana:
        host: "<Kibana url>"
```

4. Configure the `apache2` module. We need to modify the `apache2.yml` file under `/etc/filebeat/modules.d` as per our credentials. We also need to enable the `apache2` module by running the following command:

    ```
    sudo filebeat modules enable apache2
    ```

5. Start Filebeat. Before starting Filebeat, we will need to run the following command to load the Kibana dashboards:

    ```
    sudo filebeat setup
    ```

6. After setting the Kibana dashboard, we will need to start Filebeat by running the following command:

    ```
    sudo service filebeat start
    ```

In this way, we can configure the `apache2` module and can monitor its log through Kibana dashboards.

MySQL logs

We will need to install Filebeat for MySQL module as well, and we can do it in the same way we did for `apache2`. After installing Filebeat, we need to change the `filebeat.yml` configuration file for setting Elasticsearch and Kibana URLs along with the password of the Elastic user.

Once this is done, we can configure the MySQL module, using the following command:

```
sudo filebeat modules enable mysql
```

After that, we need to edit the settings from the `/etc/filebeat/modules.d/mysql.yml` file. After that, we can set up and start Filebeat.

Nginx logs

We need to follow the same steps of the `apache2` module setup:

- **Install GeoIP and user agent plugins of Elasticsearch**: Why do this same way as we did for the `apache2` module setup

- **Install Filebeat**: We do this the same way as we did for the `apache2` module setup
- **Edit Filebeat configuration**: We do this the same way as we did for the `apache2` module setup
- **Configure Nginx module**: We need to enable Nginx module from the Filebeat installation directory by executing the following command:

    ```
    ./filebeat modules enable nginx
    ```

    We also need to edit the `modules.d/nginx.yml` file as per our configuration.

- **Start Filebeat**: We do this the same way as we did for the `apache2` module setup:

    ```
    Redis logs
    ```

For the Redis module setup, we need to install Filebeat, which we can do in the same way as we did for other modules. After installing Filebeat and configuring it, we can configure the Redis module, using the following command:

```
./filebeat modules enable redis
```

After enabling the Redis module, we can edit the `modules.d/redis.yml` file as per our credentials. Once the Redis module is successfully installed, we can start Filebeat.

System logs

For configuring the system logs, we need to install GeoIP plugin, which we have already covered in previous sections. After that, install Filebeat in the same way as we did in the earlier section. Once GeoIP plugin and Filebeat are installed, we can enable the system module to capture the system logs:

```
./filebeat modules enable system
```

After enabling the system module, we can edit the `modules.d/syatem.yml` file as per our credentials. Once system module is enabled, we can start Filebeat.

Metrics

The following screenshot shows another option that we have in **Metrics**:

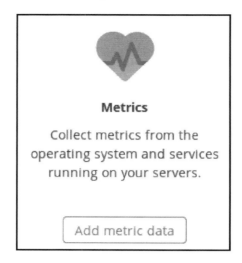

Using **Metrics**, we can fetch metrics data from our operating system and run services on the server. It has different options, as follows:

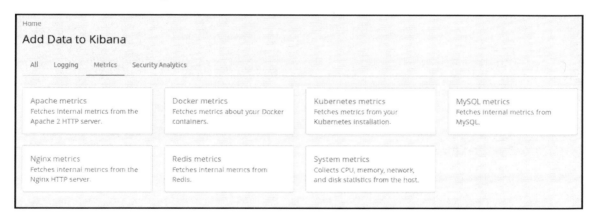

Apache metrics

Using Apache metrics, we can fetch internal metrics from Apache 2 HTTP Server. We can configure it in the following way:

1. Install Metricbeat.
2. Edit Metricbeat's configuration.
3. Enable and configure `apache` module. We need to run the following command from the installation directory:

   ```
   ./metricbeat modules enable apache
   ```

4. Start Metricbeat.

I have already covered the *Metricbeat* installation in `Chapter 1`, *Revising ELK Stack*; you may refer to that. Apache metrics are quite helpful for any web-based application, as it gives us insight into any issue that may occur in Apache web server.

Docker metrics

It fetches the metrics from our Docker containers. Docker is a program that can be used to perform operating system-level virtualization, which is also known as containerization. It can be used to run different versions of software using Docker container.

We can configure it in the following way:

1. Install Metricbeat.
2. Configure Metricbeat.
3. Enable and configure the `docker` module. We need to run the following command from the installation directory:

   ```
   ./metricbeat modules enable docker
   ```

4. Start Metricbeat.

The benefit of Docker is that developers can easily develop their code and put it to the Docker container from where it can easily be deployed. Docker metrics is quite helpful for monitoring Docker.

Kubernetes metrics

The Kubernetes Metricbeat module is used to fetch metrics from the Kubernetes. We can configure it by following these steps:

1. Install Metricbeat.
2. Configure Metricbeat.
3. Enable and configure the `kubernetes` module. We need to run the following command from the installation directory:

   ```
   ./metricbeat modules enable kubernetes
   ```

4. Start Metricbeat.

Kubernates is an open source platform, which automates deployment operations. Basically, it eliminates the manual processes during deployment and scales containerized applications.

MySQL metrics

It fetches the internal metric data from MySQL server. We can configure it by following these steps:

1. Install Metricbeat.
2. Configure Metricbeat.
3. Enable and configure `mysql` module. We need to run the following command from the installation directory:

   ```
   ./metricbeat modules enable mysql
   ```

4. Start Metricbeat.

This way, we can configure the Metricbeat to send the MySQL metric data.

Nginx metrics

It fetches the internal metric data from Nginx HTTP Server. We can configure it in the following steps:

1. Install Metricbeat.
2. Configure Metricbeat.

3. Enable and configure `nginx` module. We need to run the following command from the installation directory:

```
./metricbeat modules enable nginx
```

4. Start Metricbeat.

Redis metrics

It fetches the internal metrics from Redis Server. We can configure it by following these steps:

1. Install Metricbeat.
2. Configure Metricbeat.
3. Enable and configure the `redis` module. We need to run the following command from the installation directory:

```
./metricbeat modules enable redis
```

4. Start Metricbeat.

System metrics

Using system metrics, we can fetch the internal metrics from our system such as CPU, memory, disk, and networks statistics. We can configure it by following these steps:

1. Install Metricbeat.
2. Configure Metricbeat.
3. Enable and configure the `system` module. We need to run the following command from the installation directory:

```
./metricbeat modules enable system
```

4. Start Metricbeat.

In this way, we have seen different metrics modules, which we can configure to get the metrics data and monitor it using Kibana.

Summary

In this chapter, we covered the features of X-Pack. It provides a lot of important features to the Elastic Stack, such as security then monitoring, through which we can keep an eye on the way our cluster is performing and its individual components such as Elasticsearch, Kibana, and Logstash.

Through security settings, apart from reserved users, we can create new users, edit them, and delete them. In the case of roles, we have different reserved roles, and we can create new custom roles, edit roles, delete them, and assign them to the users.

Apart from security and monitoring, we have machine learning, through which we can do a number of things effectively, such as finding anomalies in data and doing predictive analysis. Adding machine learning to Elastic Stack provides an edge, as we can do a lot more with the data. We will discuss more about machine learning in the next chapter.

In the next chapter, we will cover machine learning for Kibana, along with a single metric job, multi metric job, population job, and an introduction to advanced job. We will create a single metric and a multi metric machine learning job. We will also cover data visualizer, which provides us with more insight about our data, and after exploring the data, we can decide the field that we can analyze using machine learning.

10
Machine Learning with Kibana

It is very difficult to identify any attack or sudden peak in data graphs because, while monitoring, we used to depend on our eyes to search and trace the root cause of any problem, and to get any idea of such issues, we have to play with time pickers for setting different time ranges. We can do that by searching and discovering the trends and peaks in the graphs, but there is a tool that can help us to pinpoint these issues and let us know about any such incidents easily.

Using the X-Pack machine learning feature, we can create the jobs for any such requirements and can obtain a complete insight by identifying the outliers. It can also help us to perform a predictive analysis by reading the data available in Elasticsearch, applying algorithms and then displaying it in Kibana.

Using Elastic Stack, we can get an insight into our data, such as the amount of traffic on a website by seeing the requests per second. This information can show us the trends, such as the peak time, but if we want to get details, such as what is causing this, or the reason behind this trend, we can use X-Pack machine learning. It can provide us these details (that are hidden behind the data) and can be explored using unsupervised machine learning for Elasticsearch.

X-Pack machine learning works on time series-based data and automates the analysis process by identifying the anomaly in data. We can apply it in real time or can set it for batch processing. It uses proprietary machine learning algorithms for running the machine learning job.

In this chapter, we will cover the description of machine learning jobs involving single metric, multi-metric, population, and advanced jobs. Then, we will cover the creation of machine learning jobs in a practical way. We will also discover the data visualizer option through which we can get further insights in the data and, based on that understanding, we can decide the field to be analyzed for machine learning.

Then, we will explore the anomaly explorer option by means of which we can see the maximum anomaly score over time. It shows the anomaly as a block, which is displayed in a different color. We are going to cover the following topics in this chapter:

- The details of machine learning jobs
- The types of machine learning jobs, such as single metric, multi metric, population, and advanced jobs
- Create machine learning jobs. Here, we will see the steps for creating a machine learning job
- Data visualizer, single metric jobs, single metric viewers, anomaly explorers, multi-metric jobs, and population jobs

Machine learning jobs

In Kibana in order to run any machine learning analysis, we used to create the machine learning job and execute that in order to get the result. A job contains the configuration and meta-data information needed to perform the machine learning task.

There are one or more detectors for each job that applies the analytical function to specific fields of our data. The job also has properties that affect the anomaly consideration through types of events or entities. For example, we can specify that entities are analyzed based on other entities in data, or relative to their own previous behavior.

For running machine learning jobs, we have a UI in Kibana through which we can execute different types of machine learning jobs. We need to click on the machine learning link on the left-hand, which will open the following screen:

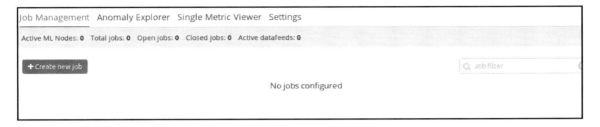

In this screenshot, we can see an empty page with a button because we have not created any job yet. By clicking on **Create new job**, we can open the index pattern page:

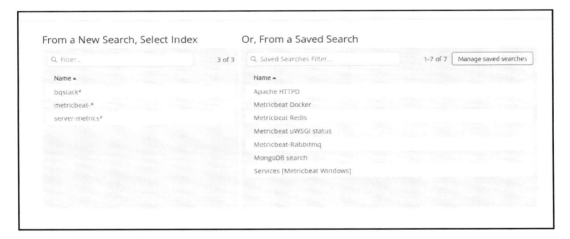

From this screenshot, we can select the index or pick from a saved search listing. I will choose the **server-metrics** index, and, for that, we need to click on the index name. The next screen will show the job creation options:

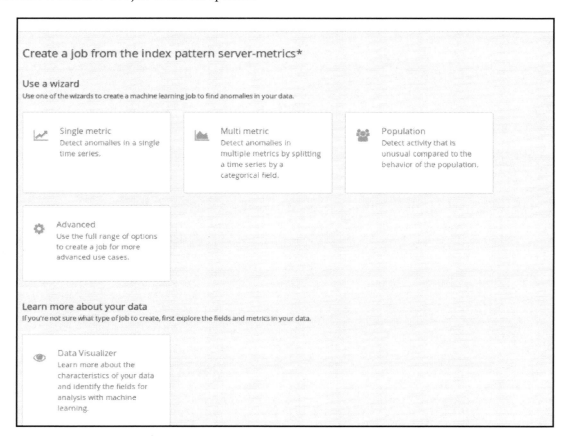

There are basically three types of jobs in Kibana machine learning.

Single metric Jobs

In a single metric job, we have a single detector to define the type of analysis that will be performed and the field that will be analyzed. Detector defines the analysis type that is going to occur, such as maximum and average. A single metric job also misses out some advanced configuration options that other job types support.

Multi-metric jobs

In multi-metric jobs, we have more than one detector and so it is more efficient for targeting multiple metrics of data rather than running multiple jobs on the same data for different metrics.

Population Jobs

A population job checks for the activities that are unusual as compared with normal activities of the population. We can mark the anomaly in data for population jobs when the routine behavior changes over time, or the behavior of events or entities differs from other entities in a specified population. The second way of finding outliers is known as population analysis.

Advanced Jobs

The advanced job defines the word "advance" as it contains multiple detectors and provides us the option to configure all job settings. We can also configure Filebeat to send access and error logs to Elasticsearch from Nginx and Apache HTTP servers for creating the machine learning jobs.

In case of any doubt regarding which type of job to create, we can use the data visualizer to understand more about the data:

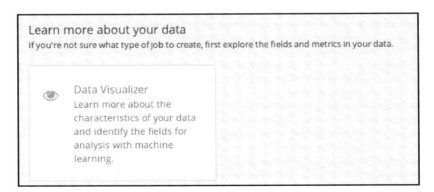

It would help us to understand the fields to which we can apply the machine learning analysis.

Create a machine learning job

We have covered different types of jobs that we can create in X-Pack machine learning, so now we will create the jobs, execute them, and then see a result of the analysis.

Before starting job creation, we have to ensure the following system requirements for running machine learning jobs:

- Elasticsearch 6.x for storing the index data on which we will perform the machine learning analysis
- X-Pack 6.x to provide the machine learning capabilities for Elasticsearch as well as Kibana
- Kibana 6.x to provide the UI for creating, executing, and obtaining the machine learning analysis results

I will show you the index pattern to be used. I am going to use the server-metrics index data in which we have the following data format:

```
"_index" : "server-metrics",
"_type" : "metric",
"_id" : "258427",
"_score" : 1.0,
"_source" : {
  "@timestamp" : "2018-04-01T01:10:00",
  "accept" : 54709,
  "deny" : 4437,
  "host" : "server_1",
  "response" : 2.3630767264,
  "service" : "app_5",
  "total" : 59146
```

The **Discover** page view screen for the Elasticsearch server-metrics index is as follows:

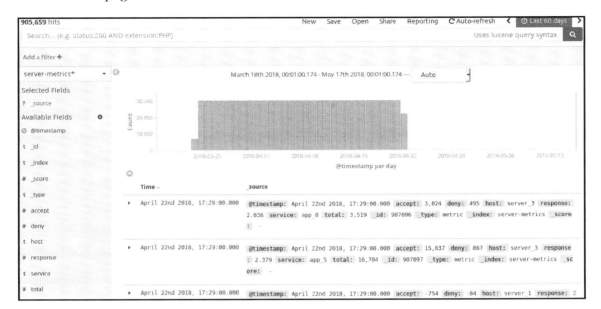

Therefore, we will be using the preceding server-metrics data for machine learning analysis. During X-Pack installation, we have created three users—`elastic`, `kibana`, and `logstash_system`—using automated tools.

Among those users, an elastic user is the admin user, and we need to log in through that user, or any other user having admin rights, to create the machine learning job.

In machine learning jobs, we provide the confrontational details and additional metadata to execute the analytical tasks. Based on these details, machine learning analytical jobs are executed, and the results are stored, which we can see.

Here, we are going to use Kibana UI for creating the machine learning jobs, but the same can be done using APIs.

We have already seen the screens through which Kibana can take the input to create the machine learning job. Using its wizard, we can create single metric, multi metric, population, or advanced types of jobs.

The following steps are for creating machine learning analysis jobs:

1. Open the web browser and type `http://localhost:5601` to open Kibana
2. Click on the **Machine Learning** link in the left-menu
3. Click on the **Create new job** button from the page
4. Click on the index name from **From a New Search, Select Index listing**
5. Click on any type of job that you want to execute such as single metric, multi metric, population, or advanced, based on requirement
6. If you are not clear about which type to choose, then please pick the **Data Visualizer** option from the bottom of the page
7. Perform the field analysis and pick up the suitable job
8. Execute the job and do the analysis after running the machine learning job

Data visualizer

We can use the data visualizer to understand more about the data. For this, we need to click on the **Data Visualizer** link from the following block:

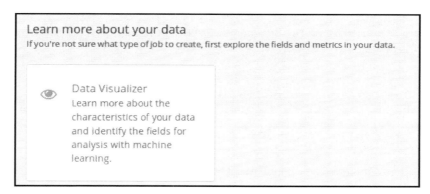

This option tells us more about the characteristics of the data, through which we can identify the fields to apply for machine learning analysis.

The following screenshot shows the screen that will be opened after clicking on the **Data Visualizer** link:

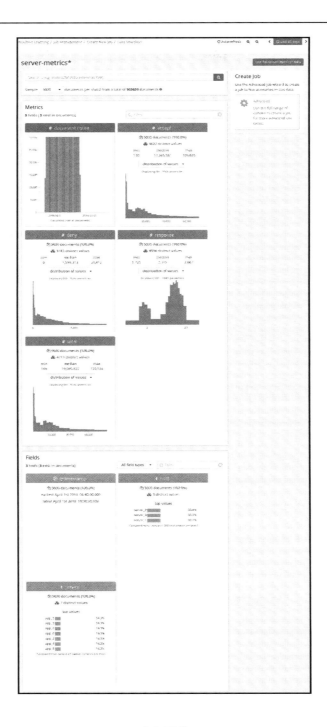

In this screenshot, we have a search box to search the index for any search criteria. Below that search box, we have a document per shard drop-down from where we can change the count of documents for each shard used for visualization. As we have a relatively smaller amount of sample data here, we can use all for the number of records per shard. For large datasets, we can decrease this value to increase the performance and decrease the load.

We have the following two sections for the fields of the index:

- **Numeric fields**: This contains all numeric fields, such as the number of documents in a selected time period, and minimum, mean, median, maximum, and distinct values.
- **Non-numeric fields**: This contains different types of non-numeric fields, such as `keyword`, `date`, `text`, `geo_points`, and `ip`. For the `date` field, we have the earliest and latest dates with the number of documents.

For host fields, it provides the distinct value count and a list of top values with the percentage of documents in the selected time period.

Single metric Job

Now, we are going to create a single metric job for anomaly detection. We will check this for the total request received field by the application. As we have already discussed, there is a single detector in a single metric job. This detector defines the types of analysis to perform, such as avg, max, and min.

To create a single metric job, we need to follow these steps:

- Click on the **Create new job** button on the machine learning page.
- Select the index pattern for machine learning. Here, we will the pick server-metrics index of Elasticsearch.
- From the **Use a wizard** section, we need to click on the **Single metric** option:

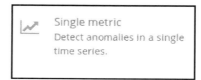

- Now, we need to provide the aggregation, field, and bucket span in order to run the single metric job. We will use sum for aggregation and field as the total to obtain the total number of machine learning analysis requests. Bucket span specifies the time frame, and then the aggregation is done. So here, after every 10 minutes, the sum of the total fields would be taken and aggregated.

- Click on the date time picker to pick the appropriate duration for the analysis. Here, we can take quick time, relative date range, or any absolute date range. After changing the date range, we need to click on the **Go** button.

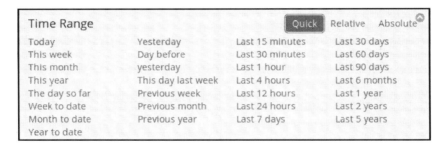

- Now, we can click on the execute icon next to the **Bucket span** field. This will open the graph with additional fields, such as **Name**, **Description**, and **Job Groups**.

In the preceding screenshot, we need to fill in the job name, and here it is `access-metric`. This name has to be unique for each cluster; additionally, we can provide the job description and job groups, which is optional. After filling in all these details, we need to click on the **Create Job** button. It shows the **Analysis running** message with a loader to show the job running duration.

Once the job is successfully executed, we get the message **Job access-metric created**. Below that, there are two buttons—**Reset** and **View Results**. The **Reset** button is there to reset the job, whereas the **View Results** button will show the machine learning analysis result:

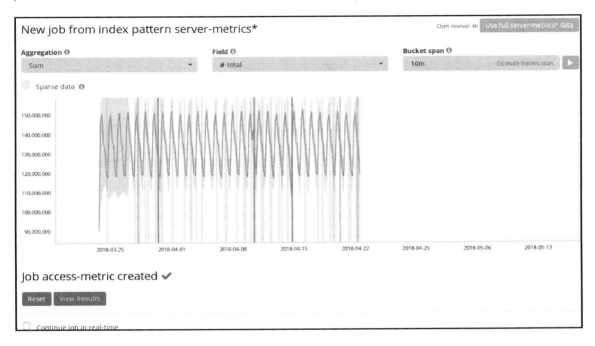

When the job is created, the graph is converted with a visual representation on top of the graph to represent the progress of the machine learning result.

By clicking on the **View Results** button, we can open the results page:

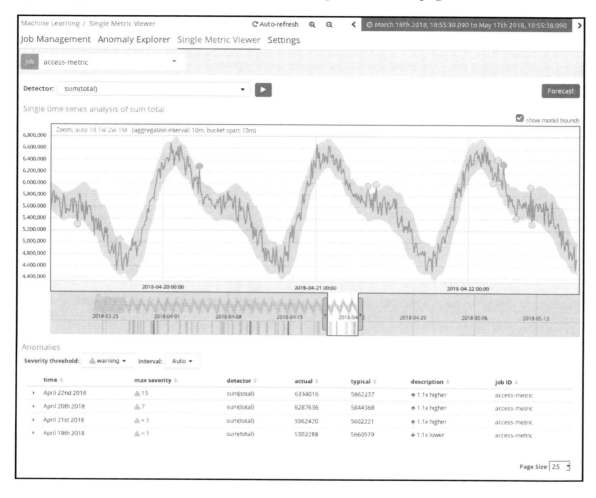

We can move the slider to below the red mark to check the anomaly in the data. You can see a view of anomaly in the following screenshot:

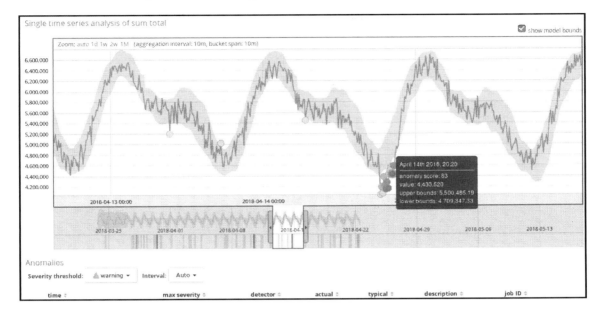

In this screenshot, we can see the red dots showing anomalies. Here, we can see date, anomaly score, value, lower bounds, and upper bounds.

Following graph, we have the tabular view for anomalies with the expand button that enables you to see the details:

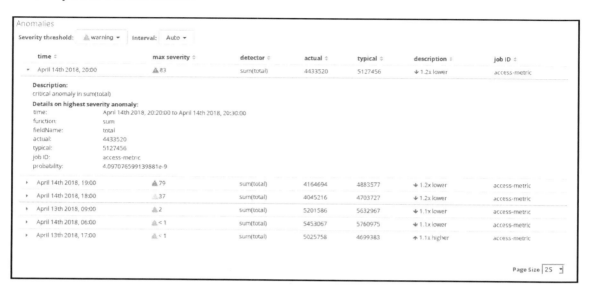

In this screenshot, the table shows the time, max severity, detector, actual, typical, description, and job ID columns and their values in the different rows.

To forecast trends, we need to click on the **Forecast** button above the graph on the right-hand side. It will open a popup to select the duration of the forecast:

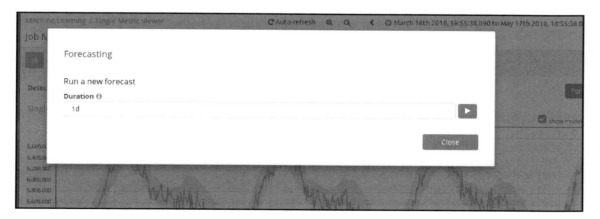

In the popup, we can fill in the duration, for example, 5d for 5 days, and then click on the **Execute** button. We can click on the **Close** button to close this window.

Once we click on the execute button, it will run the algorithm to process the result and shows the future-predicted trends in a different color, which we can see in the following screenshot:

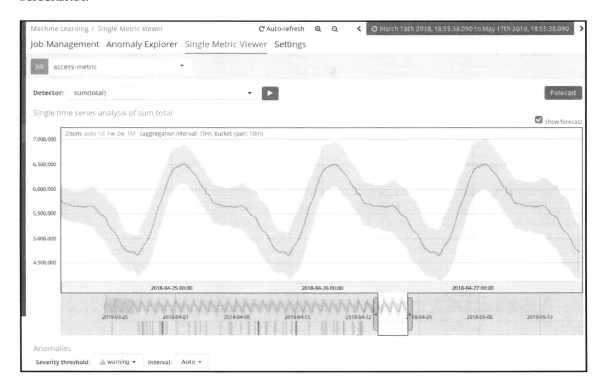

In this screenshot, we can see the future trend graph with a surrounded area marked. This surrounded area shows us the possible variation in the prediction. The leaner the area is, the better the prediction can be.

We can move the slider on the time range to change the graph view as per the selected time range. In the following screenshot, we can see the slider that can move in any direction, and, based on its location, the main graph changes, and we can get the details for that time frame. The anomaly table will be displayed below the graph to get the anomaly details.

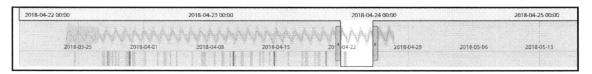

Here, we can create, execute, and analyze a single metric job. In the same way, we can create different jobs for analyzing multiple fields.

Managing jobs

After creating the job, we can get them under section to manage jobs on the **Machine Learning** page. For that, we need to click on the **Job Management** tab on the machine learning page. This will open the following screen:

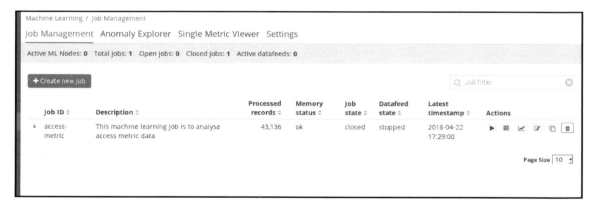

In the preceding screen, we can see the job details about the job that we just created. The details are as follows:

- Job ID
- Description
- Processed records
- Memory status
- Job state
- Datafeed state
- Latest timestamp
- Actions

We can expand the view by clicking on the expand button before the `job ID` field to open the detailed view. On the detailed view, we have the following tabs.

Job settings

Under job settings, we have three sections—general, actions, and node. The general section shows us the **job_id**, **job_type**, **job_version**, **groups**, **description**, **create_time**, **finished_time**, **established_model_memory**, **model_snapshot_retention_days**, **model_snapshot_id**, **results_index_name**, **state**, and **open_time**. Under actions, we have a **Close Job** button to close the job, whereas **node** shows the name of the node. The following screenshot shows the view of the **Job Settings** tab:

Job config

Job config shows us the configuration used to run the analysis. It shows us the detectors, analysis config (**bucket_span**, **summary_count_field_name**), analysis limits (**model_memory_limit**), and data description (**time_field**, **time_format**). The following screenshot shows the view of the **Job config** tab:

Datafeed

The **Datafeed** tab shows us **datafeed_id**, **job_id**, **query_delay**, **indices**, **types**, **query**, **aggregations**, **scroll_size**, **chunking_config**, and **state** fields. The following screenshot shows the view of the **Datafeed** tab:

Counts

On the **Counts** tab, we have the following different counts: **job_id**, **processed_record_count**, **processed_field_count**, **input_bytes**, **input_field_count**, **invalid_date_count**, **out_of_order_timestamp_count**, **empty_bucket_count**, **sparse_bucket_count**, **bucket_count**, **earliest_record_timestamp**, **latest_record_timestamp**, **last_data_time**, and **input_record_count**. Along with counts, we have model size stats, which include **job_id**, **result_type**, **model_bytes**, **total_by_field_count**, **total_over_field_count**, **total_partition_field_count**, **memory_status**, **log_time**, and **timestamp**. The following screenshot shows a view of the **Counts** tab:

JSON

The **JSON** tab view displays the JSON data of complete job-related details. The following screenshot shows a view of the **JSON** tab:

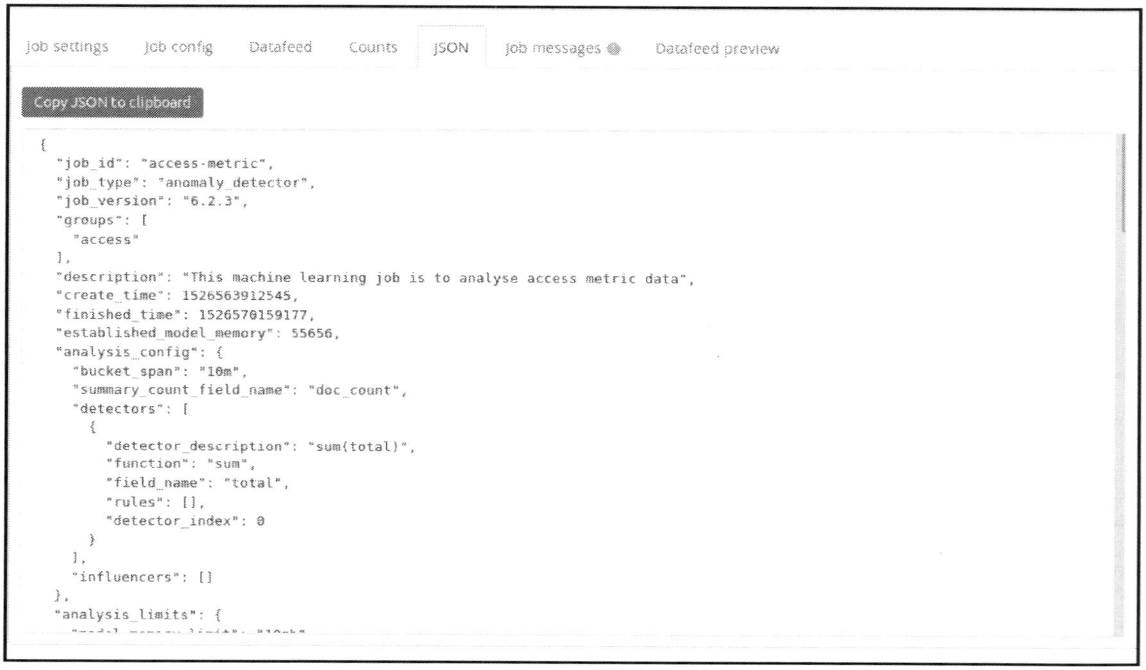

Job messages

Job messages shows the timewise log messages. These are quite helpful as they provide us with the log messages through which we can understand the complete flow for the job creation. The following screenshot shows a view of the **Job messages** tab:

Datafeed preview

Datafeed preview shows us the JSON view for the aggregated document data. The following screenshot shows a view of the **Datafeed preview** tab:

```
Job settings    Job config    Datafeed    Counts    JSON    Job messages ●    Datafeed preview

Refresh

[
  {
    "total": 7483,
    "@timestamp": 1490276400000,
    "doc_count": 1
  },
  {
    "total": 7890,
    "@timestamp": 1490304960000,
    "doc_count": 1
  },
  {
    "total": 367659,
    "@timestamp": 1490328240000,
    "doc_count": 10
  },
  {
    "total": 7359,
    "@timestamp": 1490333520000,
    "doc_count": 1
  },
  {
    "total": 54896,
    "@timestamp": 1490362080000,
    "doc_count": 1
  },
  ,
```

Anomaly explorer

Anomaly explorer shows the maximum anomaly score over time. It shows the anomaly in a form of blocks as a time frame display where anomaly boxes are displayed in a different color. By clicking on these boxes, we can get the details of the anomalies in the form of a graph and tabular view. The following screenshot shows a view of anomaly explorer.

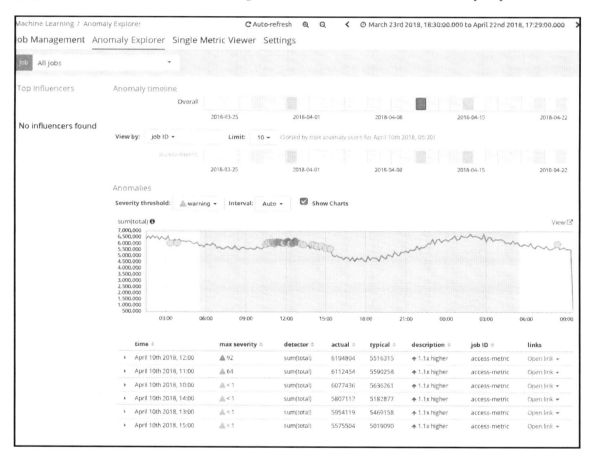

Single metric viewer

Single metric viewer shows a chart over time that shows actual and expected values. Along with the chart, it also shows the anomaly table. It is the default page for the single metric job result and only available for single metric jobs. The following screenshot shows a view of the single metric viewer:

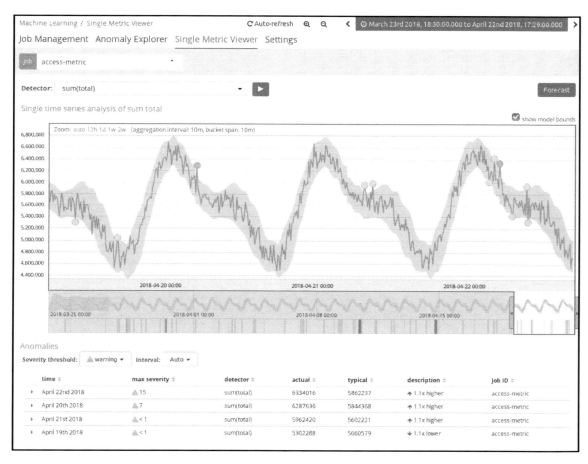

Multi metric job

Using multi metric jobs, we can create complex jobs with multiple detectors. In a single metric job, we focus on a single field since, in the previous example, we have analyzed total requests, but what if we also want to see other fields such as average response time or the maximum number of denied requests. We can do that in a single metric job by creating three different jobs for three fields, but this can easily be handled in a single multi-metric job by combining all of these fields. A multi-metric job has better scalability in comparison with different single metric jobs.

Now, if we want to analyze the request received and the response time using multi-metric job, we need to follow these steps:

1. From the **Use a wizard** screen, click on the **Multi metric** option:

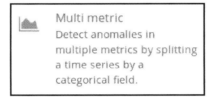

2. Set the configuration as per the following setting:
   In the fields, set **High mean** opposite **response** and **Sum** opposite **total**. Choose **Service** against **Split Data** and **10m** in the **Bucket span**:

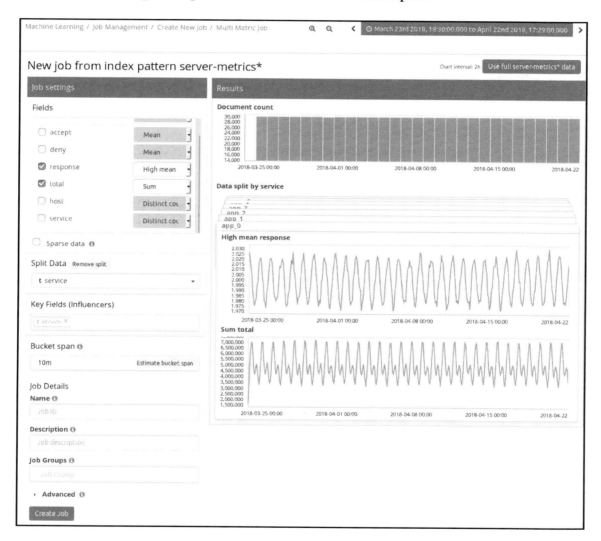

3. Then, add the unique job name, and optionally, the description and groups. After adding these details, click on the **Create Job** button. This will execute the machine learning multi-metric analysis and will show the message **Job server_metric_multi created** as I have given the job name as `server_metric_multi`. We can see the result in the following screenshot:

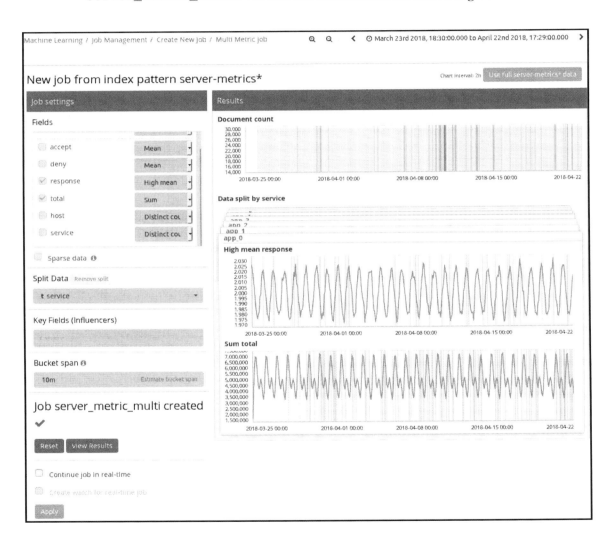

4. After executing the machine learning job, we can see that two graphs high mean response and sum total are generated for each service.

Explore multi metric job result

To view the multi metric analysis result, we need to follow these steps:

1. Open the machine learning page by clicking on **Machine Learning** in the left menu.
2. Click on the **Anomaly Explorer** link in the top menu.
3. This will open the anomaly explorer page.
4. Click on **Job** drop-down to select the group and jobs and then click on the **Apply** button. This will filter the results accordingly:

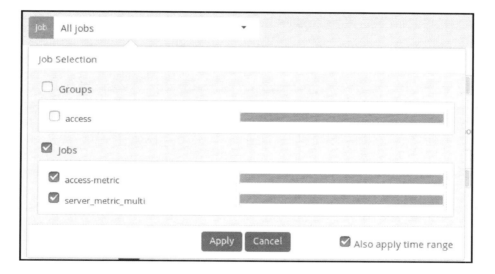

5. After clicking on the **Apply** button, we get the following anomaly explorer view:

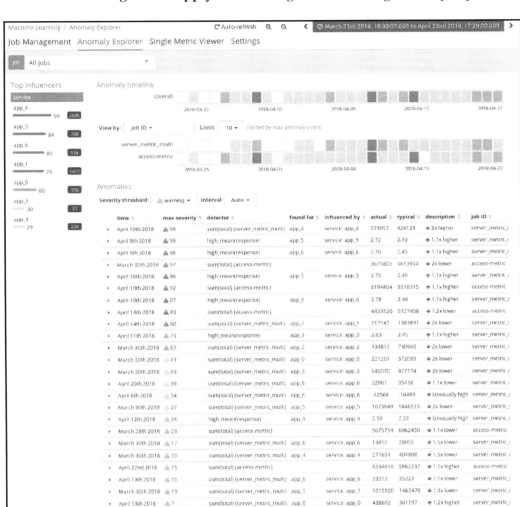

6. We have an overall anomaly timeline on top, and it shows the maximum anomaly score for that section for that time frame. We can change the time duration using the time picker in the top right-hand corner to obtain the details for any specific duration.

7. In the left section, we have a list of top influences for all anomalies shown for the selected period of time. This list also has the maximum anomaly scores aggregated for each influence.

8. In the swim lane, we can click on any section to get more details about the anomalies, as shown in the following screenshot:

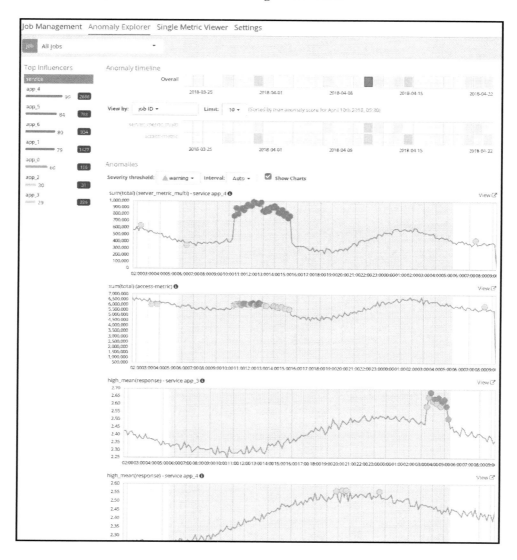

In this screenshot, I have clicked on the red block from the overall anomaly timeline and it has opened the anomaly detail graph through which we can gain further insights about the anomaly.

9. In the top right-hand of every graph, we have the 'View' link, which opens the graph in the single metric viewer.

From there, we can perform all those operations supported in a single metric job such as forecast. Forecast is already explained in a single metric job.

Population job

Population analysis builds a profile of normal trends and then identifies if an individual behaves abnormally in comparison with the population. In order to execute a population job, we need to follow these steps:

1. Click on **Population** job from the **use a wizard** option.

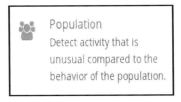

2. This will open the population analysis page. Now add the job setting parameters to run the job. For example, I have added **Accept** as **sum**, **Total** as **mean** and **Bucket span** as **15m**. Then, you need to specify the job name and other optional details such as description.

3. After filling in these details, click on the **Create job** button to create the job.

4. Once the job is created, we can see the success message in the left-hand pane with the **Reset** and **View Results** button. The following screenshot shows the successful job creation screen:

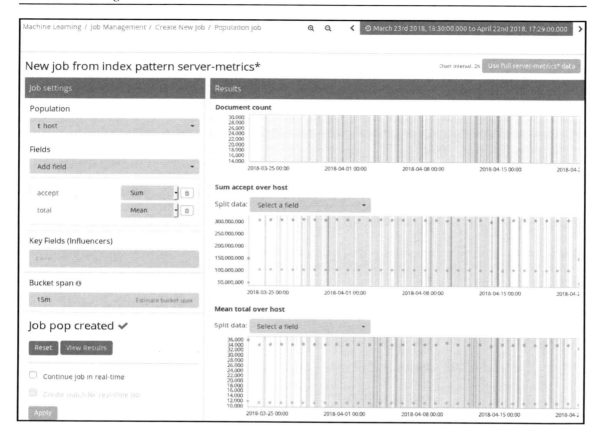

5. Now we can click on the **View Results** button to view the result of the population analysis.

6. It opens the **Anomaly Explorer** screen, as already explained in the multi-metric job section.

Advanced job is also similar to another job with the additional configuration options. In advanced job, we can edit job details, analysis configuration, data feed, and JSON data.

Summary

In this chapter, we covered machine learning jobs through which we can find anomalies in data, and, based on the analysis, it can forecast future trends. It uses the proprietary software for unsupervised machine learning to perform these analyses.

It has different types of jobs, such as single metric job, where we can analyze a single field at a time, a multi metric job, where we can combine more than one field in a single job to analyze, a population job, where it creates a format with a normal range of field data and, whenever any value goes beyond the range of the population, it marks the anomaly, and finally an advanced job, where we have more customization options and where we can tweak the job as per our requirements.

Apart from these different types of jobs, it is quite obvious that sometimes, we would not be able to decide the right type of job for the given problem in hand. For those scenarios, we have a data visualizer, which we can use to get insights into our data and can identify the fields suitable for machine learning.

After going through a description of these jobs, we covered the practical aspects of job creation and explained the step-by-step ways of creating different types of job and then how to analyze the results after executing the job. I hope that this chapter has clarified for you all the complete machine learning aspects of Kibana.

In the next chapter, we will encounter different use cases of Kibana and explore important features of Kibana that we have not yet discussed. In the beginning of the chapter, we will cover time-series data handling using conditional formatting in order to format the data plot as per the given condition. Using tracking trends, we can create a data trend using moving averages on data. Then, we will cover a visual builder, which provides us with the option to use the Timelion features using regular Kibana UI. Finally, we will see how to use GeoIP for Elastic Stack in order to plot data on maps by adding the location fields using the IP address field of the data.

11
Create Super Cool Dashboard from a Web Application

In previous chapters, we saw how we can create a dashboard to monitor key performance indicators. In this chapter, you will learn how to create web application dashboards using application database. Here, we are going to discuss how to pull the data from RDBMS using Logstash and push it to Elasticsearch and then use the data in Kibana to create the dashboard.

Basically, I am going to explain how we can use Logstash to pull the data from the RDBMS and then send this data to Elasticsearch, from where we can read it in Kibana to create the dashboard. This approach is quite interesting as we are not making any change in the application to get the data but simply using the JDBC connector of Logstash that provides us the facility to pull the data directly from any RDBMS just by writing the queries after connecting to the database server.

For this type of dashboard creation, we need to create a star schema table and pull the data into it from other tables, the same approach we use to apply for reporting. Once that is done, we can use JDBC connector to pull the data using queries in Logstash. Logstash pulls the data from RDBMS, and we can configure it to send the data directly in Elasticsearch. Then, we can create the index pattern in Kibana to use that index in order to create the dashboards.

The following diagram depicts the architecture we are going to use here:

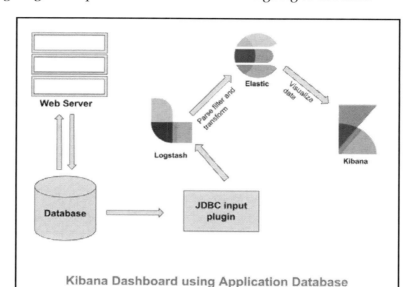

The preceding diagram shows a web server that is connected to a database server for read and write operation. We are using **JDBC input plug in** of **Logstash** to fetch the data from database by writing queries. This data is then sent to **Elastic**, and **Kibana** uses that data to create the dashboards. So, first of all, we need to understand how JDBC input plugin works.

JDBC input plugin

JDBC input plugin is there to fetch data from any database with the Logstash JDBC interface. It has a built-in scheduler that can be set to fetch the data at regular intervals without affecting the application that is connected with the database. We can also run a one-time query to fetch the data from a database.

Each column of a record converts into field, and each row converts as a resultset that can be inserted as a document in Elasticsearch. JDBC driver library is not shipped with this plugin, and we need to explicitly pass the path of the driver using the `jdbc_driver_library` configuration of the plugin. We are going to discuss many features of JDBC input plugin here.

Scheduling

We can schedule the Logstash input through JDBC input plugin. There is a specific syntax using which we can set the schedule frequency. The syntax for JDBC input plugin is quite similar to `cron`. Look at the following example:

```
"* * * * * " => runs every second
"30 2 * * *" => runs as 2:30AM
"10 22 * * *" => runs at 10:10PM
```

In the preceding example, we can see different schedules that can be created using JDBC input plugin scheduler option. Schedulers are very important for JDBC input plugin as the values in tables are updated regularly, and we need to run the queries with a scheduler to fetch the most recent records.

Maintaining the last SQL value

JDBC input plugin also maintains the last SQL value of a query. This is a very good feature as Logstash maintains the last index value and when we run the query next time it fetches the records whose ID is greater than last index value. In this way, Logstash ensures the incremental updates rather than every time reading from the first record of database table. This plugin maintains the `sql_last_value` parameter in a metadata file that is stored in the configured `last_run_metadata_path`. When we execute a query, this value is updated with the current index of the SQL query. When the query is executed next time, when we execute the Logstash pipeline, the value of `sql_last_value` is picked from the file and assigned to the query. Don't worry if you still have confusion regarding `sql_last_value`, I will explain it through the practical examples. We also have to set the `use_column_value`, `tracking_column`, and `tracking_column_type` parameters for using the `sql_last_value` option in a given query. The following expression shows the way we apply `sql_last_value` in our query statement:

```
statement => "SELECT blg.* FROM `blog_blogs` as blg where blg.id >
:sql_last_value order by blg.create_date"
use_column_value => true
tracking_column => id
tracking_column_type => "numeric"
```

The preceding expression shows the query in which we have compared `blg.id` with `sql_last_value`, and this value is set using the `tracking_column` parameter that is set as `id` and its type is set as numeric using the `tracking_column_type` parameter. In this way, we can create the queries and set the column through which we can fetch the incremental values such as the `id` or `timestamp` field.

Fetch size

Fetch size can control the size of data we can pull at a time. Sometimes when we are going to work with a large dataset, it is very important to set the fetch size; otherwise, the plugin will crash. In JDBC input plugin, we can control the fetch size using the `jdbc_fetch_size` configuration option. By default, this plugin has no fetch size, so it depends on the driver's default fetch size.

Configuring Logstash for database input

I am taking the example of a blog website that is built using a MySQL database. Basically, we are going to configure Logstash using JDBC input plugin to connect with a MySQL database. After connecting to the MySQL database, we will run the query to fetch the records from the database and will push that record into the Elasticsearch index.

Basically, a blog website is running using the data from the MySQL database and I don't want to change anything in my application, but I still want to get the insight of the blog data. This is an ideal situation where Elastic Stack can do the magic, as we just need to connect to the MySQL database and run a query to get the data; once the data is in, we can create a query that can be scheduled to get the new and updated records. Once this architecture is in place, we can test it by inserting a new record into the database and ensuring that record is also inserted into Elasticsearch.

Once we are getting the data from the MySQL database into Elasticsearch, we can create the dashboards in Kibana as per our requirement. I have already explained the Logstash installation process in the first chapter, so please refer to that for installing Logstash. Now, let's start the process by creating the Logstash configuration file.

We need to create the Logstash configuration file inside the `/etc/logstash/conf.d/` directory. So, let's create a file as `blog.conf` and write the code as follows:

```
# file: blog.conf
input {
    jdbc {
        jdbc_driver_library => "/usr/share/logstash/mysql-connector-
java-5.1.23-bin.jar"
        jdbc_driver_class => "com.mysql.jdbc.Driver"
        # mysql jdbc connection string to our database, mydb
         jdbc_connection_string => "jdbc:mysql://url-of-
db:3306/db_name?zeroDateTimeBehavior=convertToNull"
        # The user we wish to execute our statement as
        jdbc_user => "username"
        jdbc_password => "password"
```

```
        schedule => "* * * * *"
        # our query to fetch blog details
        statement => "SELECT blg.*, concat(au.first_name, ' ',au.last_name)
as name,au.email as email, cc.category_name, cc.category_image FROM
`blog_blogs` as blg left join auth_user as au on au.id = blg.author_id left
join category_category as cc on cc.id = blg.category_id where blg.id >
:sql_last_value order by blg.create_date"
        use_column_value => true
        tracking_column => id
        tracking_column_type => "numeric"
    }
}
output {
    elasticsearch {
        hosts => "http://127.0.0.1:9200"
        index => "bqstack"
        document_type => "blogs"
        }
}
```

In the preceding Logstash configuration file, we have an input and output section. Under the input section, we are connecting to the MySQL database for fetching the data, and under output, we are sending that data to the Elasticsearch cluster. Under the input section, we have `jdbc` block in which the first option is `jdbc_driver_library`, which tells the JDBC driver library path. As I have already explained, the JDBC input library does not contain the JDBC driver, so we need to download it and then provide the path under the `jdbc_driver_library` parameter. Next is `jdbc_driver_class`, where we need to provide the driver class, and then we need to provide the JDBC connection string. For the connection string, it has a syntax where we have to provide the DB type, URL of database, port of database, database name, and then we need to set username and password parameter of database.

Once these database connection-related parameters are set, we can set the scheduler by setting the schedule parameter, and then comes the actual query that we are going to execute on the connected database. The statement parameter is there to write the query; in this query, I have compared the blog ID with `sql_last_value`, which is dynamic and refers to the `id` column of the table. After each query execution, the value of `sql_last_value` is updated and set in the file. The next time the query is executed, this value is picked from the file. We are providing the data type of the tracking column along with the tracking column name; as `id` is a numeric value, I have given it as numeric for the `tracking_column_type` parameter.

Under the output section of Logstash, we have configured Elasticsearch. For pushing the data into Elasticsearch, we need to provide the host location for hosts parameter, index name for index parameter, and document type for the document_type parameter. Once the Elasticsearch configuration is done, the output of the MySQL query will be pushed to the bqstack index of Elasticsearch.

In this way, we have configured Logstash to connect MySQL using JDBC input plugin, execute the query to fetch the data, and push it into Elasticsearch index. Now, we have done the required changes in the Logstash configuration file, but, to apply these changes, we need to execute Logstash using the following command on Ubuntu:

```
/usr/share/logstash/bin/logstash -f /etc/logstash/conf.d/blog.conf --
path.data=/tmp/bq
```

In the preceding expression, we are executing the logstash command on the /etc/logstash/conf.d/blog.conf file; also, the data path is set at /tmp/bq, which is required to write additional data from Logstash. This is a one-time command, after running which the scheduler will start working, and as per our scheduler entry, the query will be executed every second.

We can do the cron entry to autostart the Logstash configuration execution once the system restarts. We need to run the following command for opening the crontab in Linux:

```
crontab -e
```

The preceding command opens the crontab file, where we can write the following entry to ensure that, after the machine restarts, the Logstash configuration is executed, and JDBC input plugin scheduler starts executing the queries to fetch the data from the database:

```
@reboot /usr/share/logstash/bin/logstash -f /etc/logstash/conf.d/blog.conf
--path.data=/tmp/bq
```

The preceding `crontab` entry starts with `@reboot`, which works after each machine restarts after we have given the expression to execute the Logstash configuration.

In this way, we have executed the queries and stored the table data into the Elasticsearch index. Also, we have scheduled the query to run every second and pull whenever a new record is inserted into the database. The query has the `id` column that we have set as `sql_last_value` to get the recent value from the file that JDBC input plugin uses to update the value after every query execution. Now, let's see the dashboard creation in Kibana where we will create an index pattern for this index and then will create the visualization and dashboard using this blog data from the MySQL database.

Creating a dashboard using MySQL data

As blog data is pushed into the Elasticsearch cluster, we need to create the index pattern in Kibana to fetch the Elasticsearch index data. To create the index pattern first of all, we need to click on the **Management** link on the left-hand menu, which will open the management page. Now, click on the **Index Pattern** tab on top links; once the page opens, click on the **Create Index Pattern** button, which will open the create index pattern page.

Now, type the Elasticsearch index name, `bqstack`, for the index pattern textbox under define index pattern. After typing the correct index name, we can see the green tick mark indicating that we have correctly mapped the index name. Now, click on the **Next** button that opens the configure settings page; here, we need to select the time filter field name from a dropdown.

A time filter field is very important as date time filter works on that field only, and we should use the appropriate field as a time filter field. Now, select default `@timestamp` as a time filter field and click on the `Create index pattern` button. After that, we can see the field listing for the index pattern with name, type, format, searchable, aggregatable, excluded, and controls columns. This listing provides us the a detailed view of index pattern where we can get the field details such as its data type and format of the field, and so on. The following screenshot shows us the field listing page of the index pattern:

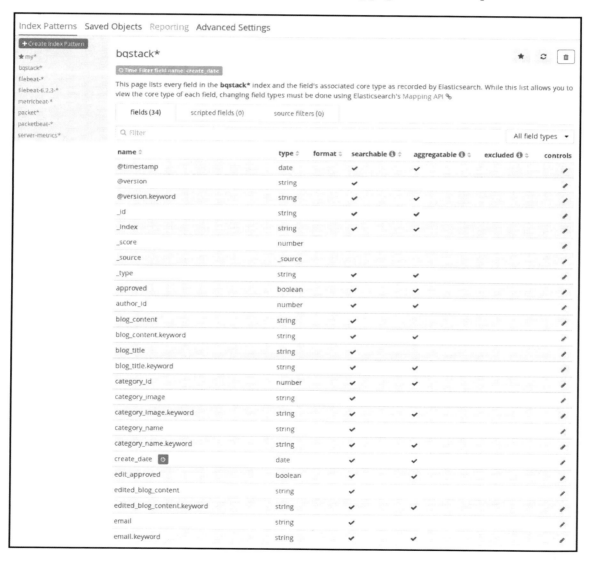

The preceding screenshot shows the files listing of the `bqstack` index pattern of Kibana. Here, we can see all fields with their attributes such as `type`, `format`, and `controls`. We can modify the format and popularity index of the field. This modification is already covered in previous chapters. The following screenshot shows the format modification of the `@timestamp` field:

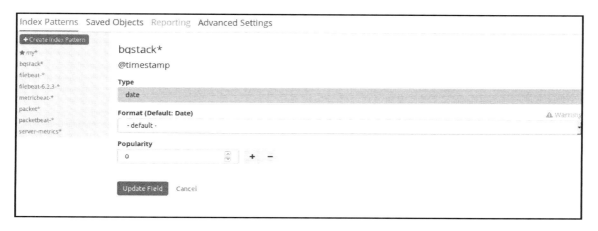

The preceding screenshot shows how we can change the format of a field, as explained in previous chapters. We can click on the star button to make `bqstack` a default index pattern. As we have successfully added the index pattern, now let's check whether we are getting the data, for which we need to click on the **Discover** tab on the left-hand menu of Kibana, which will show us the following screen:

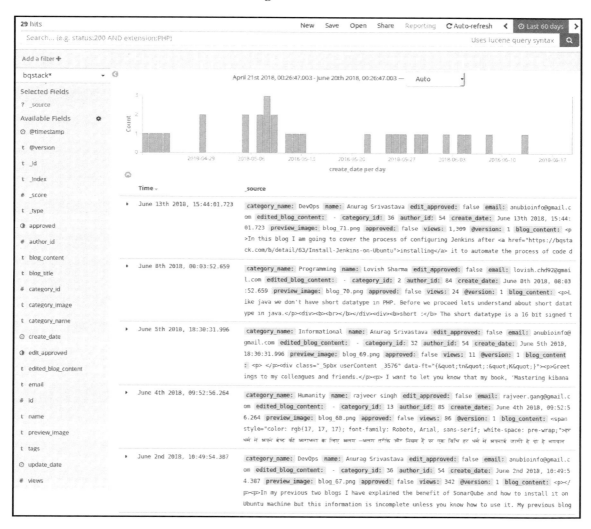

The preceding screenshot shows the `bqstack` index data pulled from MySQL database using JDBC input plugin. Now, as our data is there in the index, we need to create the visualizations for dashboard creation with key performance indicators.

Creating visualizations

We are going to create a few visualizations using the blog data and through which I want to explain the complete process so that you can get the data from any database into your Elasticsearch cluster. Using that data, you can create the visualizations and then finally a dashboard by integrating those visualizations. With this approach, we can create a parallel reporting system without making any change in the application.

Total blog and top blog count

Let's start the visualization process by creating a simple metric visualization. This metric visualization will just show the total number of blogs in the website. In any visualization tool, before creating the visualization, we have to think and ensure different types of metrics we are going to plot and then which type of visualization is going to do the job for the graph. For example, if we are going to show total number of blogs, then the metric type of visualization is best suited for that job because it shows the digits on the screen and we need to show the count of blogs in the form of digits. So, to create the metric visualization, we need to follow these steps:

1. Click on the plus icon to add the visualization
2. Click on metric box on the **Select visualization type** page
3. From the select index page, click on the `bqstack*` index pattern
4. Select the **Count** option in the **Aggregation** textbox under the **Metric** section
5. Type `Total Blogs` under **Custom Label** as we are going to show total blog count here
6. Now, click on the **Apply changes** button
7. This will show us the metric with count of total blogs
8. Click on the **Save** link on the menu at the top, give a name for the visualization, and click on the **Save** button to save the visualization

The following screenshot shows us the total blog count metric visualization:

In the preceding screenshot, we are showing total blog count with a label of `Total Blogs`. Our first visualization for the blog dashboard is created. In the same way, we also want to create a metric to show us the max views count for all blogs. The idea behind this metric is to know the most popular blog and its total views. Therefore, we need to do two changes—select the max option for aggregation under metrics, and select the views option under the field. Set the custom label as `Max Views` and click on the **Apply changes** button to create the max views metrics.

Blogger-wise blog counts

Now, I want to see the blogger with their blog count in a descending order, as this graph will immediately identify the top blogger. For this type of indicator, we can use the vertical bar type of visualization, as this bar can easily depict the blogger and their blog count in the form of vertical boxes. So, let's start creating the vertical bar in the following steps:

1. Click on the plus icon to add the visualization.
2. Click on vertical bar box on the **Select visualization type** page.

3. From the **Select** index page, click on the `bqstack*` index pattern.
4. Select the **Count** option in the **Aggregation** textbox under the **Metric** section.
5. Set the **Count** option for **Aggregation** of **Y-axis** under **Metrics.**
6. Add the **Custom Label** as `Number of Blogs` as we are going to show total blogs for each blogger.
7. Under the **Bucket** section, select the **Terms** option for **Aggregation** in **X-axis** and select the **Field** name as `name.keyword`.
8. Select the **metric:Number of Blogs** option for **Order By**.
9. Add the *x* axis custom label as `Blogger wise blog count`.
10. Click on the **Apply changes** option. This will display the vertical bar chart.
11. Now, save the chart for further use.

The following screenshot shows the vertical bar for blogger-wise blog counts in descending order:

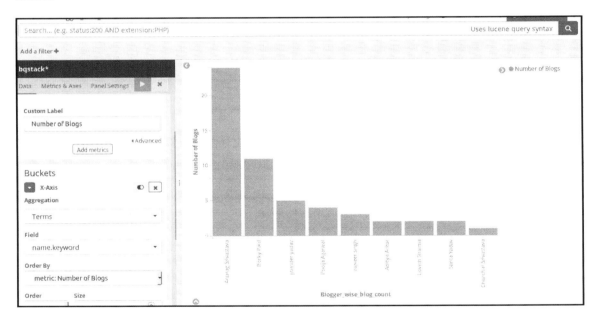

In the preceding screenshot, we can see that the bars are representing the blogger name and the block height is showing the blog count for each blogger. This type of visualization can be used for representing different categories.

Tag cloud for blog categories

We have created metrics for important counts and vertical bar for blogger-wise blog counts. Now, I am going to create cloud tags for different categories. So, for creating a category tag, we have to follow these steps:

1. Click on the plus icon to add the visualization
2. Click on the **Tag Cloud** box on the **select visualization type** page
3. From the **Select index** page, click on the `bqstack*` index pattern
4. Under the **Metrics** section, select **Count** for the **Aggregation** option
5. Add the custom label
6. Under the **Bucket** section, select **Terms** for **Aggregation** under **Tags**
7. Select `category_name.keyword` for the field name
8. Select the **Custom Metric** option under the **Order By** field
9. Now, under **Aggregation**, select **Max** as we want to order by max views for categories
10. Under **Field**, select the `views` option as we want to order by views of blogs
11. Now, click on the **Apply changes** button, which will create the tag cloud

The following screenshot shows the tag cloud for different blog categories:

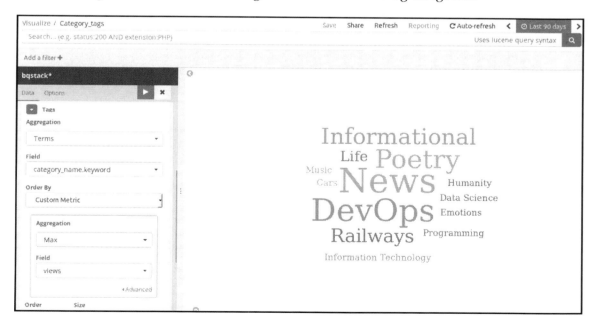

The preceding screenshot shows the tag cloud for blog categories. As we have set the order as per the blog views, the top-viewed categories are displayed in a more prominent and bigger font.

Blogger name-category-views-blog pie chart

Now, I am going to create a multidimensional pie chart where the first aggregation is blogger name, the second subaggregation is a category of the blog, the third subaggregation is the views of blog, and the fourth subaggregation is the name of blog. Pie charts are quite handy for showing multiple dimensions in a single graph. So, to create the `name-category-views-blog` pie chart, we have to follow these steps:

1. Click on the plus icon to add the visualization.
2. Click on the Pie box on the select **visualization type** page.
3. From the select index page, click on the `bqstack*` index pattern.
4. On the **Aggregation** textbox under **Metric**, select the **Count** option.
5. Add the custom label.
6. Under the **Bucket** section, select terms for **Aggregation** under **Tags**.
7. Select `name.keyword` for the **Field** name. Click on the **add bucket** link and the **split slices** link under **Bucket type**.
8. Select terms for subaggregation and `category_name.keyword` for the **Field** option.
9. Again, click on the **Add bucket** link and click on the **Split slices** link under **Bucket type**.
10. Select terms for subaggregation and views for the **Field** option.
11. Again, click on the **Add bucket** link and click on split slices link under the bucket type.
12. Select terms for subaggregation and **blog_title.keyword** for the **field** option
13. Now, click on the **Apply changes** button, which will show the image on the right-hand pane.
14. Save the pie chart visualization by giving a proper name.

The following screenshot shows us the pie chart for blog data:

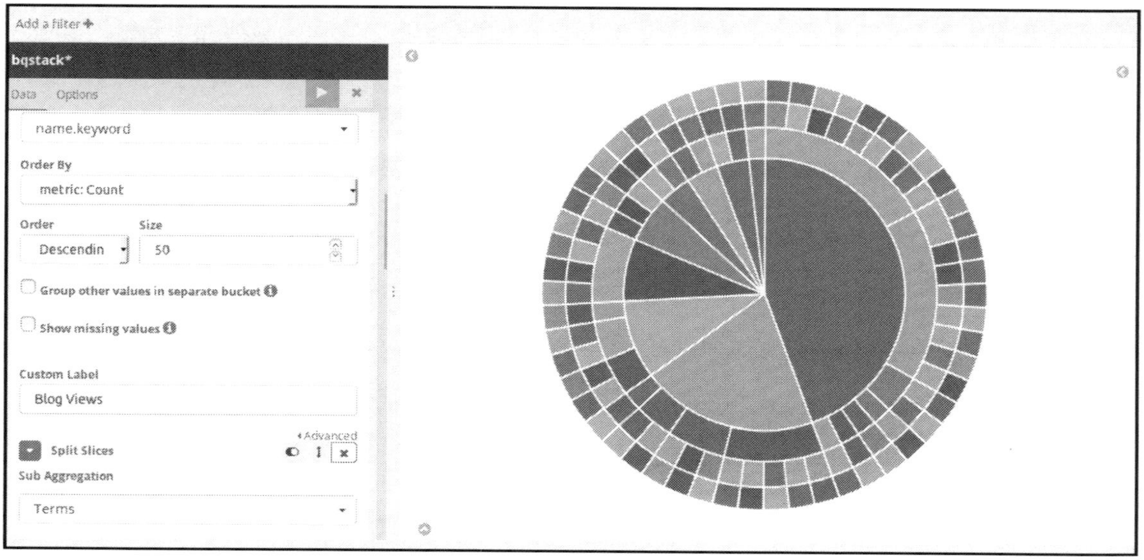

In the preceding screenshot, the inner circle shows the name of the blogger, then we have a category of the blog, the third circle from inner is the views of blog, and the outer circle is showing the name of blogs.

Tabular view of blog details

Now, we are going to create the table visualization for showing blog details in the form of rows and columns. Here, we are going to take blog title, category, blogger name, blog added on time, total views on blog, and blogger email as the columns. So, to create the table visualization, follow these steps:

1. Click on the plus icon to add the visualization.
2. Click on the **Data table box** on the select **visualization type** page under the **Data** option.
3. From the **Select index** page, click on the `bqstack*` index pattern.
4. On the **Aggregation** textbox under **Metric**, select the **Count** option.
5. Under **Buckets**, click on the **split rows** option.

6. Select terms for aggregation and `blog_title.keyword` for the **Field** type and also set the **Custom Label** as `Blog Title`.

7. Now, click on the **add sub bucket** button and again click on the **split rows** option.

8. This time, choose the field name as `category_name.keyword` and set the **Custom Label** as **Category**.

9. Again click, on the **add sub-bucket** button and then click on the **split rows** option.

10. Now, choose the field name as `name.keyword` and set the **Custom Label** as **Blogger.**

11. In the next sub-bucket option, select **create_date** as the field name and **Added On** as the custom label.

12. Next, select **views** as the field name and **Views** as the custom label.

13. At last, select **email.keyword** as a field name and **Blogger Email** as a custom label.

14. Once we are done with these field settings for the sub-bucket, click on the **Apply changes** button.

15. This will create the data table. Now, save the table by giving the proper name of the data table.

The following screenshot shows us the data table with blog details:

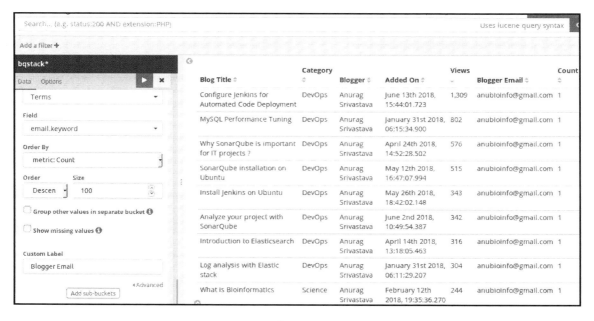

The preceding screenshot shows the tabular data for blogs where we have blog title, blog category, blogger name, blog created on, blog views, and blogger email columns.

Create dashboard

We have created some visualizations using our blog data, now let's integrate them to create the dashboard. In order to create the dashboard, we need to follow these steps:

1. Click on the **Dashboard** link on the left-hand menu.
2. Click on plus button to create the new dashboard.
3. Click on **Add button** to add the visualizations. This will open the add panel to add the visualization or saved search.
4. Under the **Visualization** tab, type the name of visualization to search the visualization and click on the name of visualization to add it on the dashboard.
5. In the same way, add all blog visualizations that we created.
6. Now resize and move the visualizations in the dashboard as per the requirement.
7. Save the dashboard by providing a proper name to the dashboard.

The following screenshot shows us the dashboard created by fetching the blog data from RDBMS using JDBC input plugin:

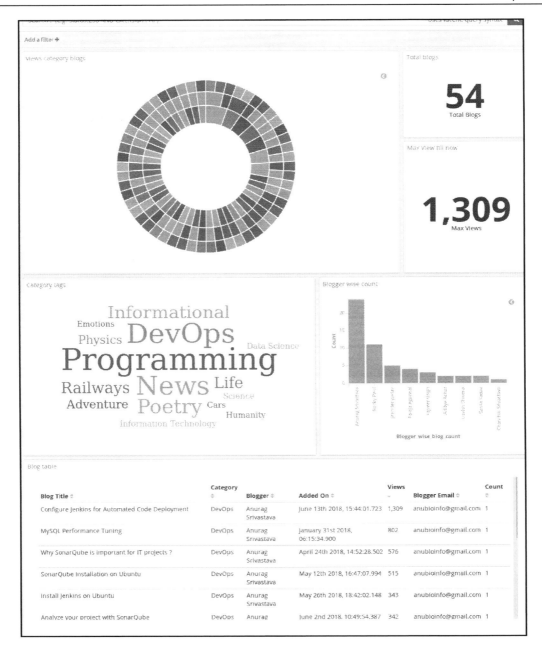

In the preceding screenshot, we can see the different types of blog visualizations such as category-wise blog views, total blogs metric, max view till now metrics, category tags, blogger-wise count, and blog table. If required, we can add more visualizations to the dashboard.

In this way, we have created visualization from RDBMS data and integrated those visualizations for creating a meaningful dashboard with key performance indicators.

Summary

In this chapter, we covered dashboard creation by directly fetching RDBMS data using the JDBC input plugin. Using this plugin, we can write the queries to fetch the data from RDBMS and save that data into Elasticsearch using Logstash pipelining.

Here, Logstash uses JDBC input plugin to query the RDBMS server directly, and after getting that data through input, it passes that data into Elasticsearch. Once the data is added into Elasticsearch, we can use that data in Kibana by creating the index pattern.

After creating the index pattern, we can create different visualizations as per our requirement and then integrate those visualizations to create the dashboard. Once the dashboard is created, we can edit and save it for further use. In this way, we covered the dashboard creation using RDBMS data.

Different Use Cases of Kibana 12

In the previous chapters, we covered various features that Kibana provides and how we can use those features for performing various tasks; for example, using Discover, we can get an insight into our data using search and filter options. Visualize can help us create different type of graphs, metrics, and data tables, and so on.

In the dashboard, we can integrate these visualizations to display the key performance indicators, save them, or share them with other users. Timelion is there to play with time series data. It provides us with the flexibility to play with different indices together, and we can apply the function chaining to get the desired output. Dev Tools are there to run Elasticsearch queries directly from the Kibana console so that we can see the request and response on the same screen and format the expression using the formatting tool.

In this way, we covered the features and methods to work with these options of Kibana. Now, in this chapter, we will explore other important features of Kibana. In the first section of this chapter, we will cover time-series data handling, where we will see how we can use conditional formatting to format the data plot as per the given condition. Using tracking trends, we can create a data trend using moving averages on data. After that, we will cover visual builder, using which we can achieve the Timelion features using the regular Kibana UI. Finally, we will see how we can use GeoIP for Elastic Stack to plot the data on a map by adding the location fields using an IP address field of data.

Time-series data handling

Time series data is the series of data points that is captured against the time order. Here, we will cover how to deal with time-series data. In Kibana, we have Timelion, which is specially designed for handling time-series data. In the previous chapter, we covered Timelion and its methods, which we can use to play with time-series data. It provides us with methods that we can chain together to get the desired output. Here, we will cover the following:

- **Conditional formatting**: In conditional formatting, we will cover how we can color-code the time-series data based on applied conditions
- **Tracking trends**: Under tracking trends, we will user the `mvavg()` Timelion function, through which we can plot a moving average graph to create a trend

Conditional formatting

Here, we will use Timelion to apply conditional logic on metricdata time-series data to track the trends with a moving average. Using this process, we can easily detect the patterns and outliers in a time series.

For this practical exercise, I will be using the metricbeat data, and to explain this process, we will pick the `system.memory.actual.used.bytes` field of data. So, first of all, I will plot the system memory used in bytes with the following command:

```
.es(index=metricbeat-*, timefield='@timestamp',
metric='max:system.memory.actual.used.bytes').label('Memory used in bytes')
```

In the preceding command, I am using the `.es()` function, which is used to query with Elasticsearch index. The first parameter of the query is index, which tells us that we are using the metricbeat index, a timefield shows that we are using `@timestamp` for time field, a metric is denoting that we are plotting on max value of the `system.memory.actual.used.bytes` field, and finally, the `label()` function is there to add the label for the field name. The following screenshot shows the response after executing this command on **Timelion**:

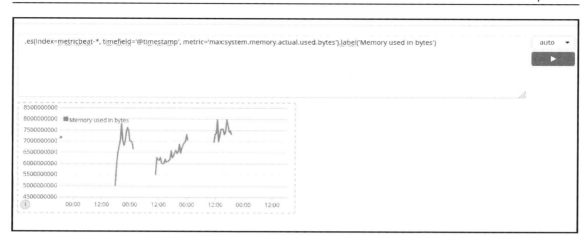

Now, by looking at the preceding chart, we can get the idea of data usage, but there is still no demarcation between normal usage, the warning threshold, and the severe threshold. So here, I will add two points on this plot and color them accordingly.

For now, let's say color the graph in yellow if the memory usage crosses 7 GB, and color the graph in red if memory usage crosses 7.3 GB. You can decide this threshold range as per your memory consumption value.

Now, as we have decided the threshold values, let's apply the Timelion logic to achieve that. For that, we can use Timelion's conditional logic using the `if()` function to compare the value with the numbers.

We have different operator values for comparison in Timelion:

```
eq : to check for equality
ne : if value if not equal to the given value
lt : less than
lte: less than or equal to
gt: greater than
gte: greater than or equal to
```

By using `if()`, we can compare each point to the threshold number and it will apply the given styling when the condition evaluates to true; otherwise, it will return false, and default styling will be applied.

As there are two threshold numbers, we can write two different styles: one with a yellow color and other with a red color. We will use the gt operator to check the condition for threshold values. We can use the following expression for applying the conditional logic to set the desired styles:

```
.es(index=metricbeat-*, timefield='@timestamp',
metric='max:system.memory.actual.used.bytes').label('Memory used in
bytes'),

.es(index=metricbeat-*, timefield='@timestamp',
metric='max:system.memory.actual.used.bytes').if(gt,7000000000,.es(index=me
tricbeat-*, timefield='@timestamp',
metric='max:system.memory.actual.used.bytes'),null).label('Memory usage
warning').color('#FFCC11'),

.es(index=metricbeat-*, timefield='@timestamp',
metric='max:system.memory.actual.used.bytes').if(gt,7300000000,.es(index=me
tricbeat-*, timefield='@timestamp',
metric='max:system.memory.actual.used.bytes'),null).label('Critical memory
usage').color('red')
```

The preceding expression shows three different parts:

- The first part is the basic expression to plot the graph against time-series
- In the second part, I have applied the if condition and inside that, I have applied the gt operator to check
  whether max:system.memory.actual.used.bytes goes beyond 7000000000; if it returns true, a warning label and a yellow color will be applied
- In the third part, I have applied the if condition and inside that, I have applied the gt operator to check
  whether max:system.memory.actual.used.bytes goes beyond 7300000000; if it returns true, a critical label and a red color will be applied

The following screenshot shows the output of the preceding expression:

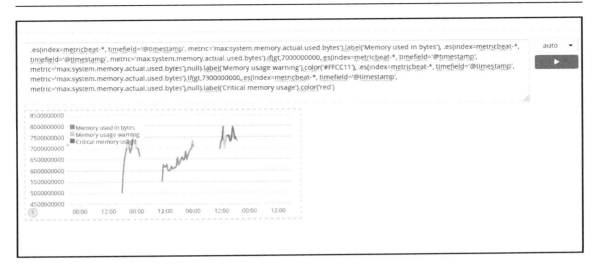

The preceding screenshot shows us the result of the conditional expression that we just applied. Here, we can see the color coding against the memory usage in bytes. For more than 7.0 GB usage, we are getting a yellow color, while for more than 7.3 GB, we are getting a red color. It is quite easy to differentiate the usage behavior using conditional color coding. We have plotted the metricbeat data and applied the color coding based on the threshold value. This can help us to easily differentiate the graph for warnings and severe conditions.

Tracking trends

Under tracking trends, we will determine the data trends with the help of the `mvavg()` function. The `mvavg()` function can be used to calculate the moving average of data over a given window. We can use the `mvavg()` function to smooth the noisy time series by calculating the moving average of a given window set. We can pass any number as a parameter to the `mvavg()` function, which represents the window of data points. So, if we consider the preceding case and want to apply the moving average on the same data, we need to execute the following expression:

```
.es(index=metricbeat-*, timefield='@timestamp',
metric='max:system.memory.actual.used.bytes').label('normal'),

.es(index=metricbeat-*, timefield='@timestamp',
metric='max:system.memory.actual.used.bytes').if(gt,7000000000,.es(index=me
tricbeat-*, timefield='@timestamp',
metric='max:system.memory.actual.used.bytes'),null).label('warning').color(
'#FFCC11'),
```

```
.es(index=metricbeat-*, timefield='@timestamp',
metric='max:system.memory.actual.used.bytes').if(gt,7300000000,.es(index=me
tricbeat-*, timefield='@timestamp',
metric='max:system.memory.actual.used.bytes'),null).label('severe').color('
red'),

.es(index=metricbeat-*, timefield='@timestamp',
metric='max:system.memory.actual.used.bytes').mvavg(10).label('moving
average')
```

In the preceding expression, there are three sections: the first for a normal plot, the second for warning situations where memory usage increases beyond 7.0 GB and is shown in yellow, and the third for severe situations where memory usage goes beyond 7.3 GB and is shown in red. In the last section, we applied the moving average with the data window size of 10 using the `mvavg()` function and added the label as `moving average`.

The following screenshot represents the output of the preceding expression:

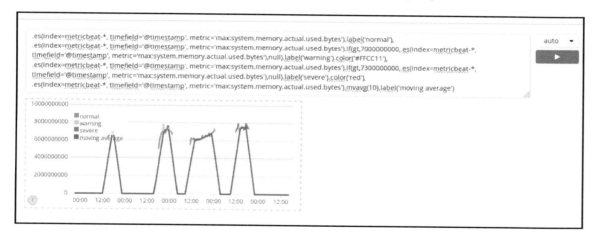

In the preceding image, we can see four different data representations:

- **Normal**: Here, we are showing the max memory usage data plot as it is, without any conditional modifications. We have applied the label as normal using the label function.

- **Warning**: In warning representation, we have used the same field and applied the if condition using the if function. Inside if, we are checking whether memory usage is more than 7 GB; if yes, apply the color as yellow and a label as a warning. We can see the yellow color in the image; it is defining the first threshold value of 7.0 GB, and we can easily get an idea when the usage goes beyond 7.0 GB.

- **Severe**: In the case of the severe label, we have applied the second threshold of 7.3 GB and when the memory usage goes beyond it, the color will change to red, as the condition has been applied where we are comparing the memory usage against the value of 7.3 GB using greater than the operator inside the if condition. Once the memory usage goes beyond 7.3 GB, the `color` function will apply a red color and the `label` function will apply the severe label.
- **Moving average**: Under the moving average section, we have applied the `mvavg()` function with the data window of 10 so that after each 10 data points, the average will be calculated and applied on the plot. Moving average is quite helpful in noisy situations, as it smoothens the noise and helps us create more meaningful graphs.

This way, we have taken the time-series data, plotted it using Kibana's Timelion, and applied conditional formatting of plots using operators inside the if condition. After conditional formatting, we created a new plot using the moving average of a data window value as 10.

A visual builder for handling time series data

Timelion is a great way to work with time series data, but it requires a learning curve since if someone knows Kibana, they can handle all features using the UI but for Timelion, they need to learn the available functions, conditional operators and chaining, and so on.

To overcome this issue, we have a **Visual Builder** under **Visualize** to work with time series data. It provides a UI to achieve the features of Timelion. Anyone can easily work on visual builder by using its easy-to-use UI and can leverage the advantages of Timelion.

To explain the **Visual Builder,** I will use the metricbeat data. We need to do the following to create the graph using visual builder:

1. Click on the **Visualize** link on the left-hand menu on Kibana
2. On the **Visualize** page, click on the **Visual Builder** box:

3. After clicking on **Visual Builder,** the following screen will open:

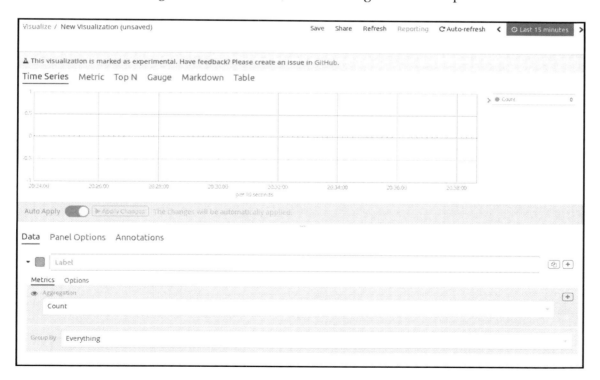

The preceding screenshot shows a blank chart with three tabs: data, panel options, and annotations:

4. Under **Panel Options**, set the index pattern as `metricbeat-*` and set the time filed as `@timestamp`.
5. Under the data tab, set the label name as per the choice.
6. Set the aggregation under **Metrics** on **Data** tab. I am using `Count`.
7. Under **Group By**, set the dropdown to **Terms** and pick the term name as `metricset.name`.
8. We can change the **Order By** and **Direction** dropdowns. After these changes, we will see the following screen:

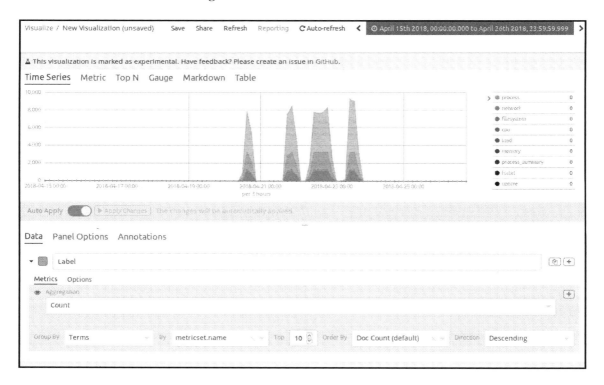

The preceding screenshot shows us the graph with metric types like process, network, filesystem, CPU, load, and so on against the time. We have the legends on the right of the graph, and by clicking on any legend value, we can filter the graph. By default, it shows all of the metric types in different colors and by hovering over the chart, we can get the details of the metric types:

1. We can play around to change the aggregation type and field to get the desired result.
2. We have an **Auto Apply** selector, using which we can enable or disable **Auto Apply**. If **Auto Apply** is disabled, we need to click on the **Apply Changes** button for applying the changes on the graph.
3. If we click on any legend value, like on **CPU**, it will filter the chart and only show the **cpu** data plot. The given screenshot shows the **cpu** filter graph:

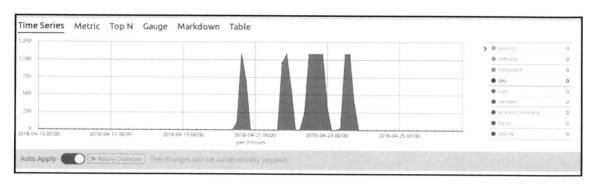

4. To refine it further, we can apply a time filter, and for that, we need to click on date time picker in the top-right corner of the page and select the desired time period. The following screenshot shows the date time picker:

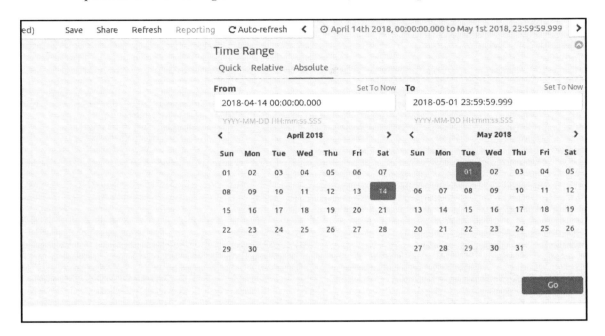

In the preceding date time picker, we can select the **Quick**, **Relative**, or **Absolute** tab and then choose the desired date range.

5. We can add more series by clicking on the add button (plus sign). I have added one more series for the `metricset.rtt` field, which is shown in the following screenshot:

In the preceding screenshot, we can see two series: in the first, we have used the `metricset.name` field, while for the other, the `metricset.rtt` field has been used. In the graph, these two series are combined, which can be seen as follows:

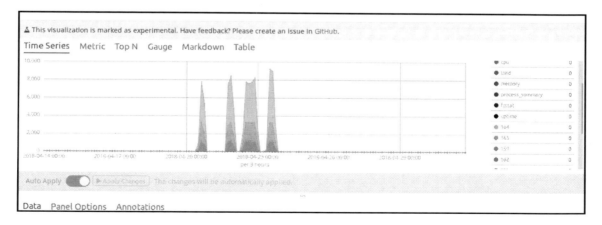

6. We can save the chart once we are done with it by clicking on the save link in the top menu
7. We can also share it by clicking on the share link in the top menu
8. This feature is still experimental in Kibana

GeoIP for Elastic Stack

GeoIP is a great feature, using which we can take beat data, normal log files, or any Logstash data and transform them with geo-locations. After transformation, we can use that data to plot a map in Kibana. We can easily get information like from where users are accessing our website.

If we are getting the IP address or hostname in the request, this information can be transformed into a latitude and longitude point, using which we can get more insight about the data.

Ingest node

We can use the ingest node for preprocessing the document before document indexing. It first applies the transformations and then pushes the document for indexing. All nodes are enabled by default for the ingest process, so they all can handle the ingest task.

If we want to preprocess any documents before indexing them, we need to first define a pipeline with a series of processors that can transform the document. We have the following ingest APIs:

- **Put Pipeline API**: Using this API, we can add or update a pipeline. The following expression shows the put pipeline example:

```
PUT _ingest/pipeline/my-pipeline-id
{
  "description" : "describe pipeline",
  "processors" : [
    {
      "set" : {
        "field": "foo",
        "value": "bar"
      }
    }
  ]
}
```

- **Get Pipeline API**: Using this API, we can get the pipeline. We can see the get pipeline in the following example:

```
GET _ingest/pipeline/my-pipeline-id
```

- **Delete Pipeline API**: We can delete a pipeline using this API. The following expression shows us the delete pipeline example:

```
DELETE _ingest/pipeline/my-pipeline-id
```

- **Simulate Pipeline API**: We can use this API to simulate a pipeline call. It helps us test the pipeline API. The following expression shows us the simulate pipeline API:

```
POST _ingest/pipeline/_simulate
{
  "pipeline" : {
    // pipeline definition here
  },
  "docs" : [
    { "_source": {/** first document **/} },
    { "_source": {/** second document **/} },
    // ...
  ]
}
```

So, that was the introduction of ingest APIs, using which we can preprocess data before indexing it. This is quite useful, as we can transform any type of data as per our requirements. Now, we will again move to GeoIP and see how pipelines can transform the data for GeoIP implementation. To use the GeoIP features, we need to first install the geo-ip plugin, which is not included by default with Elastic Stack, so we need to run the following command on all nodes:

```
sudo /usr/share/elasticsearch/bin/elasticsearch-plugin install ingest-geoip
```

The following screenshot shows the installation of the ingest-geo-ip plugin:

```
user@KELLGGNLPTP0184:~/Downloads$
user@KELLGGNLPTP0184:~/Downloads$
user@KELLGGNLPTP0184:~/Downloads$ sudo /usr/share/elasticsearch/bin/elasticsearch-plugin install ingest-geoip
[sudo] password for user:
-> Downloading ingest-geoip from elastic
[=============================================] 100%
@@@@@@@@@@@@@@@@@@@@@@@@@@@@@@@@@@@@@@@@@@@@@@@@@@@@@@@@@@
@     WARNING: plugin requires additional permissions     @
@@@@@@@@@@@@@@@@@@@@@@@@@@@@@@@@@@@@@@@@@@@@@@@@@@@@@@@@@@
* java.lang.RuntimePermission accessDeclaredMembers
* java.lang.reflect.ReflectPermission suppressAccessChecks
See http://docs.oracle.com/javase/8/docs/technotes/guides/security/permissions.html
for descriptions of what these permissions allow and the associated risks.

Continue with installation? [y/N]y
-> Installed ingest-geoip
user@KELLGGNLPTP0184:~/Downloads$
```

After running this command, we need to restart the nodes. Now that we have installed the ingest-geo-ip plugin, let's move to the next step. Now, we will create the pipeline and apply that on the index to get the additional fields. However, before creating and applying a pipeline, it's better if we can simulate a pipeline to make it work before applying it on real data. For simulating the data, we can run this expression:

```
POST _ingest/pipeline/_simulate
{
  "pipeline" : {
"processors" : [
    {
      "grok": {
        "field": "message",
        "patterns": ["%{COMBINEDAPACHELOG}"]
      }
    },
    {
      "geoip": {
        "field": "clientip"
      }
    }
  ]
  },
  "docs": [
    {
      "_source": {
        "message": "104.194.203.69 - - [01/Apr/2017:16:21:15 +0000] \"GET
/favicon.ico HTTP/1.1\" 200 3638 \"-\" \"Mozilla/5.0 (Macintosh; Intel Mac
```

```
OS X 10_11_6) AppleWebKit/537.36 (KHTML, like Gecko) Chrome/52.0.2743.116
Safari/537.36\""
        }
    }
  ]
}
```

After running this expression, we will get the following response:

```
{
  "docs": [
    {
      "doc": {
        "_index": "_index",
        "_type": "_type",
        "_id": "_id",
        "_source": {
          "request": "/favicon.ico",
          "agent": """Mozilla/5.0 (Macintosh; Intel Mac OS X 10_11_6)
AppleWebKit/537.36 (KHTML, like Gecko) Chrome/52.0.2743.116
Safari/537.36""",
          "geoip": {
            "continent_name": "Oceania",
            "city_name": "Alexandria",
            "country_iso_code": "AU",
            "region_name": "New South Wales",
            "location": {
              "lon": 151.2,
              "lat": -33.9167
            }
          },
          "auth": "-",
          "ident": "-",
          "verb": "GET",
          "message": """104.194.203.69 - - [01/Apr/2017:16:21:15 +0000]
"GET /favicon.ico HTTP/1.1" 200 3638 "-" "Mozilla/5.0 (Macintosh; Intel Mac
OS X 10_11_6) AppleWebKit/537.36 (KHTML, like Gecko) Chrome/52.0.2743.116
Safari/537.36""",
          "referrer": """"-"""",
          "response": "200",
          "bytes": "3638",
          "clientip": "104.194.203.69",
          "httpversion": "1.1",
          "timestamp": "01/Apr/2017:16:21:15 +0000"
        },
        "_ingest": {
          "timestamp": "2018-05-31T19:29:50.286Z"
        }
```

```
            }
        }
    ]
}
```

We can do this simulation testing in Kibana using Dev Tools; the following screenshot shows the simulation:

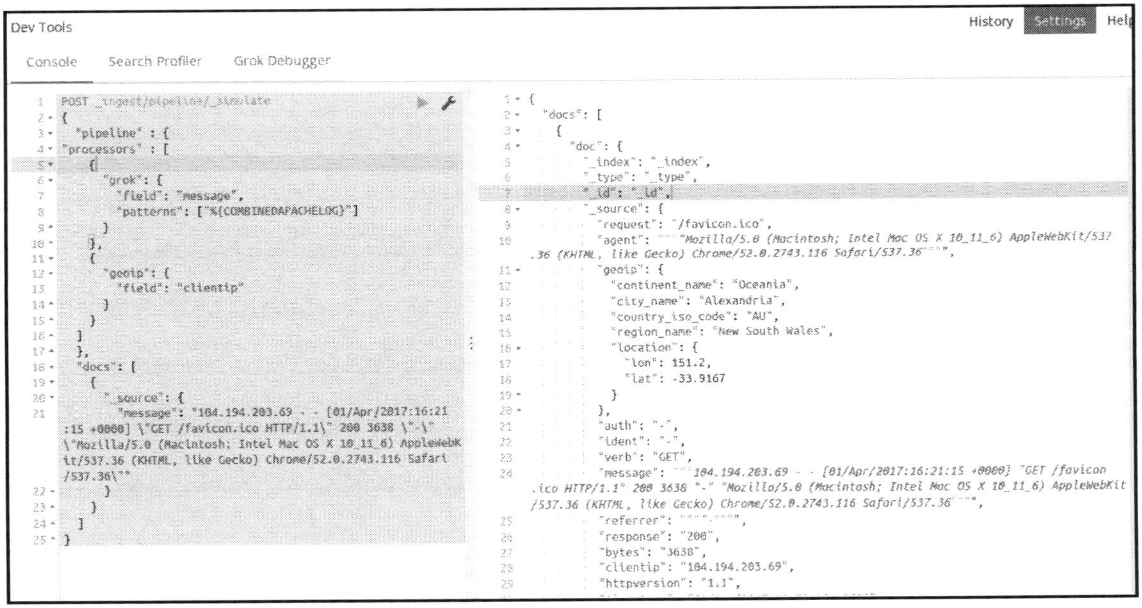

In the preceding screenshot, the left section shows the request expression, while the right section shows the response of the request.

This way, we can simulate the pipeline to test it properly before playing with actual data.

GeoIP with Packetbeat data

Now, I will configure GeoIP to process the Packetbeat data; for that, we need to create the pipeline first. A pipeline can be created using the following command:

```
PUT _ingest/pipeline/geoip-info
{
  "description": "Add geoip info",
  "processors": [
    {
```

```
      "geoip": {
        "field": "client_ip",
        "target_field": "client_geoip",
        "properties": ["location"],
        "ignore_failure": true
      }
    }
  ]
}
```

After executing this command, we will get the following response:

```
{
  "acknowledged": true
}
```

We get `acknowledged` as `true` when an expression is executed successfully. This way, we have created a new pipeline and executed it successfully. We have created the pipeline with the ID as `geoip-info`, which, on execution, will create the `client_geoip.location` field of the `geo_point` type. The `client_ip` is the output field of Packetbeat that contains the client's IP address.

We have created the pipeline for transformation, so now we need to configure the pipeline into a Packetbeat configuration file so that we can apply the pipeline on Packetbeat data before it goes to Elasticsearch. For configuring the Packetbeat, we need to open the `packetbeat.yml` file and add the following lines:

```
output.elasticsearch:
hosts: ["localhost:9200"]
pipeline: geoip-info
```

In the preceding entry, we are specifying the pipeline ID under the `output.elasticsearch` section of the Packetbeat configuration file. After adding the pipeline ID in the Packetbeat configuration file, we need to run the following command to execute the configuration changes:

```
./packetbeat -e -c /etc/packetbeat/packetbeat.yml
```

After executing the preceding expression, the pipeline will include the `client_geoip.location` field after getting the data from Packetbeat and will insert the transformed data into Elasticsearch with additional geo data that's required for map plotting. Now, the last missing link that we need to fix is Kibana, as we need to create the map plot using this data. So, in order to create a map in Kibana, we need to do the following:

1. Query elasticsearch to check whether our data is having additional location-related fields.

2. The second step is to create the index pattern in Kibana for the Packetbeat data using the index patterns option under **Management**.

3. Click on the **Visualize** link from the left menu of Kibana; this will open the visualization screen, from where we can create different types of visualizations.

4. Click on the add new visualization button (plus sign); this will open a new screen with different types of visualization creation options.

5. From the different available options, click on **Coordinate map** under the **Maps** option. This will open a screen with an option to choose the index pattern to use.

6. Click on **packetbeat-*** from the **a new search, select index** listing. This will open a default map screen with options to configure. The following screenshot shows us the default map page:

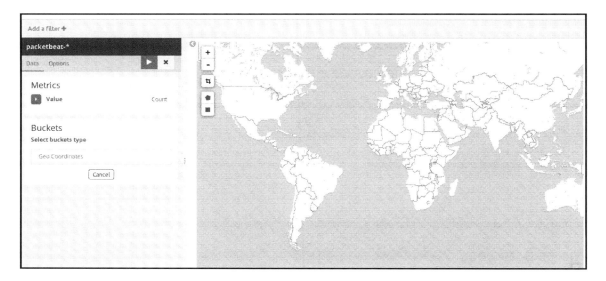

7. Under the metrics heading, select the count options for value. We can use any different aggregations, such as average, min, max, and more.

8. Under the buckets option, select Geohash for aggregations and under field, choose `client_geoip.location`.

9. Click on the **Execute** button after setting the mentioned details to see the changes on the map. The following screenshot shows us the map display:

10. In the preceding screenshot, we can see circles with different sizes and colors. In the bottom-right corner, we have the legend display with different colors. Based on the locations of the data, they are shown on the map.

11. We can zoom in or zoom out of the Kibana map to get further details of the locations. The following screenshot shows the zoomed in map display:

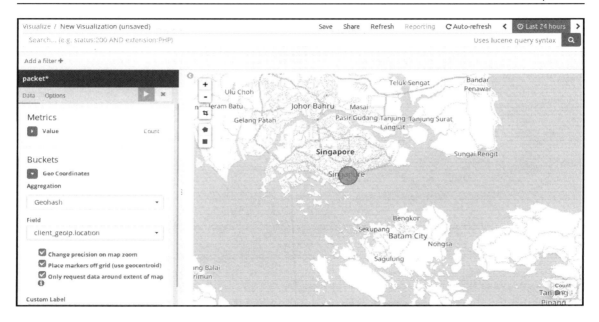

12. From the visualization options, we can change the map type. The map type provides us with different options such as scaled circle markers, shaded circle markers, shaded geohash grid, and heatmap. The following screenshot shows us the heatmap type of map:

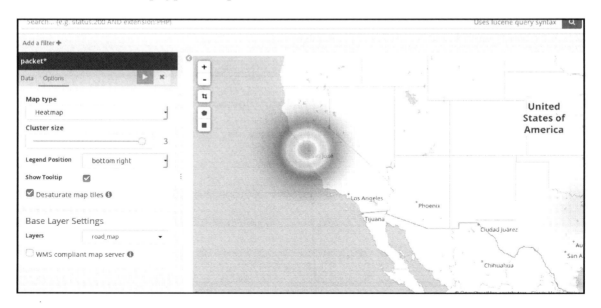

This way, we can transform any type of data by implementing the pipeline after creating them as per our requirements. This data transformation provides an edge, as the normal IP address of Packetbeat data can be used to add the location fields; also, through those location fields, we can plot that data on a coordinate map of Kibana.

Summary

In this chapter, we covered some good features of Kibana, such as time series data handling, under which we covered conditional formatting and tracking trends. Using conditional formatting, we can apply conditional formatting on data plots, such as changing the color if a data range goes beyond a threshold value or changing the label of a plot in case something changes. Under tracking trends, we covered how to smooth a plot if it is noisy, as sometimes it is difficult to get an idea about the trend, and for those situations, we can use moving average for certain block sizes to get a smooth plot, using which we can take the decisions.

After conditional formatting and tracking trends, we explored the visual builder, using which we can work on time series data without depending on Timelion. This is again a very good feature as not everyone is familiar with Timelion because of its different syntax and ways of writing expressions. Using visual builder, anyone can achieve these features of Timelion using the simple UI of Kibana.

At the end of this chapter, we covered the GeoIP for Elastic Stack. Using GeoIP, we can transform the normal data. This is because if we have the IP address in data, we can transform that data to add location fields using GeoIP. To do that, we need to install the ingest-geoip plugin. After that, we can create the pipeline, test it, and apply that pipeline for any data source input like we did for Packetbeat data by setting it in the Packetbeat configuration file and executing an expression to execute the changes. Once this is done, Packetbeat will take the data, transform it as per the pipeline, and insert it into Elasticsearch. Later, we can use that Elasticsearch data in Kibana to plot it on the map. So, using this feature, we can transform any data as per our requirements.

13
Creating Monitoring Dashboards Using Beats

In the last chapter, we covered the dashboard creation using Logstash, where we were pulling the data from RDBMS and pushing it to the Elasticsearch cluster. After that, we were showing the dashboard in Kibana by reading the Elasticsearch data. In this chapter, we will cover dashboard creation using Elastic Beats, which also provides us with the option to import built-in dashboards.

There are different Beats that provide us with metrics from different servers, such as the following:

- **Packetbeat**: This gives us the details about the network packets. It is a lightweight network packet analyzer that sends packet data to Logstash or Elasticsearch.
- **Filebeat**: Filebeat is used to send file data , such as logs. It runs on the server and periodically checks for any change in the log file; when there is any change, it sends the log to Logstash or Elasticsearch.
- **Metricbeat**: This is used to collect metrics for memory usage, CPU usage and disk space, and so on.

Apart from these Beats, we have Heartbeat and Winlogbeat, but we will focus on Packetbeat, Filebeat, and Metricbeat for creating the dashboard. Beats has given us the luxury to get these details from a different server directly into Logstash or Elasticsearch, and we need not configure these data sources to take the metrics.

In this chapter, we will cover how, after configuring the Beats, we can pull the data and create the visualizations and dashboards for monitoring the key performance indicators.

Configuring the Beats

First, we will cover the configuration of different Beats in order to get the metric data into Elasticsearch directly or using Logstash, based on our requirements. The following flowchart shows us the way through which Beats ship the data to Logstash or Elasticsearch and then we can plot into Kibana using that data:

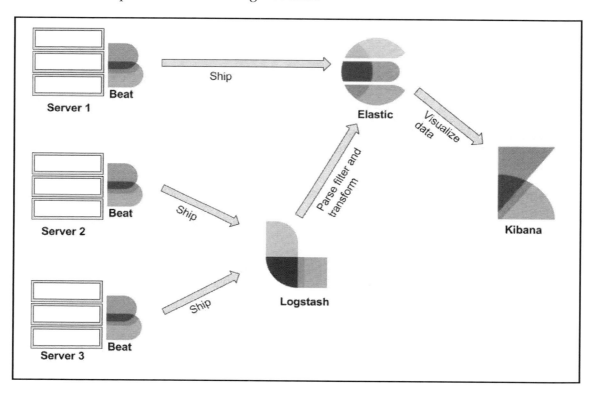

We will configure Filebeat, Metricbeat, and Packetbeat so that these Beats can send the data to the central Elasticseach cluster or Logstash. Once this process is started, we can use the Elasticseach data to create different visualizations and can then integrate those visualizations to create the dashboard. So, let's start the Beats configuration.

Filebeat

Filebeat is a lightweight data shipper that can be used to forward the logs and files data. Filebeat reads and forwards the log lines and in case of any downtime, it remembers the locations and resumes from that location once everything is back online:

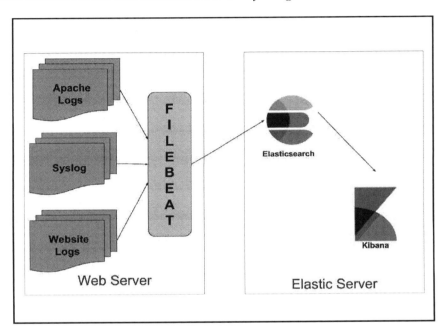

Filebeat has internal modules for Apache, NGINX, MySQL, audit and system, and so on, using which we can get the metrics from these applications through a single command. Back-pressure sensitive protocol works when we ship data from Filebeat to Logstash or Elasticsearch; this protocol assures that if Logstash or Elasticsearch are busy in pushing data, it notifies the Filebeat to slow down its read process.

 Back-pressure sensitive protocol is a mechanism that works when the queue is full, and in this mechanism, Logstash puts back pressure to the input for stalling the inflow of data and helps Logstash to control the data flow at the input stage itself.

Configuring Filebeat

After installing Filebeat, we need to configure it for sending log data to Elasticsearch or Logstash.

 The steps to install Filebeat are mentioned in Chapter 1, *Revising ELK Stack*.

In this chapter, we will skip the Logstash part and send the log data directly to the Elasticsearch cluster. So, for configuring Filebeat, we need to open the filebeat.yml file, which we can open using this command:

```
sudo vim /etc/filebeat/filebeat.yml
```

The preceding command will open the filebeat.yml file for editing. Filebeat has predefined default values for different configurations, which we can change as per our requirements. So, to configure Filebeat to send the log data, we need to define the single prospector for a single path; for example, to read various logs from the /var/logs location, we can define the following prospector:

```
filebeat.prospectors:
- type: log
  enabled: true
  paths:
    - /var/log/*.log
```

In the previous expression, we are setting the Filebeat prospector, in which we are defining the type as log, enabling it and providing the path of the log directory. This path tells Filebeat to fetch all files with the .log extension, inside the /var/log directory.

In case we want to read the log files from any location other than /var/log/, we have to create a new prospector and provide the path of the location. If we want to target all files from all different directories inside the /var/log/ directory, we need to give the following path:

```
paths:
    - /var/log/*/*.log
```

The preceding path tells Filebeat to check the files inside /var/log/ and then all directories inside the log directory for their files with an extension of .log, so in this way, we can target all log files inside the /var/log/ directory.

There are different ways to enable the modules in Filebeat:

- We can enable Filebeat modules using the `filebeat.yml` file. We need to make the following changes on the `filebeat.yml` file:

```
filebeat.modules:
- module: nginx
- module: mysql
- module: system
```

- We can enable the module from the `modules.d` directory. We can enable the modules by running this command:

```
sudo filebeat modules enable apache2
```

If we want to see enabled and disabled modules, we can run the following command:

```
sudo filebeat modules list
```

- We can enable the module along with the `filebeat` command execution. When we want to run a specific module, we can do it by passing the `--modules` flag. This module-enabling process is session-specific and quite handy when we want to run a specific module for a particular session only. The following command shows the module-enabling process:

```
sudo filebeat -e --modules nginx,mysql,system
```

After that, we need to provide the Elasticsearch credentials inside the file. The following section shows us the Elasticsearch block under the `filebeat.yml` file:

```
# Array of hosts to connect to.
hosts: ["localhost:9200"]
# Optional protocol and basic auth credentials.
#protocol: "https"
username: "elastic"
password:  "yourpassword"
```

Here, we need to provide the host location for Elasticsearch server.

> I am referring to the localhost, as my Elasticsearch is installed on my local machine, but if it is installed on a different machine, we need to provide the URL of that machine.

We need to provide the `username` and `password` of Elasticsearch in case authentication is enabled for Elasticsearch. We can leave this as commented in case authentication is not enabled. Once this is done, we can start the Filebeat service.

In case we want to set up the default Filebeat dashboard for Kibana, we need to configure it by configuring the `setup.kibana` endpoint:

```
setup.kibana:
  host: "localhost:5601"
```

In the preceding expression, we are providing the host URL of Kibana. I have configured Kibana on `localhost`, but if you have configured it on another server, you need to provide the Kibana URL of that server.

Once we have completed these configurations, Filebeat will start sending data into Elasticsearch in the default index as `filebeat-*`; for example, `filebeat-6.2.3-2018.06.07`. We can verify the index name by referring to the list of indices in Elasticsearch using the following command:

```
curl -XGET "http://localhost:9200/_cat/indices"
```

Once we get the Filebeat index in the listing, we can get the details of that index by typing this command:

```
curl -XGET "http://localhost:9200/filebeat-6.2.3-2018.06.07/_search"
```

After running the preceding command, we can get the following response:

```
{
  "took": 5,
  "timed_out": false,
  "_shards": {
    "total": 3,
    "successful": 3,
    "skipped": 0,
    "failed": 0
  },
  "hits": {
    "total": 91285,
    "max_score": 1,
    "hits": [
      {
        "_index": "filebeat-6.2.3-2018.06.07",
        "_type": "doc",
        "_id": "Dr4i22MByi9VfmHrn07x",
        "_score": 1,
        "_source": {
```

```
        "@timestamp": "2018-06-07T04:39:24.855Z",
        "offset": 32411,
      "beat": {
          "hostname": "ANUGGNLPTP0184",
          "name": "ANUGGNLPTP0184",
          "version": "6.2.3"
        },
        "prospector": {
          "type": "log"
        },
        "mysql": {
          "error": {
            "thread_id": "0",
            "level": "Note",
            "message": "Shutting down plugin 'INNODB_FT_INDEX_TABLE'",
            "timestamp": "2018-06-07T04:39:24.855267Z"
          }
        },
        "source": "/var/log/mysql/error.log",
        "fileset": {
          "module": "mysql",
          "name": "error"
        }
      }
    }
  ]
}
}
```

This way, we have successfully configured Filebeat to send data to the Elasticsearch cluster. Once the data is in Elasticsearch, we can configure the index pattern into Kibana, as I explained in the previous chapters.

Metricbeat

Metricbeat is a lightweight data shipper that sends the system and service metrics. It can send the data from CPU, memory, NGINX, Redis, MySQL, and so on. We can deploy it on any operating system to connect with Logstash or Elasticsearch; after that, it reads the system level metrics and sends them to Logstash or Elasticsearch. It has different modules for Apache, NGINX, MongoDB, MySQL, PostgresSQL, and so on, using which it reads the metric data from `software.output.elasticsearch`.

Configuring Metricbeat

The first step is to enable the Metricbeat modules and specify the metric sets for different modules. Metricbeat accepts default system metrics if we leave the default configuration.

There are different ways to enable the modules in Filebeat. We will discuss them in a bit.

Enabling the modules using the metricbeat.yml file

We can enable Metricbeat modules using the `metricbeat.yml` file. We need to make the following changes to the `metricbeat.yml` file:

```
metricbeat.modules:

#------------ Apache Status Module ------------------
- module: apache
  metricsets: ["status"]
  period: 1s
  hosts: ["http://127.0.0.1/"]

#------------ MySQL Status Module ---------------
- module: mysql
  metricsets: ["status"]
  period: 2s
  hosts: ["root@tcp(127.0.0.1:3306)/"]
```

Enabling the modules from the modules.d directory

We can enable the modules by running this command:

```
sudo metricbeat modules enable apache mysql
```

If we want to see enabled and disabled modules, we can run the following command:

```
sudo metricbeat modules list
```

We need to specify the IP address of Elasticsearch in case we want to send the metric data directly to Elasticsearch instead of sending it to Logstash:

```
output.elasticsearch:
  # Array of hosts to connect to.
  hosts: ["localhost:9200"]
```

We can use the default dashboard of Metricbeat for Kibana. To configure the default dashboard, we need to configure the endpoint of Kibana:

```
setup.kibana:
  host: "localhost:5601"
```

In case we are using authentication for Elasticsearch, we need to provide the username and password of the Elasticsearch user along with the host address:

```
output.elasticsearch:
  # Array of hosts to connect to.
  hosts: ["localhost:9200"]
  username: "elastic"
  password: "yourpassword"
```

Once we have done these configurations, Metricbeat will start sending data into Elasticsearch in the default index as `metricbeat-*`; for example, `metricbeat-6.2.3-2018.06.07`. We can verify the index name by looking at the list of indices in Elasticsearch using the following command:

```
curl -XGET "http://localhost:9200/_cat/indices"
```

Once we get the Metricbeat index in the listing, we can get the details of that index by typing the following command:

```
curl -XGET "http://localhost:9200/metricbeat-6.2.3-2018.06.07/_search"
```

After running the preceding command, we can get the Elasticsearch index output for Metricbeat data. Once the index is created in Elasticsearch, we can set up the index pattern in Kibana for the dashboard creation.

Packetbeat

Packetbeat is also a lightweight data shipper that can be installed on any operating system. It is basically a real-time network packet analyzer. It captures the network traffic between application servers. Packetbeat helps us easily monitor the application issues, such as bugs or performance problems, and helps us troubleshoot them and fix them faster.

Configuring Packetbeat

I have already covered the Packetbeat installation in the first chapter, so refer to that for the installation process. To configure Packetbeat, we need to edit the `packetbeat.yml` Packetbeat configuration file; its location varies on different operation systems. On Linux, we can open the Packetbeat configuration file using the following command:

```
sudo vim /etc/packetbeat/packetbeat.yml
```

After opening the file, we need to perform the following steps.

Set the network interface for capturing the data. We can check the network devices using the following command:

```
packetbeat devices
```

The preceding command will return the device interface names. The following list shows the response of the preceding command:

```
0: wlp2s0 (No description available) (192.168.43.252
fe80::72dc:b71e:a6f9:592d)
1: any (Pseudo-device that captures on all interfaces) (Not assigned ip
address)
2: lo (No description available) (127.0.0.1 ::1)
3: enp0s25 (No description available) (Not assigned ip address)
4: nflog (Linux netfilter log (NFLOG) interface) (Not assigned ip address)
5: nfqueue (Linux netfilter queue (NFQUEUE) interface) (Not assigned ip
address)
```

After getting the list, we can choose the device to capture the data using Packetbeat. We can set the device interface using the following command:

```
packetbeat.interfaces.device: 0
```

The aforementioned command sets the first option for the network interface. We can also specify the device interface name instead of the ID:

```
packetbeat.interfaces.device: eth0
```

In this way, we can set the device interface by providing the ID or name.

If we are using any specific port, we need to add it under the protocol section of the `packetbeat.yml` file. If we are not specifying the port numbers, it will take the default one for each protocol:

```
packetbeat.protocols:
- type: icmp
  # Enable ICMPv4 and ICMPv6 monitoring. Default: false
  enabled: true
- type: http
  # Configure the ports where to listen for HTTP traffic. You can disable
  # the HTTP protocol by commenting out the list of ports.
  ports: [80, 8080, 8000, 5000, 8002]

- type: memcache
  # Configure the ports where to listen for memcache traffic. You can
disable
  # the Memcache protocol by commenting out the list of ports.
  ports: [11211]

- type: mysql
  # Configure the ports where to listen for MySQL traffic. You can disable
  # the MySQL protocol by commenting out the list of ports.
  ports: [3306]

- type: pgsql
  # Configure the ports where to listen for Pgsql traffic. You can disable
  # the Pgsql protocol by commenting out the list of ports.
  ports: [5432]
```

We need to specify the IP address of Elasticsearch in case we want to send the metric data directly to Elasticsearch instead of sending it to Logstash:

```
output.elasticsearch:
  # Array of hosts to connect to.
  hosts: ["localhost:9200"]
```

We can use the default dashboard of Metricbeat for Kibana. To configure the default dashboard, we need to configure the endpoint of Kibana:

```
setup.kibana:
  host: "localhost:5601
```

In case we are using authentication for Elasticsearch, we need to provide the `username` and `password` of the Elasticsearch user, along with the host address:

```
output.elasticsearch:
  # Array of hosts to connect to.
  hosts: ["localhost:9200"]
```

```
username: "elastic"
password: "yourpassword"
```

Once we have done these configurations, Packetbeat will start sending data into Elasticsearch in the default index as `packetbeat-*`; for example, `packetbeat-6.2.3-2018.06.07`. We can verify the index name by referring to the list of indices in Elasticsearch using the following command:

```
curl -XGET "http://localhost:9200/_cat/indices"
```

Once we get the Metricbeat index in the listing, we can get the details of that index by typing the following command:

```
curl -XGET "http://localhost:9200/packetbeat-6.2.3-2018.06.07/_search"
```

After running the preceding command, we get the Elasticsearch index output for Packetbeat data. Once the index is created in Elasticsearch, we can set up the index pattern in Kibana for the dashboard creation.

Beats are very handy, lightweight, and are easy to set up on any server. They are designed to do specific type of jobs; for example, Filebeat handles the file data, Metricbeat reads system metrics, and Packetbeat reads packet data. So in this way, based on our requirements, we can pick the specific Beat and then fine tune inside that Beat to enable the required modules. So here, we have configured Filebeat, Metricbeat, and Packetbeat to send the data on Elasticsearch indices. Now we will use this data to create the visualizations and dashboard.

Creating visualizations using Beat data

We have configured the Filebeat, Metricbeat, and Packetbeat to send the data from different servers to the Elasticsearch cluster and created the index pattern for them in Kibana. Now, we will create the visualization in Kibana in order to create the dashboard.

Visualization using Filebeat

We have already configured the index pattern for Filebeat data, so now, first of all, we need to verify the data in Kibana and for that, we can click on the **Discover** tab of Kibana. The following screen gives us the **Discover** view of the Filebeat data:

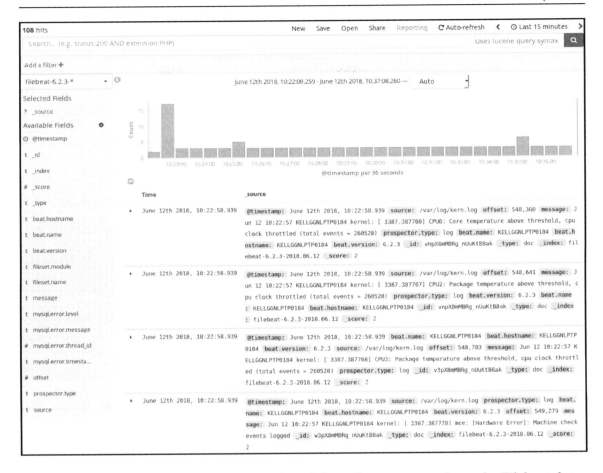

The preceding screenshot shows the data for Filebeat. So now, as we have the Filebeat data in Kibana, we can create the visualizations, and, for that, open the **Visualize** tab of Kibana. Click on the plus button to add a new visualization, and then click on the vertical bar to create a vertical bar using the Filebeat data. From the index selection screen, select the Filebeat index that opens the new visualization screen from where we can actually create the chart. So now, I will create a pie chart for Apache error level, which can be error, warning, or notice. This graph can help us understand the ratio of error levels in Apache.

To create the visualization from the Filebeat data, we need to do the following:

1. Click on the **Pie** chart under basic charts. This will open the select index page.
2. Click on the **filebeat-*** index for selecting the Filebeat index.
3. Under metrics, select the aggregation as count.
4. Set the custom label for the count; for example, `count of entries`.
5. Under buckets, select terms under aggregations.
6. Select `apache2.error.level` under field.
7. Add the label for the field; for example, **Apache error level**.
8. Click on the **Apply Changes** button. This will create the pie chart for **Apache error level**.
9. Click on the **Save** button on the top menu, give a name such as `filebeat_apache_error_level`, and click on the **Save** button to save the visualization.

The following screenshot shows the output of the pie chart we just created:

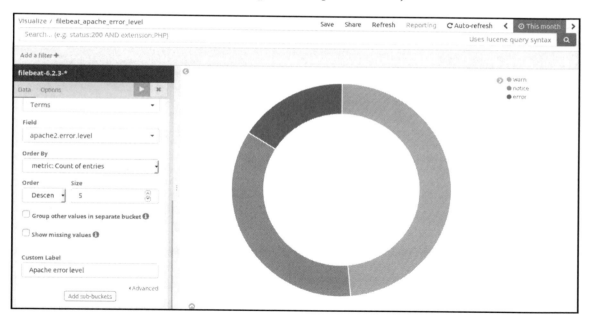

In the previous screenshot, we have a donut type pie chart that we can customize using the **Options** link. We have the legend in the right corner to show the different error levels of Apache.

In the same way, we can create different visualizations using the Filebeat data. I will not create other graphs in Filebeat, but you may try using other stats of the Filebeat data, such as MySQL, NGINX, and more.

Visualization using Metricbeat

So as we have checked the data for Filebeat, we can do the same for Metricbeat by opening the **Discover** link of Kibana and verifying that the data is there in the selected time period. Once the data is verified, we can move to the visualize link on Kibana and click on the plus button to open the create visualization page. We need to select the index name, and this time, we need to choose the Metricbeat index from there. Here, we will create a heat map for CPU usage; to create a Metricbeat heat map, we need to do the following:

1. Click on the **Heat Map** option from basic charts type.
2. Select the **metricbeat-*** index from the index selection page.
3. Under metrics, select average for aggregation, and under field, select **system.cpu.user.pct**.
4. Give this a label, such as CPU usage.
5. Under bucket, for *x* axis, select data histogram under aggregation. In field, select **@timestamp**.
6. For *y* axis, select terms for subaggregation and under field, select beat.name.
7. Give it a label, such as Hosts.
8. Click on the **Apply Changes** button. This will create the pie chart for **Apache error level**.
9. Click on the **Save** button in the top menu, give a name, such as metricbeat_cpu_usage, and click on the **Save** button to save the visualization.

The following screenshot shows the heat map chart for CPU usage using Metricbeat data:

The legend shows the percentage of CPU usage using the intensity of the color. Using this heat map, we can easily identify the timings when CPU usage was increased to more than normal.

Visualization using Packetbeat

Now we will create a visualization using the Packetbeat data. Before starting the graph creation, ensure that the Packetbeat data is available under the index pattern of Kibana, and this can be easily done by clicking on the **Discover** link of Kibana. After verification, click on the **Visualize** link in the left menu on Kibana. Now, click on the plus button to open the create visualization page; after that, we need to select the index name, and this time, we need to choose **Packetbeat index** from the index listing page. This time, I want to create a data table to show the slow queries of MySQL. To create the data table, we need to do the following:

1. Click on the **data table** option under **Data**.
2. Under metrics, select average for aggregation and response time for field dropdown.

3. Change the custom label to `Response time`.
4. Under buckets, select terms for aggregation and query for the field dropdown.
5. Select **metric:Response time** for the **Order By** field.
6. Change the custom label to **MySQL query**.
7. Click on the **Apply Changes** button. This will create the pie chart for **Apache error level**.
8. Click on the **Save** button on the top menu, give a name, such as `packetbeat_mysql_responsetime`, and click on the **Save** button to save the visualization.

The following screenshot shows us the data table for MySQL slow queries based on the response time for MySQL queries:

Here, we have a table with MySQL queries with their respective response times in descending order. This information is quite helpful, as we can take these queries and optimize them individually to increase the MySQL performance.

In this way, we have created one visualization for each beat type; Filebeat, Metricbeat, and Packetbeat. Now we will create a dashboard by integrating these visualizations.

Creating the dashboard

Now, as we have created the visualizations using different Beats, let's integrate them to create the dashboard. You can create the visualizations as per the requirements and can add them to the existing dashboard.

For creating the dashboard, we need to do the following:

1. Click on the **Dashboard** link in the left menu to open the dashboard page.
2. Click on the plus button to add a new dashboard. This will open the blank dashboard with a message saying **This dashboard is empty. Lets fill it up**.
3. Click on the **Add** button on the page or the **Add** link in the top menu.
4. This will open the **Add Panels** page with visualizations and the saved **Search** tab.
    1. From the **Visualization** tab, search the visualization and click on the visualization you want to add.
5. So, I am adding `filebeat_apache_error_level`, `metricbeat_cpu_usage`, and `packetbeat_mysql_responsetime` visualizations.
6. After adding the visualizations, click on the **Save** button in the top menu, and after giving a name to the dashboard, click on the **Save** button to save.

The following screenshot shows the dashboard with the three visualizations that were created using different Beats:

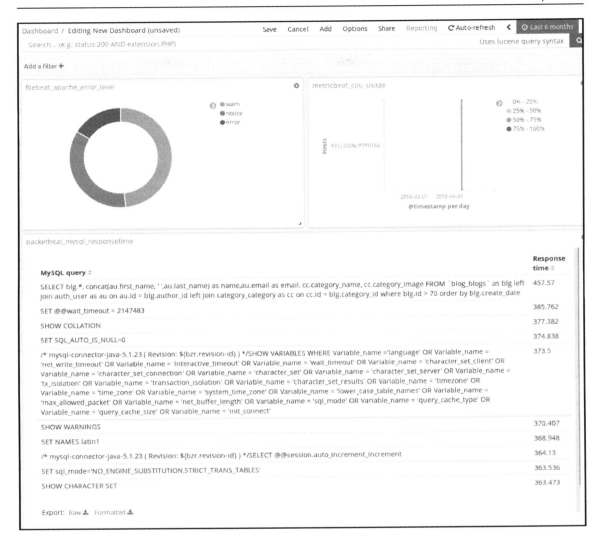

The first visualization is a pie chart for the Apache error level using the Filebeat index data, the second visualization shows the heat map for CPU usage using the Metricbeat data, and the third is a data table showing slow MySQL queries using the Packetbeat data.

This way, we have explored the visualization and dashboard creation using Beats data.

Importing Beat dashboards

Beats have predefined Kibana dashboards that we can import directly for showing inside the Kibana dashboard. By using a Beat executable, we can import the dashboards and index pattern for that Beat. Now, I will cover how we can import the dashboards in different Beats.

Importing dashboards in Filebeat

We need to run the following command for importing Filebeat dashboards and index patterns in Kibana:

```
filebeat setup
```

The preceding command will load index mapping, Kibana dashboards, and machine learning jobs if they have been created. We can pass the flag in the previous command. For example, if we only require dashboards, we can pass the following command:

```
filebeat setup --dashboards
```

We can pass --help if we want the details about the Filebeat setup command:

```
filebeat setup --help
```

Importing dashboards in Metricbeat

We have to run the following command for importing Metricbeat dashboards and index patterns in Kibana:

```
metricbeat setup
```

The preceding command loads index mapping, Kibana dashboards, and machine learning jobs if they have been created. We can pass the flag in the preceding command. For example, if we only require dashboards, we can pass the following command:

```
metricbeat setup --dashboards
```

We can pass --help if we want the details about the Metricbeat setup command:

```
metricbeat setup --help
```

Importing dashboards in Packetbeat

We need to run the following command for importing Packetbeat dashboards and index patterns in Kibana:

```
packetbeat setup
```

The preceding command loads index mapping, Kibana dashboards, and machine learning jobs if they have been created. We can pass the flag in the preceding command. For example, if we only require dashboards, we can pass this command:

```
packetbeat setup --dashboards
```

We can pass `--help` if we want the details about the Packetbeat `setup` command:

```
packetbeat setup --help
```

This way, we can import the dashboards directly into Kibana from Beats. This is quite handy, as the prebuilt dashboards include all the major key performance indicators, and we can use them as per our requirements.

Summary

In this chapter, we covered how we can create visualizations and dashboards using Beats data. At the beginning, I explained how we can configure Filebeat, Metricbeat, and Packetbeat for sending data into Elasticsearch or Logstash.

After getting the data into Elasticsearch, we can create the index pattern for each Beat. Once the index pattern has been created, we can verify the data using the Kibana **Discover** option. After getting the data in Kibana, I explained how to create the visualizations and dashboards by integrating the visualizations.

At the end of the chapter, I explained the process to import index pattern and dashboards directly into Kibana from Filebeat, Metricbeat, and Packetbeat. So basically, this chapter was all about Beats and the usage of Beats for dashboard creation and import.

14
Best Practices

In this chapter, we will cover best practices for Elastic Stack. These practices are very important to optimize Elastic Stack performance and to avoid security threats. Elastic Stack best practices are there to ensure that we follow the proper ways for data handling in Logstash, Elasticsearch, and Kibana. There are different aspects where we need to ensure best practices, such as avoiding large documents and unrelated data in the same index and returning large result sets.

We will cover different aspects of, and best practices for, Kibana, Elasticsearch, and Logstash. In this chapter, we will cover why a test environment is required for our Elastic Stack setup, why we should pick the right time filter field, and why we should avoid indexing large documents. After that, we will discuss sparsity and different ways to avoid it, such as normalizing the document, avoiding unrelated data in the same index, and avoiding different document types in an index.

Requirement of test environment

We should always create a test environment to test changes before applying them to the production environment, so that, if any change breaks the Elastic Stack setup, we can stop it at the testing level without affecting the production environment. Also, we can use it as a playground to test trivial or nontrivial things, and once it is successful, we can easily replicate it on the production setup.

In Elasticsearch Stack, we have different configuration options to tweak and change some features of the setup and, sometimes, can also break the running application, so it is very necessary to test changes on the test environment first before applying them on the production setup once it is successful on the test environment.

Apart from configuration settings, we have APIs in Elasticsearch, with which we can play around, and once what is tested, we can then just do the same on production setup as well. There are so many things to consider, such as visualization creation in Kibana. We should perform visualization on the test environment first before doing it directly on the production environment.

Picking the right time filter field

We created the index pattern in Kibana to access Elasticsearch index data, and during index pattern creation, we will need to provide the timestamp field using which we can apply time-based filters and manipulations in Kibana. In any document, we can have multiple timestamp fields, so it is quite important to pick the right field.

The following screenshot shows the time filter field name selection screen where we select the field using the drop-down option. The time filter field is basically used to apply a time filter on different options of Kibana such as **Visualize**, **Discover**, **Timelion**, or **Dashboard**.

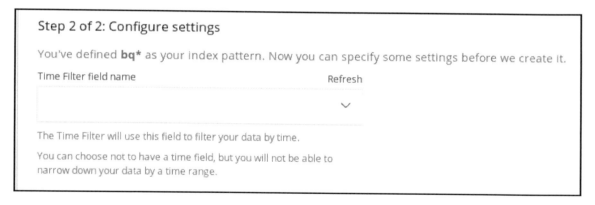

For example, consider that we have year-wise population data and different date fields, such as the population capture date, `create_at`, and `update_at field` in that data. Now, if we need to filter the data on the basis of population capture year, then we should pick capture date as the default time filter field, as this may help us to apply the time filter directly on that field. So, it is quite important to think for a while before just picking any time filter field during index pattern creation.

Avoiding large document indexing

We should avoid indexing large documents since Elasticsearch has a default maximum content size, and if we try to index a document that crosses this limit, Elasticsearch will refuse to index the document. Elasticsearch's default maximum length for any document is 100 MB, and it is defined using the following configuration:

```
http.max_content_length
```

Although we can increase the default `max_content_length` in Elasticsearch, it is not recommended to increase the limit. Large document sizes increase network load, and we will lose the benefit of Elasticsearch because the main advantage of Elasticsearch lies in the search capabilities and speed that it provides. If we index a large document, it puts stress on memory usage, disks, and also on the network.

 We have the Lucene maximum content limit, which is about 2 GB.

It is required to understand the data that we are going to index before indexing it into Elasticsearch, such as categorizing it in order to conclude the unit of information we are going to index. We need to decide at the document-level breakup of data and then try to find out the size of each document we expect in the future.

Take the following example of a book: assume that we need to index a book in Elasticsearch to make it searchable, so one approach is to create a document for the complete book, which is a bad approach. We need to check the size of the book, and depending on that, we can either put each of its chapters as a document, or paragraphs of chapters as a document to index. Once this is decided, we can have a property in the document that will identify the chapter or book it belongs to. Similarly, we can decide for other data sources, because deciding the level for document creation in Elasticsearch is quite important before indexing the document because it is quite difficult to change the document again once we have indexed it. Also, don't make it so small that individual document-level information becomes meaningless.

In this approach, we are breaking a large document into smaller documents, which not only fixes the issue of large documents but also enhances the search experience. Whenever we perform search operations, they will be faster and will provide more detailed results since they will be listed in different paragraphs, which are listed for given search criteria. So, based on the Elasticsearch maximum document size, that is, 100 MB, we can plan our document and can get the maximum benefit from indexing.

Avoiding sparsity

Elasticsearch is a search engine that is built on top of Lucene and passes data to Lucene for storage and searching. Lucene data structures can perform in a better way if the data is stored in dense form; for example, all documents with the same type of fields can create a dense storage rather than storing different types of field in a single document. Lucene identifies documents with `doc_id`, which has an integer value and varies from 0 to total number of documents in the index. This is how Lucene recognizes Elasticsearch document in the index. These `doc_id` elements of Elasticsearch documents are used to communicate with Lucene's internal APIs.

For example, if we execute a match query on any term, Lucene will produce an iterator of `doc_ids`. These `doc_ids` elements are used to compute the score for the document in the search by retrieving the value of the norm. One byte is reserved for each document to store the norm value, and this is the current norm lookup implementation in Elasticsearch and Lucene. For any `doc_id`, this norm value can be retrieved by reading the byte at the `doc_id` index.

This is quite an efficient way and helps Lucene to quickly access the document's norm value by reading the byte data, but it has an overhead, as it has to maintain the storage of one byte for every document, whether or not that document is empty, and that is the biggest disadvantage of this approach. So, if we talk in a more practical way, let's say we have x documents in an index; the norm will require one byte of storage per field even if the field is a small fraction of the document in the index. So, as we have x documents, and each document has some fields, then the storage required for the norm will be one byte multiplied by the field count and then the document count.

We have discussed the impact of sparsity on storage requirements because it is quite a notable impact, but apart from that, it has other impacts as well such as indexing speed and search speed. Indexing and searching speed are impacted because bytes where there are no field in the documents still need to be written during indexing, and then they will be skipped during the search, so this creates an unnecessary extra overhead. It is normal to have a small number of sparse fields in the document, but if it becomes the rule rather than the exception, then we will lose index efficiency. So, we should try to take sparsity into consideration during indexing, as this is a very common issue that can affect our performance at a later stage. Sparsity also impacts inverted index performance. Now, let's take a look at some important ways to avoid performance hits through sparsity. There are different ways to avoid sparsity such as avoiding unrelated data in the same index, normalizing the document structure, or avoiding types. Now, we can discuss the following measures to remove sparsity in detail.

Avoiding unrelated data in the same index

We should avoid adding unrelated data structures in a single index, as this may increase sparsity. So if we are facing a situation where we need to put different types of document in a single index, it's better to break the index into two different indices and put the documents in respective indices.

Based on the document size, we should also consider sharding and assign fewer shards to those indices where the overall document count is less in number in comparison to other indices. This applies to only those cases where we are trying to put documents of different types into the same index, and because of that we could increase the unnecessary storage. In this way, we will increase sparsity.

So, whenever we index a document, we ensure that this is going to sit in an index with similar types of document. This way, we can decrease sparsity and can optimize the Elasticsearch cluster to get the maximum output from it. Similar types of document in an index reduce the unnecessary space requirement and provides better performance to Elasticsearch.

Normalizing the document

Although we should avoid putting different types of document in the same index, still if it is required to put them in a single index, there are few things that we should take into consideration such as normalizing the fields so that we can easily perform any operations on them. For example, consider that we have a date field on which we can perform any operation, and in one document, this date field is timestamp while in an other field this date field is create_date. Then, this will be a problem when performing any operation on the date field for these situations.

Refer to the following example where we have two documents in the index; in the first document, the date field is create_date, whereas in the other, the date field is timestamp:

```
[{
        "_index": "bqstack",
        "_type": "blogs",
        "_id": "EQJnGWQBnhG38eKPq5Bo",
        "_score": 1,
        "_source": {
            "category_name": "Railways",
            "name": "Rocky Paul",
            "edit_approved": false,
            "email": "rocky.paul.9867@xyz.com",
```

```
                    "edited_blog_content": null,
                    "category_id": 24,
                    "author_id": 75,
                    "create_date": "rocky.paul.9867@abcd.com"
                }
            },
            {
                "_index": "bqstack",
                "_type": "blogs",
                "_id": "EwJnGWQBnhG38eKPq5Bo",
                "_score": 1,
                "_source": {
                    "category_name": "Cars",
                    "name": "Rocky Paul",
                    "edit_approved": false,
                    "email": "rocky.paul.9867@abcd.com",
                    "edited_blog_content": null,
                    "category_id": 35,
                    "author_id": 75,
                    "timestamp": "2018-05-09T13:28:20.917Z"
                }
            }
        ]
```

If we have not normalized these fields, then during the search it will pick only those documents where the field is defined and will leave other documents with a different field name.

So, to avoid these issues, we can rename one document field name to match it with an other document's field of the same type. This will increase Elasticsearch performance, and we can get the results from the whole document in the event we perform any operation on such a type of fields.

Avoiding types in Indices

Document types provide us with an option through which we can store multiple tenants in a single index. However, it is again a problem because if we have different fields in different documents types, then putting them in a single index will again increase sparsity because, by using the document type again, we are putting different fields in a single index. So, do not create a type if there is a variation in document field, and for those situations, it is always better to create a separate index rather than a document type.

In the following example, we have the same problem as described previously—the only difference is the document type, as we have two different document types in both documents, and they are part of the same index:

```
[{
        "_index": "bqstack",
        "_type": "political_blogs",
        "_id": "EQJnGWQBnhG38eKPq5Bo",
        "_score": 1,
        "_source": {
            "category_name": "Railways",
            "name": "Rocky Paul",
            "edit_approved": false,
            "email": "rocky.paul.9867@xyz.com",
            "edited_blog_content": null,
            "category_id": 24,
            "author_id": 75,
            "create_date": "rocky.paul.9867@abcd.com"
        }
    },
    {
        "_index": "bqstack",
        "_type": "tech_blogs",
        "_id": "EwJnGWQBnhG38eKPq5Bo",
        "_score": 1,
        "_source": {
            "category_name": "Cars",
            "name": "Rocky Paul",
            "edit_approved": false,
            "email": "rocky.paul.9867@abcd.com",
            "edited_blog_content": null,
            "category_id": 35,
            "author_id": 75,
            "timestamp": "2018-05-09T13:28:20.917Z"
        }
    }
]
```

In the preceding code, we have an index with two document types, political_blogs and tech_blogs. Also, there is a field name mismatch for the date. Now, in this situation, it is better to break the type into two separate indices rather than putting them inside a single index in the form of a document type.

So, these are some of the ways in which we can remove sparsity from an Elasticsearch index and optimize its performance.

Avoiding wildcard searches

Wildcard searches are useful when we don't know the exact search text and know only certain parts of the text. So, in that case, we will provide some text plus a wildcard character to get all the matches to partial text and also the text against the wildcard characters, which can be numbers of characters or can be without any character limit, which again depends on the type of the wildcard we have used. Take a look at the following example where we want to search for the name of a blogger, but we do not remember the exact name and only knows that it starts with pa and ends with l:

```
GET /_search
{
    "query": {
        "wildcard" : { "name" : "pa*l" }
    }
}
```

On executing this search, Elasticsearch will return all the results with the name starting with pa and ending with l, such as paul. This is a good feature and quite helpful in those situations where we do not know the exact search text.

Now, let's return to the problem part and understand why we should avoid wildcards in certain situations. Wildcard queries are costly, as additional computation is required to scan documents. Now, if we have a large dataset, then this can stall the system and can decrease Elasticsearch performance. When we use Kibana to search on Elasticsearch, we have more ways to perform the search, and we can execute a full wildcard search without typing even a single character. Now, in this case, we are fetching the complete dataset in the form of a result set, and if the data size is large, then it is going to consume a lot of memory and can stall the system. So, it is not advisable to use wildcard searches on Elasticsearch if the data size is large.

Summary

In this chapter, we covered different best practices that we should follow for Elastic Stack. This is quite a general approach, and it may be possible that this practice is not related to the type of architecture you have, so it is quite important to understand the architecture of your Elastic Stack. Apart from that, apply the best practices as per your data size and the environment you are using.

For example, your Kibana setup is working on a production environment and everything is working fine, and now you suddenly make some changes to your Kibana configuration settings from the **Management** tab, and it breaks everything. So, to avoid these situations, you need to test any configuration changes on the test environment first.

We also covered the issue of sparsity and how it can consume memory even when your document field has no data. Then, we discussed different ways to reduce sparsity such as avoiding unrelated data in the same index, normalizing the document, and avoiding different document types in an index. We also discussed how to avoid wildcard searches if we have a large dataset in Elasticsearch.

Other Books You May Enjoy

If you enjoyed this book, you may be interested in these other books by Packt:

Learning Elastic Stack 6.0
Pranav Shukla, Sharath Kumar

ISBN: 9781787281868

- Familiarize yourself with the different components of the Elastic Stack
- Get to know the new functionalities introduced in Elastic Stack 6.0
- Effectively build your data pipeline to get data from terabytes or petabytes of data into Elasticsearch and Logstash for searching and logging
- Use Kibana to visualize data and tell data stories in real-time
- Secure, monitor, and use the alerting and reporting capabilities of Elastic Stack
- Take your Elastic application to an on-premise or cloud-based production environment

Mastering Elastic Stack

Yuvraj Gupta, Ravi Kumar Gupta

ISBN: 9781786460011

- Build a pipeline with help of Logstash and Beats to visualize Elasticsearch data in Kibana
- Use Beats to ship any type of data to the Elastic stack
- Understand Elasticsearch APIs, modules, and other advanced concepts
- Explore Logstash and it's plugins
- Discover how to utilize the new Kibana UI for advanced analytics
- See how to work with the Elastic Stack using other advanced configurations
- Customize the Elastic Stack and plugin development for each of the component
- Work with the Elastic Stack in a production environment
- Explore the various components of X-Pack in detail.

Leave a review - let other readers know what you think

Please share your thoughts on this book with others by leaving a review on the site that you bought it from. If you purchased the book from Amazon, please leave us an honest review on this book's Amazon page. This is vital so that other potential readers can see and use your unbiased opinion to make purchasing decisions, we can understand what our customers think about our products, and our authors can see your feedback on the title that they have worked with Packt to create. It will only take a few minutes of your time, but is valuable to other potential customers, our authors, and Packt. Thank you!

Index

.es function parameters 130

A

advanced job 245
advanced settings
  about 196
  dateFormat 198
  dateFormat dow 199
  dateFormat tz 198
  defaultIndex 199
  search queryLanguage 197
  search queryLanguage switcher 197
  xPack defaultAdminEmail 197
anomaly explorer 265
Apache Access Log 10
Apache Lucene 7
application performance monitoring, X-Pack 231
area chart
  about 78, 90
  creating 91

B

bar chart
  about 77, 86
  creating 88, 90
basic charts, visualization
  about 79
  heat maps 80
  line, area, and bar charts 79
  pie chart 80
Beat dashboard
  importing 338
  importing, in Filebeat 338
  importing, in Metricbeat 338
  importing, in Packetbeat 339

Beats
  about 7, 11, 18
  configuring 320
  Filebeat 11, 21, 321
  Heartbeat 22
  Metricbeat 11, 19, 325
  Packetbeat 18, 327
  Winlogbeat 22
bucket aggregation 81
bucket aggregation, bar chart
  about 87
  date histogram 87
  date range 87
  filters 87
  histogram 87
  IPv4 range 87
  range 87
  significant terms 87
  terms 87
bucket aggregation, pie chart
  about 81
  date histogram 81
  date range 82
  filters 82
  histogram 82
  IPv4 range 82
  range 82
  significant terms 82
  terms 82

C

chainable methods
  .abs() 134
  .avg() 132
  .bars() 136
  .color() 137
  .derivative() 135

.divide() 134
.label() 137
.legend() 138
.log() 134
.max() 133
.min() 133
.movingaverage() 138
.multiply() 135
.precision() 140
.range() 140
.sum() 131
.trend() 139
about 131
conditional formatting 298
Console
about 158
Auto indent link 161, 163
Copy as cURL 160
Editor 158
multiple requests 163, 167
Response pane 158

D

dashboard
cloning 112
creating 29, 39, 40, 42, 43, 100, 294, 336
creating, MySQL data used 283, 286
CSV data, exporting from visualization 49
customizing 44
Elasticsearch request, obtaining 50
Elasticsearch response, obtaining 50
Elasticsearch statistics, obtaining 50
exploring 113
filters, adding 115, 117, 118
saved version, sharing 111
search query 113
sharing 110
snapshot, sharing 111
time filter, applying 119
title, changing by customizing panel 45
visualization colors, changing 46
visualization, deleting 46
visualization, editing 44
visualization, moving to full screen 46
visualization, resizing as requisites 48

visualizations, clicking on 122, 124, 125
visualizations, dragging 48
visualizations, dropping 48
data metric
about 78, 92
creating 92
data source functions 141
data table
about 78, 93
creating 93
data visualizer 248, 250
data, visualization
about 80
goal and gauge 80
metric 80
table 80
data
discovering, Kibana Discover used 58
Kibana, configuring to read Elasticsearch index
with packet logs 62, 64
Packetbeat, configuring to push packet data into
Elasticsearch 59, 60
visualizing 77
date field 190
demo visualizations
creating, with Apache log data 36, 38, 39
document indexing
avoiding 343

E

Elastic 278
Elastic Stack (ELK Stack) 7
Elasticsearch 6.1.3 MSI
URL, for downloading 13
Elasticsearch monitoring 216, 217, 220
Elasticsearch, data source functions
about 142
offset, setting for data sources 145
static/value 142
world bank 143
Elasticsearch
about 7, 9, 12
installing, TAR file used 12
installing, with Debian package 13
installing, with Homebrew 13

installing, with MSI Windows installer 13
installing, with RPM package 13
ELK Stack
  about 8
  Beats 11, 18
  Elasticsearch 9, 12
  installing 12
  Kibana 11, 15
  Logstash 9, 14
  use cases 24

F

fields
  date field 190
  geographic point field 190
  managing 187
  number fields 191
  string field 189
Filebeat
  about 11, 319, 321
  configuring 322, 323
filter field
  picking 342

G

geographic point field 190
GeoIP
  for Elastic Stack 309
  ingest node 309, 311
  with Packetbeat data 313, 316
graphical user interface (GUI) 13
Grok debugger 175, 177

I

index pattern
  about 180
  creating 181, 183
  default, setting 185
  deleting 186
  fields, managing 187
  fields, refreshing 185

J

JDBC input plugin

about 278
fetch size 280
scheduling 279
SQL value, maintaining 279
job
  configuring 259
  counts 261
  datafeed 260
  datafeed, previewing 264
  JSON 262
  managing 258
  messages 263
  settings 259

K

Kibana Discover
  about 54, 56, 58
  Elasticsearch query DSL 70
  exploring, to access packet data 65, 66
  field data statistics 74
  filter 72
  required fields, displaying 67
  save and open searches 73
  time filter, applying 69
  used, for discovering data 58
Kibana monitoring 222, 223
Kibana v6.1.3
  URL, for downloading 17
Kibana
  about 7, 11, 15, 278
  configuring, to Elasticsearch index 32, 34, 35
  installing, .tar.gz used 16
  installing, Debian package used 16
  installing, on Windows 17
  installing, rpm used 16

L

log data
  outputting, into Elasticsearch 31
logging, X-Pack
  about 232
  Apache logs 233
  MySQL logs 234
  Nginx logs 234
  system logs 235

Logstash
about 7, 9, 14
apt package repositories, using 14
configuring, for database input 280, 281
configuring, to fetch data from Apache log file
  30, 32
yum package repositories, using 15

M

machine learning job
about 242, 244
advanced job 245
anomaly explorer 265
creating 246, 247
data visualizer 248, 250
job, managing 258
multi metric job 245, 267, 269
multi metric job result, exploring 270, 272
population job 245, 273, 274
single metric job 244, 250, 252, 255, 257
single metric viewer 266
machine learning, X-Pack
about 229
other options 229
maps, visualization
about 80
coordinate map 80
region map 80
markdown 78
markdown visualization
about 96
creating 97
metric aggregation 81
metric aggregation, bar chart
about 86
average 86
count 87
max 86
median 86
min 87
percentile 87
percentile ranks 87
standard deviation 87
sum 87
top hit 87

unique count 87
metric aggregation, pie chart
about 81
count 81
sum 81
unique count 81
Metricbeat
about 11, 319, 325
configuring 326
module, enabling from modules.d directory 326
module, enabling metricbeat.yml file used 326
metrics, X-Pack
about 236
Apache metrics 237
Docker metrics 237
Kubernetes metrics 238
MySQL metrics 238
Nginx metrics 238
Redis metrics 239
system metrics 239
monitoring, X-Pack
about 215
Elasticsearch monitoring 216, 217, 220
Kibana monitoring 222, 223
multi metric job
about 245, 267, 269
result, exploring 270, 272
MySQL data
used, for creating dashboard 283, 286

N

non-numeric fields 250
number fields 191
numeric fields 250

O

other items, visualization
markdown widget 81
tag cloud 81

P

Packetbeat
about 18, 319, 327
configuring 328
pie chart

about 77, 81
creating 82, 83, 84
dimension, adding 85
population job 245, 273, 274

Q

queries
aggregation profile 172
profiling 168, 169
query profile 170

R

Relational Database Management System
    (RDBMS) 25
reporting 200

S

save and open searches, Kibana Discover
result, opening 73
result, saving 73
share result 74
saved objects
about 192
dashboards 193
searches 194
visualizations 195
security settings, X-Pack
about 224
roles 226, 228
users 224
security
about 200
roles 201
users 202
single metric job 244, 250, 252, 255, 256
single metric viewer 266
sparsity
avoiding 344
document, normalizing 345
types, avoiding in index 346
unrelated data, avoiding 345
stage
demo visualizations, creating with Apache log
    data 36, 38, 39
Kibana, configuring to Elasticsearch index 32,

34, 35
log data, outputting into Elasticsearch 31
Logstash, configuring to fetch data from Apache
    log file 30, 32
setting up 29
string field 189

T

tag cloud
about 78
creating 94, 96
test environment
requisites 341
time series
about 80
timelion 80
visual builder 80
time-series data handling
about 298
conditional formatting 298
trends, tracking 301
Timeline expression 129
Timelion autorefresh 154
Timelion graph
saving 146, 148, 150
Timelion interface 128
Timelion sheet option
about 151
deleting 152
Timelion
function reference 153
help link 152
keyboard tips 153
trends
tracking 298, 301

U

use cases, ELK Stack
data, visualizing 26
e-commerce search solutions 26
full text search 26
log management 24
security alerting 25
security monitoring 25
web scraping 25

V

visual builder
  for time series data handling 303, 306, 309
visualization, dashboard
  blog details, tabular view 292
  blogger name-category-views-blog pie chart 291
  blogger-wise blog counts 288
  creating 287
  tag cloud, for blog categories 290
  total blog count 287
visualization
  arranging 103
  creating 78
  creating, Beat data used 330
  creating, Filebeat used 330, 332
  creating, Metricbeat used 333
  creating, Packetbeat used 334
  dashboard, saving 110
  dashboard, sharing 110
  data, displaying 107, 108
  full screen, displaying 106
  modifying 109
  moving 103
  other items 81
  removing 105

  resizing 104
  sharing 78, 97
  time series 80

W

Watch Payload 202
watch
  about 202
  advanced 203, 206
  creating 203
  deleting 208
  threshold alert 203, 204
wildcard searches
  avoiding 348
world bank
  about 143
  country 143
  indicator 143

X

X-Pack
  features 214
  installing 212
  installing, into Elasticsearch 212
  installing, into Kibana 213

Made in the USA
Lexington, KY
26 May 2019